Framing Education as Art

The Octopus Has a Good Day

Framing Education as Art

The Octopus Has a Good Day

JESSICA HOFFMANN DAVIS

Teachers College, Columbia University
New York and London

All Octopus drawings created by Emerson Davis, Age 4.

Published by Teachers College Press, 1234 Amsterdam Avenue, New York, NY 10027

Library of Congress Cataloging-in-Publication Data

Davis, Jessica Hoffmann, 1943–
    Framing education as art : the octopus has a good day /
    Jessica Hoffmann Davis.
        p. cm.
    Includes bibliographical references and index.
    ISBN 0-8077-4578-2 (cloth : alk. paper) — ISBN 0-8077-4577-4 (pbk. : alk. paper)
        1. Arts—Study and teaching (Elementary) 2. Arts and society. 3. Arts and children. I. Title.
    LB1591.D38 2005
    372.5—dc22   2004063675

ISBN 0-8077-4577-4 (paper)
ISBN 0-8077-4578-2 (cloth)

Printed on acid-free paper
Manufactured in the United States of America

12   11   10   09   08   07   06   05   8   7   6   5   4   3   2   1

For Will
whose artistry on so many fronts
inspires and sustains

Contents

Acknowledgments

I am grateful for the mentorship of my mother, Anna Hoffmann, director of the Hoffmann School, whose vision of education and art was seamless. For their essential and joyful contributions to the life and content of this work, I thank my artful children and grandchildren: Joshua, Susan, Emerson (illustrator of this work), Malcolm, Alexander, Frances, William, and Benjamin. For all they've taught me and is everywhere reflected herein, I am grateful to the extraordinary artful educators in the Harvard Graduate School of Education's (HGSE) Arts in Education (AIE) Program. For helping to make that program and therefore much of the thinking in this volume possible, I thank my dear colleague Professor Howard Gardner, our visionary dean Professor Jerome Murphy, my many distinguished colleagues at HGSE and at Project Zero, our creative and dedicated friends Patricia Bauman, John Landrum Bryant, and the dauntless members of the AIE Program Advisory Councils. I am grateful to Bobette McCarthy for her assistance in early preparation of the manuscript and appreciate contributions to its development from Mary Benefiel, Professor Gertrude Hoffmann Bolter, Charlotte Dixon, Rubén Gaztambide-Fernández, Adriana Katzew, Professor Sara Lawrence-Lightfoot, Kristen Greer-Paglia, Scott Ruescher, Elisabeth Soep, Tiffanie Ting, and Barry and Pamela Zuckerman. I am indebted to the generous funders who supported the research described in these pages: the Bauman, Cummings, Dodge, Ford, Julian and Warhol Foundations, as well as the National Arts Learning Collaborative. I especially appreciate at Teachers College Press the sage guidance of Carole Saltz and Catherine Chandler and the skillful production and promotion oversight of Karl Nyberg, Jessica Balun, and Nancy Power.

Introduction

NAMING THE QUEST

After a long morning at my computer, I was delighted by my 4-year-old grandson's appearance on my lap. He looked with curiosity at the computer screen and asked, "What are you doing?" "I'm writing a book," I replied. "What's its title?" Emerson asked earnestly. "*The Arts in Education: Generative Tensions.*" Without a minute's reflection, he confided, "It's not a good title." "Why not?" "Well," he explained politely, "I like a title that's a little more interesting." He thought for a moment. "Like *The Octopus Has a Good Day.*"

Of course Emerson was right. A title like *The Octopus Has a Good Day* tells the reader what the book is about in a way that *Generative Tensions* doesn't begin to do. I wanted to write a book that demystifies a subject too often associated with "magic." The fearsome magic of the arts, the precious territory of the few, the knowledge base of the elite—these are all concepts I preferred to rewrite than to reinforce with a forbidding title like *Generative Tensions.* Embracing the example provided by the *Octopus* title, I began to think the title, as a metaphor, might serve my purposes well.

An octopus has eight tentacles. The artistic domains that are particularly featured in educational scenarios appear in at least eight versions (painting, sculpture, music, drama, dance, poetry, photography, and film). The arts reach their long arms into specialized and multi-arts classrooms, disciplinary and interdisciplinary initiatives, arts-based and non-arts exercises and projects, within and beyond the limits of the school day. Like an octopus spreading its tentacles, arts education enters school from outside in through visiting artists and performances, and from inside out through field trips to cultural institutions of at least eight varieties (museums, concert halls, community centers, public art spaces, artist studios, galleries, dance stages, and theaters).

Arts learning in community venues reaches beyond those settings into young people's academic performance, entrepreneurial initiatives, school attendance, professional pursuits, collaborative endeavors, selection of role models, and explorations of personal/ intrapersonal and cultural/cross-cultural values. Within a school curriculum, the arts appear in general education in at least eight ways—as arts based, infused, expanded, pre-professional, extracurricular, aesthetic, or cultural education. The octopus with its eight tentacles and far-reaching sprawl serves well as a metaphor for the arts in education. Indeed, I have learned that the octopus has three hearts and a highly developed brain; these points of information only make the metaphor more apt.

Even as the translucent tones of the octopus change as it moves through the water, the arts have held a fluid and often tenuous role in the education of children in the United States. In the last 50 years, educators have moved away from the once prevalent view of the arts as useful because they help children to express emotions and to release tensions. Current advocates suspect that the "emotive" view kept art education on the fringe of life in school, differentiating it from the more academic and essential disciplines. More recently, there has been interest in claims that the arts actually improve intellectual performance, develop critical thinking skills, and prepare children for effective roles in the workplace. The hope is that these less "touchy feely" benefits may help secure for the arts a more central role in schooling and a more equal status to that of other academic disciplines.

Whatever the shape of the rationale, the arts seem always to need some reason beyond their own processes and products to make them worthy of real time in the school day. Why must we argue for a place for activities that provide singular shape and expression to our understandings as human beings? Shouldn't the arts be the most revered of subjects simply because they connect us to our unique and various cultures as well as to the shared culture of humankind? Advocates bemoan the ongoing need for redefinition of the function of arts learning and the seemingly constant role of the arts as outsiders, only occasionally or superficially welcomed on to center stage of the drama of school. But schools do not exist in a vacuum; their perspectives and value systems reflect the priorities and biases of the world beyond school. On this account, one might argue that the ongoing battle waged by arts educators and advocates runs parallel to or at least reflects the struggle that art and artists face in the larger world.

Like art education, the arts and artists seem to live in an ambivalent twilight, both as the luminous visionaries and trendsetters of culture and as the dark outsiders to mainstream life. Is the impact of such apparent contradiction frustrating and enervating? Or does the quest for continued self-reflection and redefinition provide some energy and quality to the life of the arts and to the field of art education? Are there benefits from the apparent tension between a view of the arts as being at the core of humanity—the best work we can do—and at the outskirts of everyday life—put aside for when there's time to play? Questions like these and the tensions or apparent contradictions that invite them affect the course of the arts in education in this country, fuel my interest in the subject, and provide the framework and direction of the discussions that lie ahead.

In the chapters that follow, I argue that it is *because* of their particular products and processes, their ongoing redefinition, and even their outsider status that the arts deserve a central place in education. I hope to demonstrate that the vexing tensions that surround the arts and the arts in education are, with apologies to my grandson, "generative"—that they ultimately propel more surely than they deter and that they may even provide to other disciplines a useful means for self-exploration and development. While the deceptively clean-cut lenses of "either and or" help to focus inquiry, real discovery lies in the messy layered spaces in between. Challenging disciplinary boundaries and embracing personal themes and multiple interpretations, the arts provide a way for education to benefit from the salient differences that abide among various cultures of learning and confound attempts to standardize curricula and assessment. My hope is that readers will find in this book useful fodder for their own understandings of the role and potential of the arts in education and for their open-ended consideration of the ways in which education writ large is and can be more like art.

FRAMING THE JOURNEY

I have been involved in the arts in education for almost half a century. I have taught art to children in school and in community education, worked as a practicing artist in illustration and design, and served as an arts administrator and advocate in the community and in higher education. More recently, as a cognitive developmental psychologist, I have studied development in artistic production and perception as well as effective pedagogy in schools, community art centers, and art museums. At the Harvard Graduate School of Education where I founded and for many years directed the Arts in Education Program, I designed a course of study intended to lead students on a focused tour of the challenging, beleaguered, and inspirational realm of the arts in education. The map of that journey has helped chart the course of action for this volume and for the perspectives, queries, and suggestions it contains.

The road is lined with discoveries from my research, personal life, and work, and it bears the patina of advocacy and affection for this field. While I refer throughout to the "arts" writ large, I focus most frequently on the visual arts because of my experience and research in this area and because they are (along with music) the most frequently taught in our schools. Following the example of works of art, my text is filled more with questions than answers in hopes of inspiring the same. While I personify doubters of the efficacy of the arts, nowhere do I waste a breath on that music teacher who told us to move our lips and not sing, that dance teacher who made our bodies feel oversized, or the visual arts teacher who scribbled over our first attempts at life drawing. Instead, I attend here to one telling of the many positive things there are to learn and emulate from both the triumphs and trials of art, art making, artists, artist teachers, contexts for arts learning, and our children—every one of whom is an artist. In a broader landscape in which the arts in education are too frequently isolated or ignored, I choose to tell the story in this way.

I have chosen as our tour guide and pathfinder a representative child whom, with deference to our working metaphor, I am calling Octavia. Although she is a fictive character, the stories she tells are derived from empirical evidence from my research and/or pedagogy. Octavia's artistic development from pre- to high school serves as a beacon along the way. A collage of voices of artists, scholars, and researchers lend ballast to my own. Works of art from various domains add depth to our traveling and layers to our vision of the whole. Each juncture in this journey is marked by a different generative tension, variously understood as a false though dueling dichotomy, complex challenge, and/or key debate in the arena of the arts in education. Illuminating pivotal perspectives and intersecting roadways, the tensions are nowhere intended to frame a comprehensive view of the whole.

MAPPING THE TERRAIN

The generative tensions are introduced and considered within four contexts: (1) *The Artistic Process*, in which we consider the traditional conflict between thinking and feeling; (2) *The Child as Artist*, in which a tension is found between romance and reason; (3) *The Arts in Education in School*, in which justification challenges celebration; and (4) *Arts in Education in the Community*, in which we consider two very different sites of arts learning, the Mighty Muse (the art museum) and Safe Haven (the urban community art center). In the fifth and final chapter, "Framing Education as Art," I revisit and pull strands across each of the four contexts, framing the space in between and across the generative tensions as paradigms for non-arts learning. The following brief descriptions introduce in greater detail the various contexts and tensions that organize the content and direction of this book.

Chapter 1 concerns the artistic process, the nature of artistic activity, and the tension inherent in its relative relationship to feeling and/or thinking. In literature, education, psychology, and philosophy, a view of the arts as dedicated to the expression of emotion may seem in opposition to a view of art as the realization of highly refined thought. On the one side, the arts are seen as irrational, magical, comprised of emotion presented in a work to be experienced by the audience. The other side of the conversation holds that the arts represent complex processes of thought, opportunities for making and finding meaning, with even the construction of expression regarded as a cognitive achievement. What differences in general regard for the arts or determination of a place for the arts in education might derive from either perspective or from the dynamic between them? The feeling/thinking dynamic serves as a virulent thread, collecting nuance and power, throughout each of the contexts that we consider.

Chapter 2 examines the notion of the child as artist and provides an overview of the interest in children's artistic productions on the part of psychologists, educators, artists, and art critics. Embracing the *romance* side of the tension here, artists (in the modernist tradition) were so taken with children's art that they were known to copy it directly in their work. In apparent *reason*-driven contrast, psychologists have investigated the similarities, differences, and implications of a comparison between the work of young children and adult artists. What does the comparison say about our respective regard for artists or children? What do we learn about children, art, and development from the study of child art? What are the differences in educational practice that results from an appreciation versus a dismissal of early artistry?

In Chapter 3, we situate the child as artist within the context of school, and move to a discussion of the history and content of art education in the United States. In this context, we consider the persistent tension between *justification* and *celebration*. Throughout the history of this field there have been changing rationales for including the arts in curriculum. Goals range from the cultivation of marketable skills for a developing industrial nation, to the education of the whole child, to the training of creative and critical thinkers. Regardless of the particular justification for inclusion, the arts have rarely been celebrated on their own as essential parts of general education. Against this backdrop, we consider the eight ways in which the arts find themselves in mainstream education and we examine schools that focus on the arts as outposts where a celebration of the arts drives curriculum and enriches communities of learners. What do we learn of the range and potential of the arts from the frameworks in which they are justified and from the settings in which they are celebrated?

In Chapter 4, we look beyond school walls into the broader community for more examples of the reach and potential of the arts in education. Situating the generative tension in community-based institutions, we examine on the one hand learning as it is represented by and delivered in art museums, those *mighty muses* that seek to shape and preserve culture. Alternatively, we look to the lessons of urban community art centers, most often started and directed by professional artists, with a history of working successfully with and providing *safe havens* for disenfranchised students. What do we learn about the arts in education from the mighty muse's focus on object-based learning or the safe haven's focus on student-based learning?

In a closing tapestry, I revisit and operationalize the discoveries of the first four sections, exploring the space "in between" each generative tension as a lens through which general education can be considered. My concluding reflections are dedicated to the book's primary premises: (1) that the tensions that fuel and confound the arts and the arts in education, made as they are more of questions than of answers and of multiple rather than singular points of entry, are in the end more surely assets than obstacles; and (2) that the time has come to stop packaging the arts in the same tight wrappings that arguably work for other subjects and instead find new ways for other subjects to package themselves in the generous colors of the arts.

Toward these ends, I conclude with suggestions of ways for non-arts subjects to engage in the same sort of integrative boundary crossing, industrious self-reflection, and ongoing redefinition that has been the challenge and duty as well as the triumph and promise of the arts in education. In doing this, I evoke the inspirational work of artful[1] educators and offer as entry points to cross-disciplinary learning a string of arts related open-ended questions. It is said that in the blurry-edged, multilayered presentations that characterize the arts, clear truths can be discerned. In this last section, I benefit from the work of theorists and advocates who have braved this ground and add my voice to those of the many educators who embrace the ragged contours of human realities in place of the apparently clean borders of right and wrong answers. Throughout it all, it is my hope that this text will help to give the octopus its long awaited and well-deserved good day.

NOTE

1. In my use of the term "artful" educator, I thank Professor Peter Kivy for warning me of the unintended connection readers might make with the crafty attitude of Dickens's artful dodger and note as possible inspiration for the term the Bernstein Institute's Artful Learning approach, which is described in Chapter 3.

1

The Artistic Process

OCTAVIA ONE

Four-year-old Octavia sits at a small table. Yesterday's *New York Times* provides protection for the table's surface and backdrop for a large piece of white paper. Each mold of an adjacent muffin tin is carefully filled with different colored paint. Where batter would be poured, there is clear red, smooth yellow, lucid blue, leaf green, night black, and navel orange. A Mason jar of water holds a long-handled brush; the paper towel to the right serves for mopping wet edges.

"White. A blank page or canvas . . . so many possibilities." In his musical *Sunday in the Park with George*, composer and lyricist Stephen Sondheim places these words in the voice of his protagonist, the 19th-century neoimpressionist painter George Seurat (Sondheim & Lapine, 1991, p. 174). The words seem apt for the eager expression on Octavia's face, the anticipation of creating in this open space something that was not there before—something entirely new, newly defined by the hand, head, and heart of this ready young artist. "The challenge," Sondheim's Seurat tells us, "to bring order to the whole through design, composition, balance, light, and harmony" (pp. 17–18).

A dip of the brush in red and an outlined rounded sphere is boldly implanted in the center of Octavia's page. The red brush is dutifully swirled in the water and dabbed on the towel before its enthusiastic entry into the tin's clear blue circle of paint. Two smaller outlines within the open red circle suggest eyes, a dab in the center for eyeball, a half lid—and lashes now carefully etched (if somewhat blurrily) along the rim of each lid.

The young artist seems to know exactly what she is doing as she produces these two dramatic eye shapes that seem both familiar and entirely fresh. The brush, now ready for more color, is gingerly dipped into the green. Octavia notes briefly that she has skipped the rinsing step, but seems more interested in the depth that has been added to the green as she slaps the color broadly around the perimeter of what now is clearly a face.

"I loved it at the zoo." Octavia speaks softly, adding a yellowish shape to the left of the colorful rendering of what must be her own image. An oval torso-like sphere directly attached to the face is framed in a triangle that seems dresslike. Two vertical lines (in the purplish shade that the brush now carries from its unrinsed forays through the muffin tray) descend from the base of the triangle and are resolved into small solid circles or shoes. Horizontal arms emerge to right and left, each branching into five spidery digits. A smile is added to the face. The soft whisper: "They're in cages . . . " accompanies the application of vertical black lines across the yellow-brown animate creature that has emerged to the side wearing the same smile and bearing the same lidded eyes as the little girl front and center in the painting.

The colors in the various sections of the tin now bear a similar hue—but Octavia dips from one to the other as if aware of some special importance in each variation of sloppily mixed color. The unwashed brush is now dabbling a background all over the blank spaces of the paper. Dot, dot, dot, dot, dot, dot, dot, dot, dot—Sondheim's music would punctuate the activity well. The rhythm of the staccato tone Sondheim linked to Seurat's process of applying tiny dots of color to canvas would aptly accompany Octavia's latest activity as she fills in the background of her painting with what? Leaves? Rain? Dots?

Octavia is excited as she encounters the heavily painted image, looking to left and right, now adding a brownish green line at the bottom . . . balancing it with another at the top. The young artist seems completely engaged, lost somehow in the all-consuming exchange of brush to paint to paper, making and responding in a single fluid action. The painting is dark and dense and filled with energy and interest.

The water in the Mason jar is brown. The once-pristine muffin tin is covered with paint—the clear red, now brown; the smooth yellow, now brown, and ditto for the lucid blue, leaf green, night black, and navel orange. These colors are now both more and less than what they once were—all integrated into a balanced if muddy format that suggests both a specific experience and a more general sense of delight. Covered herself with bits and shades of paint, Octavia looks at her work with an obvious sense of satisfaction and an assertive attitude of completion. "Done," she says with certainty, ready to move on to whatever comes next, perhaps never to look again with interest on this particular creation.

How did this young artist decide that she was finished—that the work was "done"? Did she run out of space? Young children will often paint on top of what's there until they feel the product is complete or they will reach for more paper and create image after image until they feel the process is done. But when they are there, they know their work (product and process) is, even if only for now, finished—completed, whole. This is what adult artists work toward and recognize as well: the aesthetic whole of balanced color, form, content, and feeling. This is what Sondheim's George describes as he separates himself from the rest of the world to do his work, "finishing a hat . . . look, I made a hat . . . where there never was a hat" (pp. 66–67). Both the hat itself and the making thereof.

INTRODUCTION TO THE GENERATIVE TENSION: THE ARTISTIC PROCESS—FEELING/THINKING

What great source of inspiration or need fuels the work of child and adult artist? Is the process driven by the thoughtful reconstruction of inner experience, the simple need, as New York artist and educator Betty Blayton Taylor would say, "to turn thoughts into things" (Davis, 1991c)? Or is this process ultimately a passionate human mandate to communicate feelings beyond the limited terrain of one's own being? Is art the purview of humanity's sensory corporeal or rational cerebral self?

Discussions of the extent to which art is a matter of thinking or feeling have persisted throughout time and held important implications for our relative valuing and determination of a place for the arts in education. Historic concerns over the conflicting forces of head and heart may have been replaced with modern views of relatively autonomous or mutually informative parts of the brain governing the varying functions of emotion and reason. But whatever the contextual turn, these persistent tensions not only engage and perplex philosophers and neuroscientists, they hold enormous weight in the content of arts educational discourse. The respective views of art making as the free expression of experienced emotion or the disciplined result of mindful reflection anticipate relative regard for the arts as therapeutic extraneous extracurricular activities or serious vehicles for teaching and learning worthy of more centrality in the curriculum.

Debates abound among critics, artists, and scholars over what art is and isn't, is and isn't for, and even whether it exists at all as something apart from everyday life and living (see Dissanayake, 1988). Across cultures, understandings of the place, function, and essentiality of art differ greatly, as do views of artistic activity as, for example, a solitary creative or collective political endeavor. Within these various and far-reaching strands, a most relevant dynamic persists between our relative regard for the artistic process as a connected and essentially communicative human need or an autonomous essentially cerebral human potential. Against the vast landscape of discourse on the who, what, where, and why of art, the generative tension between thinking and feeling helps to focus a discussion of the nature of the artistic process and its relation to education. Let's begin with feeling.

THE ARTISTIC PROCESS—FEELING

Communicating Emotion

At the end of the 19th century, Russian author Leo Tolstoy expressed what might be called a "communicative" view of art—envisioning works of art as ensconced in "felt and to be felt" emotion. In his classic treatise *What Is Art?* Tolstoy eschewed traditional views of art (or of the aesthetic) as necessarily concerned or associated with beauty. Instead, he described the artistic process as a medium through which the artist conveyed "by means of movements, lines, colors, sounds, images" a feeling that he or she had experienced so that others could experience it as their own. Tolstoy describes the process as a vesting or infecting of the work with emotion: "Art is that human activity which consists in one man's consciously conveying to others, by certain external signs, the feelings he has experienced, and in others being infected by those feelings and also experiencing them" (1898/1995, p. 40).

Tolstoy was writing *What Is Art?* (1898/1995) about the same time that George Seurat was painting *A Sunday Afternoon on the Island of La Grande Jatte* (1884, see Plate 1) on which Sondheim's musical, created 100 years later, is based. Seurat's canvases were filled with light and color and the use of tiny dotlike particles that rendered in blurry detail the intense imprint of encountered sensation that fellow neoimpressionist painters of his era sought to capture. Tolstoy's novels were lush in detail, portraying historic and religious episodes, depicting personal struggles between good and evil, filled everywhere with the image of human beings as noble loathsome joyful romantic suffering journeymen. Against this backdrop of human limitation and potential, Tolstoy envisioned the communication of feeling from one individual to another as a virtuous and socially ameliorative endeavor—a cultivation of a sort of shared "humanhood" that could amount to a personal, powerful, and unifying truth.

Tolstoy was tortured by conflicting forces surrounding religion and by inequities such as the coexistence of the homeless and the wealthy, and of the unjust and the moral. He ultimately rejected church, politics, and private property for his view of the good: "That which no one can define, but which defines everything else" (1898/1995, p. 52). The breaking of boundaries in his thinking and writing pressed Tolstoy to the margins. Just as the sensory, experientially based works of the Impressionist painters initially repelled 19th-century critics, Tolstoy's provocative views were highly controversial. Indeed, because of the suspicion and rejection of the Russian censors, the first publication of *What Is Art?* was in English (p. xxvii).

Social consciousness and human communication loom large in the vision of artistry that Tolstoy prompts us to unfold. But perhaps of most importance to our thinking/feeling discussion is Tolstoy's unapologetic acknowledgment of emotion at the heart of artistic/literary endeavor. The vision of a subjective, humanistic, experiential truth, not unlike the one Impressionist painters sought to display, is offered as more real than any attempted version of objective reality. Where Tolstoy evoked the centrality of felt emotion transferred through art from producer to perceiver, the impressionists dismissed the clear delineations of representational painting for a blurrier portrayal of a less definable but ultimately more faithful "felt" reality. And just as Tolstoy's view of emotion in art is deepened by his dense philosophic ruminations, so is Seurat's emotive edgeless presentation informed by his scientific reflections on the range of possibilities for putting paint on canvas.

Drawing on writings about color theory in the end of the 19th century such as Ogden Rood's *Modern Chromatics* (1879), neoimpressionists of that era explored the technique of "divisionism" or the application of small dashes of color to achieve an optical effect of pure color. Reflecting his creative development of such thinking, Seurat's painting of *La Grande Jatte* was the first in which the term "pointillism" was evoked because of his use of small points or dots that decomposed the image and left it for recomposing by the human eye. For both Tolstoy and Seurat, then, careful cross-disciplinary study (of philosophy and science, respectively), as well as thoughtful constructive reflection contributes actively to their creative processes. Nonetheless, these intellectual forays are ultimately employed in the service of art as the conveyance of personal powerful and even persuasive emotion. It is as if head and mind recognize the supremacy of heart and feeling.

This almost reverential view of human emotion as the purpose and function of art (even as it may be informed by theoretical reflection) has informed understanding and initiated conflict throughout history. The Greek philosopher Aristotle describes the thoughtful ways in which tragedy inspires fear or pity and poetry provides pleasure by drawing on and serving the human predilection for imitation and harmony. Aristotle's notion of "catharsis"—the experience through theater and expulsion in life of profound and potentially devastating emotions—speaks to an almost functional emotive aspect for great art. In tragedy, the everyday individual in the audience feels one with the great historical hero on stage and is both enlarged and relieved by the shared emotional artistic encounter. Contemporary therapeutic lenses illuminate in these ancient works modern dilemmas such as the Oedipus or Electra complexes (Freud, 1900) that speak across circumstance and time to the continuum of human feelings embodied by art. Addressing this continuum, Aristotle places poetry above history, saying, "Poetry tends to express the universal, history the particular" (1951, p. 35).

Art as Contagion

In book ten of Plato's *Republic*, the authoritative and visionary Greek philosopher Socrates seems less celebratory of the emotional aspects of art, condemning the "contagion" of the arts for its evocation of pleasure and pain and for feeding and watering "passions instead of drying them up" (1953, p. 647). Situating our thinking/feeling tension in the "ancient quarrel between philosophy and poetry," Socrates is suspicious of the unruly boundaries of emotion and advocates for "the part of the soul which trusts to measure and calculation" (p. 645). That touted part of the soul would seem to be driving 21st century educators who have created a climate of accountability that ultimately favors teaching the testable and devaluing, rather than celebrating, that which is beyond measure.

In the arena of right and wrong answers around which schooling and educational testing have thrived, mind is prioritized over heart, reason over romance, and the neatness of supposed objective accuracy over the messiness of unruly subjective experience. Where Seurat's hand-painted dots create a complex blended sensorial veracity, educators have sought the clarity of ruler-drawn straight lines. In the separating of disciplines for study in school, those hard-edged subjects that most apparently address empiricism and intellect (like science and math) have held an almost inviolable centrality in the education of our children. Alternatively, "softer" subjects that more overtly address our students' feelings and fears, like art, music, poetry, and dance, struggle for time within the school day. Art education historian Arthur Efland marks the underlying distinction, "that there are certain subjects that are good for thinking (logic and mathematics) whereas the cultivation of feelings [lies] mainly in the arts" (1996, p. 52).

There are those who attribute the rejection of the softer subjects in American schools to the international space race competition initiated in 1957 when the Russians launched the world's first artificial satellite. Surely this accomplishment put an enormous pressure on schools to educate our children in math and science so that we could compete in the momentous arena of outer space. Nearly 50 years later the struggle concerns literacy, and the indispensability of teaching children how to read, write, and demonstrate those skills through standardized testing. While arts advocates responsively point to something they call "literacy in the arts," or "visual" or "cultural" literacy, the mandate for teaching essential and measurable skills threatens to render dispensable those activities that address the infection, experience, and reexperience of emotion.

The history of art education in the United States reveals that, regardless of changing educational values and needs, the arts have always struggled (and most often unsuccessfully) for a central place in the curriculum. When defended as agents to sharing emotion, the arts plummet in their curricular appeal; and curricular discussions of the conciliatory or socially ameliorating potential of human emotion shared through art are few and far between. That said, there have been luminaries in the field, such as the educational philosopher Maxine Greene, who have contributed greatly to an understanding of the potential of art education to increase the moral and social consciousness of students. In her eloquent and artlike treatises, Greene states that the arts "awaken" students, and "free them to respond not only to the human condition which we all share but to the injustices and the undeserved suffering, and the violence and the violations." Greene suggests that the arts may inspire students "to respond and endeavor to repair" (2001, p. 129).

But too often those of us who recognize and advocate for the social/humanistic importance of art in education do so in familiar arenas where the sympathies of the audience are similar to our own. Were we to carry to an unsympathetic board of education Tolstoy's message of emotive communication as a rationale for including art in the curriculum, we might not be taken very seriously. Furthermore, his numerous religious exhortations would certainly impede our cause. While his own literary works would no doubt be considered worthy of historic, philosophic, and literary attention, Tolstoy's explanations for the importance of art, laced as they are with religious intonations, would only align the subject with other practices that are forbidden in school.

Attributes of Artistry

The subject of art holds obvious connections to religion because of the prevalence of religious themes explored by artists throughout time and because of the amount, nature, and power of art used in religious contexts. Beyond that, a certain "religiosity" can be attributed to the artistic process itself because of the zeal that it inspires, the rituals associated with making and beholding, and even the churchlike quality of art museums and other spaces designated for the display and appreciation of art. There is an almost trancelike state evoked by serious art making—an intense "reverie-like" concentration that psychologist Mihaly Csikzentmihalyi has described as a state of "flow"—a concentration "so intense that there is no attention left over to think about anything irrelevant, or to worry about problems. Self-consciousness disappears, and the sense of time becomes distorted" (1990, p. 71).

This loss or realization of self, this total engagement, is apparent when artists are deep in their work. We can also see it in preschoolers so involved in their pretend play that they are unaware of adult attempts at interruption. It is apparent in the art making of young children like Octavia when the talking-painting-moving-process of creating takes over. These romanticized "swept-away" behaviors may contribute to the air of suspicion that, perhaps ironically, surrounds activities filled with such emotive power and promise. Although this sort of intensity can be experienced in the workplace or in social interactions, it is most often regarded as the "whatever it is that makes them do it" of art making. And artists are both revered and resented for engaging repeatedly in an enterprise that is both so precious and profound. Adult artists may even be likened to children at play because their work seems as engaging and transporting as the child's industrious activity of making sense of the world.

Psychologists and educators have taken these comparisons seriously and investigated at length the potential similarities between the "playful" productions of young children and the "work" of adult artists (Davis, 1991a, 1993c, 1997a, 1997b; Davis & Gardner, 1992, 1993). Similarities are cited not only in the intensity of engagement in process, but also in the expressive content of their respective artistic products. Whatever the similarities explored, distinctions between the art making of artists and children are usually drawn around the issue of intention. Seurat's intention to capture light and sensation, like Tolstoy's striving to communicate emotion are, as Tolstoy indicates, "conscious" or deliberate. But is 4-year-old Octavia consciously vesting her work with the joyful emotion she felt at the zoo? Is she, like Tolstoy, painting in order to communicate that emotion? With the dots she makes in the background of her work, is she, like Seurat, trying to capture the sensation of light? Is it intention or intuition that guides her movement?

Art historian Jonathan Fineberg has studied the role of child art in the work of modern artists. Citing an emotive link, he quotes the German painter Caspar David Friedrich, who wrote in 1830, "The only true source of art is our heart, the language of a pure childlike spirit" (Fineberg, 1997, p. 2). But the painter, Paul Klee, whose work incorporates images from child art, cautioned, "Don't translate my works to those of children. . . . They are worlds apart. . . . Never forget the child knows nothing of art; the artist on the contrary is concerned with the conscious formal compositions of his pictures, whose representational meaning comes about with *intention* . . . " (cited in Gardner, 1980, p. 8). For Klee, that intention was, as it was for Tolstoy, closely tied to emotion. Klee wrote in his diary: "I create pour ne pas pleurer [*so as not to cry*]: that is the first and last reason" (cited in Arnheim, 1969, p. 254).

The view of the artist as manipulating representational meaning with a certain and presumably effective intention may seem daunting. Where would a nascent artist begin in the process of intentional manipulation of something as loosely defined and encountered as Aristotle's fear and pity or Seurat's response to light? In this intention/emotion-driven view of art making, how does the artist begin to control the impact of the emotive content of the work? Do Klee's tears find in his work such aesthetic shape that perceivers necessarily recognize the impetus? How does Tolstoy know the reader reexperiences the very emotion with which he has "infected" his work? How can something as apparently clearly focused as intention be linked with something so amorphous as feeling? Is the communication of emotion always or even most often as the artist intends it to be received?

The Uncertainty of Intention

I remember with some angst a final solo performance I rendered in completion of a course in acting for teenagers at the American Academy of Dramatic Arts in New York. Pouring my deeply felt emotion into a tragic soliloquy from Eugene O'Neill's *All God's Children Got Wings*, I was devastated by my teacher's response. After encouraging and hearty applause, he exclaimed to my despair, "You were born for comedy. You have the stage presence of Rosalind Russell." Was the experience of feeling I'd known insufficient to the challenge of my part? Could I not summon up the appropriate emotion to invest as a performer the qualities of sadness that O'Neill had offered the audience in his words? Was my attempt laughable? Or did certain gestures and modes of presentation seem recognizable to this veteran as elements for a venue in which I'd more usefully spend my time? How can an artist be certain that the "external signs"—the gestures or "images expressed in works"—will be received as they are intended, infecting with the same strand of emotion with which they are infected?

From an emotive/experiential messy edged perspective, it would seem impossible for there to be a specific outcome—one that could be predicted with accuracy—from the dynamic between artist and audience. The audience brings an unpredictable and ever changing cadre of experience that determines its response. One reason we can repeatedly return to great works of art, music, and literature is that our changing experiential contexts allow us to find new meanings from the same artistic source. Differences in responses among readers of literature, perceivers of works of visual art, or listeners to music are affected by distinctions among contexts such as belief systems, personal experiences or, as literary theorist Stanley Fish has suggested, "social and institutional circumstances" (1980).

I am reminded in these considerations of the explanation of "expression" provided by the Iraqi architect and critic Rifat Chadirji (Davis, 1986). Chadirji shared the story of a man who walks into a museum of history, and looking in a glass case, catches sight of an ancient tool. At the edge of the tool there is a flaw, a dent. Looking carefully at that dent, the museum-goer discovers that he is deeply moved. He envisions the person making that tool, and imagines that in his careful making and for whatever reason, the maker is distracted; perhaps he thinks of his wife who is at a distance or his child who is sick. For whatever human reason, the maker of the tool has been distracted and his hand has slipped and left this mark. And thousands of years later in this museum, this museum-goer notices the mark and is moved. That, Chadirji says, is "expression"—the kind of expression we find in art: the imprint of experienced emotion discovered and reexperienced across time and place.

Of course Chadirji's perceiver may be telling the whole story. Perhaps the piece was dropped by a moving man on its way to being placed in the case. Perhaps the slip of the tool infuriated the toolmaker and made him abandon his effort, or the dent came from its contact with a failed effort at breaking stone. The significance of the story lies in the fact that perception of expression is an active process. The perceiver brings her own meaning-making capacities to whatever conversation is perpetuated across time through objects—be they crafted for practical use and/or deliberately shaped as works of art meant to convey emotion.

Tolstoy's and Klee's emphasis on the intention of the artist would place Chadirji's tool outside the realm of art where one might also find my failed attempt at tragedy. The audience for art is an important factor in any explanation of the artistic process. If it is art only when it successfully delivers emotion, the recipient of the emotion that is enclosed in the work plays an essential part in the realization of the work's artistry. In discussions of whether we can consider as art the strongly expressive drawings of young children like Octavia, the burden is always placed on the perceiver. We may be moved by, and therefore consider as art, work that the child has created for other reasons, perhaps with no artistic intention at all.

Debates over the display as art of objects that were not created as such—for example, sacred objects created for use in tribal rituals—represent heated controversy in current museum settings (see Karp & Wilson, 1996). What is lost if an object that is used in one culture for sacred activities is only appreciated by another culture for its aesthetic aspects? What if the object was not designed to be art and to be valued for those "special effects" that convey emotion or, evoking another aesthetic context, for its beauty? Who decides what is and can and should be art? Who has the right to appreciate a hammer or tool as one would appreciate a painting or work of literature? Who can rightly name as art the zoo painting of a 4-year-old child just because it seems to embody and perhaps therefore to evoke emotion?

While the uncertainty of intention clouds the issue, the communication of emotion persists—if not as an articulated mandate for art, at least as an expectation or assumption. Contemporary poet laureate Mark Strand extoling the historic work of Andrew Marvell, explains, "Something beyond knowledge compels our interest and our ability to be moved by a poem" (2000, p. 41). In describing the realist paintings of 20th-century American artist Edward Hopper, Strand could be speaking of Seurat's expressive achievements when he says the works "transcend the appearance of actuality and locate the viewer in a virtual space where the influence and availability of feeling predominate" (2001, p. vii).

But this responsive feeling space, this "something beyond knowledge," like the potentially off-putting intensity of art making, can as easily add to an air of disdain as to a reverential celebration of art. Do I want to be moved? Do I fear the emotion a work may evoke? Do I believe, as Tolstoy does, that the ability to unite through emotion a maker and perceiver is at the heart of the artistic encounter and at the heart of the promise art holds for bringing human beings together in unified and empathetic action? Does art make real, relevant, and even essential the truth of a shared humanity that is most often only and surely sufficiently discussed in religious and philosophical treatises? Dare we even suggest that art is about love?

Tolstoy ends his essay on this very topic:

> The purpose of art in our time consists in transferring from the realm of reason to the realm of feeling the truth that people's well-being lies in being united among themselves and in establishing, in place of the violence that now reigns, that Kingdom of God, that is of love—which we all regard as the highest aim of human life. Perhaps in the future science will open to art still newer, higher ideals, and art will realize them: but in our time, the purpose of art is clear and definite. The task of Christian arts is the realization of the brotherly union of men. (1898/1995, p. 167)

Historical Context

Whatever art's travels since Tolstoy's 19th-century reflection, the challenge voiced in the passage above that science might open to art still "higher" ideals persists today. History abounds with examples of science informing art and art informing science. Philosopher Israel Scheffler (1991), in his wonderful essay, "In Praise of the Cognitive Emotions" challenges the ferocity of the distinctions made between the two. He asserts, "Cognition cannot be cleanly sundered from emotion and assigned to science, while emotion is ceded to the arts, ethics, and religion. All these spheres of life involve both fact and feeling; they relate to sense as well as sensibility" (p. 3).

Whether falsely or usefully polarized, these alternative "spheres of life" hold strong attractions for artists working to brave new terrain, and there is much to learn from artists' efforts to integrate both areas into their work. Indeed, the natural merging of art and science in the work of Renaissance artist Leonardo da Vinci (who explored both domains with passion and vision) provides models for modern interdisciplinary curricula in schools and after-school programs (Chiu, 2000). Art teachers in schools are invariably the ones who are asked to uncover links between arts and non-arts courses, as if there was some shared knowledge that, as artists, they naturally attend to both. No matter the extent to which art and science are poised in opposition in a thinking/feeling dynamic, their commerce and interrelationship enhance the work of artists and give rise to new understandings and realizations of art.

In Sondheim's *Sunday in the Park with George*, the second act moves from the bucolic 19th-century park portrayed in the Seurat painting to the 20th-century New York art scene. Here the great-grandson of

Seurat, a "kinetic sculptor" (like the cyber artists that abound in electronic studios and on the Internet today) is working with laser light to create a "chromolume" that he hopes will shock and transform the thinking of those art critics and patrons who ultimately decide whether work is creative (see Davis & Gardner, 1997; Gardner, 1993; Csikzentmihalyi, 1996). The anguished young Seurat, like his great grandfather inventing pointillism, is "playing" with light and trying to do something "new." Evoking the essentiality of human expression, the pointillist Muse/mistress, Dot, speaks across time to her discouraged progeny: "Anything you do, let it come from you. Then it will be new" (Sondheim & Lapine, 1991, p. 171).

From the rich romantic period at which Tolstoy wrote and Seurat painted, artistic movements have embraced a variety of changing perspectives on the form and content of artistic expression. A modernist ethic (about 1859–1970) sought to extend traditional boundaries and canonical understandings of what is art. A postmodernist movement (starting about 1970 to present) goes further still and attempts to erase boundaries, deconstruct authority, and question instead what isn't art. Emotion is addressed directly in the classical portrayals found in representational narrative paintings where sad stories and their unfortunate protagonists are displayed with articulate visual detail. But emotion may be more vividly portrayed in the subtle luminescence of impressionist and postimpressionist paintings where the clear-cut edges of literal representation, as in *La Grande Jatte*, are made blurry by the moving effects of color and light.

Where the impressionists played with softening the edges of literal representation, a group of modernists rejected completely the need for art to present literal versions of individuals, objects, or events. The modernist era introduced abstract work that appears at first glance to refer to nothing beyond its own aesthetic features or frame. This new direction can be seen in the work of the modernist painter/abstract expressionist Mark Rothko (see Plate 2). Rather than tell a literal story, Rothko presents as the metaphoric subject of his work stacks of simple blocks of muted color that serve as agents to the expression and evocation of emotion. In a lecture at the Pratt Institute in New York in 1958, Rothko said of his work, "My current pictures are involved with the scale of human feeling, the human drama, as much of it as I can express" (cited in Horsley, 1998–1999, p. 4). The details of expression differ; but from the earliest classic representational paintings to the nonrepresentational triumphs of the modernist period, emotion has remained high on the list of what to portray. On another occasion, sounding much like Tolstoy, Rothko said that his paintings were "not art." Finding the category limiting, he said that what he was involved in was "communication on an exalted level of experience" (p. 8).

In a postmodern work of art such as an installation in a museum of checkbook stubs or toy airplanes—where traditional understandings of what and how art represents experience have been exploded or left behind, one might ask what place emotion can possibly hold. Does the excitement the viewer feels knowing the artist may be hiding behind a door in the gallery filled with toy planes count as emotive content for the work? What if some of the checks have been written to doctors or hospices? Can the checkbook stubs serve the same expressive function as Chadirji's ancient tool? Can the arrangement of objects (usually thought to be the province of a curator) count as artistic process when the individual doing the arranging is an artist? When the viewer has to think hard about the what and the why of a work of art, she may seem less available to the emotive content or effect of the piece. When the expected lines (such as the frame of the canvas or the proscenium arch of the theater) between art and life are erased or redrawn, where can or do we find familiar markers such as intention, expression, and communication?

Social Reconciliation

The landscape of postmodern art is heavy with the shadow of AIDS, the peril of social injustice, the escalation of terrorism, and the exploitation of technology. Arguably, the exploration of such issues in minimal metaphoric statements or elaborate performance pieces is almost a priori an intense and humanistic endeavor. Conceptual artists will even label the queries or the "talk about" art as art, whether the words find resolution in durable materials or not. But work that plays in the margins with the limit and power of words and resonates with the tenor of finally heard feminist voices newly defines rather than functions apart from an emotive view.

An example of such transformative effect can be found in conceptual/performance artist Suzanne Lacy's and media maven Leslie Labowitz's 1977 performance piece, *In Mourning and in Rage*. In this performance, an example of what Lacy calls "new genre public art"

(1995), ten women, whose faces were concealed behind black draped fabric hanging from headdresses that made them seven feet tall, stood in a row before the Los Angeles City Hall. They represented the ten victims of Los Angeles's Hillside strangler and served as an artistic protest to urban violence against women. The women's chilling arrival in a hearse set the stage for rewriting the image of vulnerable female mourners into that of dark and lofty champions. Mourning and rage were the emotions with which the artists had infected the piece and hoped the audience would reexperience responsively.

The artists accompanied the performance of the piece with television appearances educating the public on the details and extent of the injustices that the work addressed (Sayre, 1997, p. 60). The emotive content of the piece was powerful, even as its ideological and informational intent was clear. When the literal boundaries of the art object are replaced with conceptual or process-based entities, the conversation becomes increasingly complex. The postmodern artist crosses boundaries between negotiating product, process, education, humanism, ethics, inquiry, and critical perspective. Throughout it all, the voices conversing through art struggle on with issues of heart and mind.

Tolstoy's understanding of artistic communion is of a constant social truth that brings humans together through shared experience, feeling, and concern. The content of truth and experience necessarily changes over time, but the notion of communion through art persists. Lacy and Labowitz's performance piece can be seen as a direct response to Tolstoy's call for artistic communication to replace "the violence that now reigns." Nonetheless, the immediacy of its presentation (as nontraditional performance/art that is neither framed on a wall nor bound in a book), its presentation in the public domain (as opposed to in a theater or museum or as a removed encounter reading), and the artists' active presence in the media extending the message of the work, all challenge the traditional *distanced* view of communication (from an artist working in isolation in her studio or at her desk) through a finished work to its perceiver or reader (who most likely will never see or meet the artist).

Like views of the shape of communication through art, understandings of the ways in which artists are distanced from their audiences change over time. In nonrepresentational works of modern art, like Mark Rothko's bands of color, so easily dismissed by viewers as simplistic ("my child could have done that") or unintelligible, there was the suggestion of a "self-indulgent" or "self-serving" creator who was not afraid to alienate through obscurity a whole audience of viewers. Modern artists could be viewed as creating alone in self-exploration or in closed communication with small groups of like-minded aficionados who alone understood each other's work and were shaping together a particular (and "trendy") movement in art. But the same charge could have applied to the Impressionists, or to any other movement through which artists attempt to break boundaries and brave new directions in the unique and universal realm of artistic expression.

Postmodern artists like Lacy and Labowitz have struggled to free themselves from the otherness of the "closed" conversations of previous and dominant artistic movements. With work that happens in unexpected arenas and enters public conversations on pressing topics such as identity and oppression, contemporary artists actively denounce the canons of "high art" and aspire to a more pluralistic and less "privileged" discourse. But the postmodern erasure of boundaries and defiance of definition challenges user-friendly explication. For example, if whatever it is is art only because it is artists who are doing it, the definitions of art and artist becomes both more salient and illusive. In debunking classical canons and challenging the notion of a canon itself, postmodernists have been suspected of unwittingly creating newly forbidding albeit alternative sets of artistic tenets (see Markowitz, 1991).

Modernist art critic Suzi Gablik in *The Re-enchantment of Art* (1991) celebrates the work of a number of postmodern artists as a tangible bridging of the boundaries between artist and audience, a literal and veritable enactment of communication as art. Like Lacy and Labowitz, the artists that Gablik describes see the freedom of their movement as an opportunity literally, and as their art, to effect social change through direct relationships with or even in direct service to their audience. Gablik recounts the work of a young artist who, working in consultation with homeless people, hand-crafted shopping carts of softer wire that could better negotiate street travel and were individualized according to needs identified by the homeless beneficiaries whose trust the artist had gained.

While not solving with his creations the problem of homelessness, this young artist's work draws attention to a pressing issue and speaks to the possibility and importance of communication. For Gablik, communion and social responsibility can in this way be imprinted literally on a work of art. She acknowledges that these contemporary artists are working, as artists throughout history have done, at the margins of society and art. But Gablik, also sounding a bit like Tolstoy, describes these innovators as "prototypes who embody the next historical and evolutionary stage of consciousness, in which the capacity to be compassionate will be central not only to our ideals of success, but also to the recovery of both a meaningful society and a meaningful art" (1991, p. 182).

Looking beyond the visual, a similar strand may be found in the realm of drama in the work of Brazilian theater guru Augusto Boal (1979, 1992). Boal has broken down the classical boundaries between stage and audience and rewritten the part of the spectator as a "spect-actor" who participates in various degrees in what is going on on stage. In what Boal calls "forum theater," members of the community construct relevant theatrical encounters that enable them to reexperience emotions and events and to develop, through theater, problem-solving techniques that may hold long-standing "healing" powers.

Where in Greek tragedy, the audience member experienced catharsis alone in his or her seat, the audience member in Forum Theater is literally a member of the cast and at the center of the drama. In classrooms around this country, visiting artists introduce Boal-like methods and involve students in restorative dramatic exercises that address their most pressing personal and community issues. As example, actors from the educational theater group Urban Improv in Boston will take the classroom stage and enact a scene in which a protagonist the students' age is confronted with a challenge that is relevant to the out-of-school lives of the audience (see Spolin, 1986).

Whether it is the challenge of not giving in to rage when your mother is called a name or resisting peer pressure when drugs or alcohol are being shared, students are brought up as actors on the stage to take part in the action and, through theater, to imagine and portray alternatives for expressing their emotions. In these settings, the professional actors become deeply engaged in a back-and-forth with the audience: "What should Sam do? Should he go home?" And the active audience participation is expressed in lively conversation around what should happen next. One never hears a theatrical critique. Technical aspects of theater are beside the point. The students are not applauded or doubted for playing a role convincingly or moving well across the stage. In these settings emotion is the subject, vehicle, and objective of the activity and process-based interaction between artist and audience is made tangible and immediate.

Distanced by more than a century, Tolstoy's emotive view of socially ameliorative communication through art is not so removed from the direct contact and interaction accomplished as art by these socially responsible contemporary artists. Whether in the classroom or the broader public sphere, contemporary artists redefine the terms of the communion, even as they realize Tolstoy's noble intention of sharing both emotion and social responsibility through art. In the visual arts classroom in which a freewheeling individualistic expression of feeling is prioritized (see Lowenfeld & Brittain, 1947/1970); in the creative dance interaction in which self-image and esteem are targeted, or in conflict resolution through theater anywhere in the school, the emotive and healing aspects of the artistic process resonate throughout our current understandings of the arts and, as we will see, build both bridges and fences between the arts and education.

REVIEWING THE EMOTIVE
APPROACH TO THE ARTISTIC PROCESS

What can we carry forth from this selective review of literary and personal reflections on the relative centrality of emotion in the artistic process? Certain ancillary threads have been generated that inform our discourse and will gain more attention later on. They include the notion and implications of art-making providing a source of and medium for social reconciliation—of a communication that is central to the artistic process that has promise for positive societal change. Another thread addresses the significance of process (that "flow" like state) as an important attribute of art making. We have also in passing likened that attribute to a kind of religiosity that might evoke a fearfulness of whatever it is that entranced, engaged, and emotive artists do. At the center, however, is the view of art as *communicated feeling*—as emotion or feeling experienced by an artist given form through the modes and materials of art with the *intention* and presumable result of it being reexperienced by an empathetic audience.

Returning to the example of the painting scenario offered at the start of this chapter, do we see evidence of this emotive incentive in action? Applying these related lenses to the description of 4-year-old Octavia, we do observe a richness of feeling in the joyful way in which she applies the paint and in the sensory response she has both to the changes in her muddying colors and to the unfolding of her developing image. Octavia is deeply engaged in process. She speaks of the pleasure she feels in the story she is representing in her image ("I loved it at the zoo") and responds compassionately (the animal in the cage is smiling) to the events she explores in her piece. But even as we observe Octavia interacting with medium and image, we do not hear about or sense awareness on her part of an audience with whom she intends her work to communicate.

While Octavia may not have an audience of viewers in mind, she does seem to revel in her own reexperiencing of a well-loved visit to the zoo and in the turning of this experience into a vivid and engaging image of satisfaction and excitement. Is this activity, for Octavia, in any way the "conscious" expression of emotion—of "feeling experienced" in the past with which she is "infecting" her current work? Do we recognize the painting as filled with interest and engagement because of her investment of emotion in the work? Is there an alternative process holding sway in this 4-year-old's encounter with paint? In a new world in which alternative processes and definitions are finding their place, dare we call whatever it is Octavia is doing "making art"?

THE ARTISTIC PROCESS—THINKING

Constructing Cognition

We look to philosopher Nelson Goodman for Tolstoy's counterpoint as an advocate of a thinking or cognitive perspective with which we can contrast what we are calling the feeling or emotive approach. Goodman, who was also an art collector and educator, wrote on the subject of art a century after Tolstoy's treatise. Where Tolstoy saw art as an eternal truth, Goodman saw it as a transient state determined by the intellectual or cognitive rather than the emotive or experiential disposition of the artist and perceiver. In an essay (1978) whose title "When Is Art?" seems responsive to Tolstoy's *What Is Art?*, Goodman asserts that an artist doesn't need to feel anything to create a work of art; nor does a work of art (even one that expresses emotion) need to make a viewer feel anything at all.

Through the process of what Goodman calls "exploiting" the aesthetic potential of symbols (their ability under certain circumstances to be considered art), the thinking artist can vest a work of art with attributes that render it recognizable by a thinking perceiver as, for example, sad. Goodman's emphasis is on the work of art as a symbolic structure capable in itself, by virtue of the details of its construction, of embodying emotion. Considerations of whether the work moves a viewer to tears, self-recognition, or political action are not the substance of his concern. In our thinking approach, attention is turned to the features of a work and the ways in which those features, when the object itself is functioning as art, both refer to something outside of itself (the referent) and contain (display) aspects of the referent from within.

This emphasis is consistent with psychologist Rudolf Arnheim's Gestalt theory of expression in which he identifies "expression as an inherent characteristic of perceptual factors" (1966b, p. 64). This description necessarily includes among entities capable of conveying expression, inanimate objects. A weeping willow, Arnheim explains, looks sad because "the shape, direction, and flexibility of willow branches convey the expression of passive hanging" (p. 64). Secondarily, an attentive perceiver associates that "passive hanging" with human sorrow. This distinction is in line with Goodman's statement that "the properties a symbol expresses are its own property" (1976, p. 86). Whether in nature's chance construction of the willow or in the artist's deliberate construction of a heavy hanging flower, the expression of emotion is situated in the object's symbolic potential not in a distraught producer or a tearful perceiver.

What is fundamental here is that the work of art itself and as a construction is manipulated by the artist as a deft user of symbols, consciously making a symbolic connection, for example, between the gestalt of a given emotion and the work itself. Whether he is Rothko or Seurat, Goodman's thinking artist is thoughtfully adjusting aesthetic aspects such as line and composition so that emotion is perceived as exemplified by that work. You will note that Tolstoy also asserted that the artist intentionally employed "movements, lines, colors, sounds, images." The distinction lies in the respective roles assigned to artist and perceiver and the end in view for the work.

The artist's question, from a thinking perspective, is not "How do I feel?" but "Of what is the expression or manifestation of a given feeling made?" And the thinking perceiver of art's question is not "How does this work make me feel?" but "What emotion is expressed in this work?" A thinking artist may consciously use the willow tree not only as a symbol for sorrow, but as an opportunity for his or her use of drooping passive lines in drawing, weighted tones in writing, or heavy gestures in dance. The thinking artist and perceiver are figuring things out, exploring representation as a process of making and finding meaning.

A thinking manipulator of symbols is attentive to the referential possibilities for works of art and strives for complexity in that regard. A work can all at once represent an individual occurrence of an emotion, the more general gestalt of that emotion, and even serve in itself as an example of that emotion ("that painting is sad"). These complex references are the triumph of the thinking maker of art. On the feeling side, there is the suffering artist whose pain spills into his work and is everywhere evident to a sympathetic and moved audience; on the thinking side, there is the skilled manipulator of symbols deciding (perhaps on a day on which she feels perfectly happy) to create a piece (through her knowledge of the various ways in which different representative elements can work) that is recognizable by a thoughtful audience as sad. Where the feeling artist struggles to communicate, the thinking artist conspires to construct. Where for the feeling artist, thought is harnessed in service of emotion, for the thinking artist, emotion is a vehicle for demonstrating the prowess of thought.

Earlier on, I offered Paul Klee's diary entry "I create *pour ne pas pleurer*: that is the first and last reason" as a simple statement of the role of process in an emotive approach. In the context of a feeling perspective, the statement refers to the therapeutic nature of art—the release of emotion that artistic production apparently can provide for both creator and audience. Rudolf Arnheim points instead to artistic content when he explains the same excerpt from a cognitive perspective. He writes, "It is evident that Klee's drawings and paintings could serve so great an artist and so intelligent a human being as an alternate to weeping only by clarifying for him what there was to weep about and how one could live with, and in spite of, this state of affairs" (1969, p. 254). The alternative of intellectual investigation over emotive release perhaps inadvertently highlights the space in between.

In a similar vein, Nelson Goodman might have rewritten Tolstoy's statement that "The purpose of art in our time consists in transferring from the realm of reason to the realm of feeling . . . " Goodman's version might read, "The purpose of art in our time consists in transferring from the realm of feeling to the realm of reason. . . . " For Tolstoy, the intention is to inspire empathetic action through the provocation of human emotions. The medium is feeling. For Goodman the intention is to provoke intellectual reflection though the manipulation of symbols. The medium is thinking. The transference of human emotion to symbolic referent is marked by symptoms that can be recognized by the discriminating mind of a thoughtful human being.

Art as a When

Interestingly, where Goodman speaks of "symptoms," Tolstoy speaks of "infection." It may be a coincidence of terminology or an accident in translation from Russian. But across both theorists there is this notion of illness, of a state or physical condition evoked by or insinuated into a work of art. It suggests, on first reading, a views of art as, like health or disease, driven by forces beyond our reach and capable of taking us over, getting us down, or even manifesting itself as a kind of irrationality or madness. This view of wanton irrationality is in line with Socrates' assertion that the arts can induce a loss of reason and present a challenge to rational demeanor and to the appreciation of high ideals. Indeed, Socrates as well used for artistic communication the term "contagion." The view also anticipates abiding suspicions of art classrooms as containing chaotic activities that invite a level of excitement and autonomy not welcome in disciplined schools.

But Goodman's view of symptoms of the aesthetic is far from that of a rapturous or wild view of infection. Goodman in fact derides what he calls "tingle" theory in art (1976), that "way all over" that some say art makes them feel. Instead, Goodman's use of the term is meant to illustrate that a work's status as art is relative and transient, "it comes and goes," depending, like illness and wellness, on the degree to which certain symptoms present (1978, p. 70). Fever may let me know that I am not well; and it may pass or become more or less severe. Similarly, intense coloration may draw my attention to a painting and to more or less extent and for more or less time engage my interest in exploring what I perceive as meaning in the image. These symptoms then concern the amount and kind of attention that works of art require or invite from the viewer or audience. I can walk by or attend to the ten women in front of the Los Angeles Court House. I can dismiss as meaningless the painting by Rothko or see it as inviting a different

kind of attention and need for analysis than a painting in which meaning can be literally read from the story that is depicted.

For Goodman, works of art are symbolic structures that refer in particular ways to the things and/or ideas they represent. It is the nature
of that reference (recognized by an active perceiver) that exhibits the
symptoms that Goodman says prevail *when* a work is functioning as
art. As an example of the *when*, Goodman contrasts the lack of attention
we give a stone lying in a driveway with the observation of detail we
might direct toward that stone if it were illuminated on a pedestal in
a museum. Ignored features or properties of the stone demand attention *when* it is displayed in the museum setting. A Rembrandt painting
used to shelter someone from the rain functions in that circumstance
as protection, not art (1978).

Consider Andy Warhol's well-known 1962 screen-printed image,
Campbell's Soup Can, created a decade before Goodman wrote "When
Is Art?" At a recent retrospective of Warhol's work at the Museum of
Modern Art, I could hear some viewers laughing at that image, dismissing as "non-art"—something more fit for a billboard or a grocery
shelf—the commercial icon that apparently fascinated Warhol. "It isn't
even pretty. I wouldn't hang that in my home." But others studied the
image carefully, its placement on the page or wall, the making of the
familiar unfamiliar, the excitement of confronting this world-famous
piece.

Did Warhol make the Campbell soup can art by asking viewers to
attend to it in his presentation? Did the viewers who attended so carefully make the soup can image art while those who ignored it did not?
Would viewers of the show now go out into the world as the British
art historian Ernst Gombrich suggested museum-goers might, with a
"painter's eye, or more technically speaking with a painter's mental
set" (1960, p. 306) and now look at soup cans and other things in their
daily lives as sources for or examples of art? And what of the package designer who designed the Campbell soup can? Was it his or her
design that made the can a subject for a work of art or the place of
Campbell soup in the lives and advertising experiences of American
consumers? Could that soup can at the same time function as art and
not as art? Do any of us consider how that Campbell's soup can makes
us feel?

When works are considered art, Goodman tells us, they ask more of
the perceiver than a functional decoding or technical reading of their

meanings (1978). You can decode a line in a cardiogram by attending to the precise points it touches in order to obtain data that describe a patient's medical condition. But if you put that same line in a painting of a mountain range, you may find its importance lies in its very construction. A thick bold line will contribute to a difference in the meaning represented in the painting than a thin or watery one. The viewer attends in the case of the painting to properties of the line itself rather than to the data points of information to which it refers. And one viewer may detect a different significance from the wateriness of the line than would another. Aesthetic symbols do not invite precise, right or wrong responses. Aesthetic symbols have messy edges that invite multiple interpretations (see Langer, 1953).

Symptoms of the Aesthetic

Accordingly, in terms of Goodman's symptoms, works, when they are functioning as art, display one or all or some combination of the following features which have to do with their symbolic functioning, or the ways in which they refer to the meanings they represent: (1) *syntactic density,* or a "thickness" of presentation that requires interpretative rather than literal reading or decoding; (2) *semantic density,* or "complexity" of reference indicating fine differences in meaning that require attention to detail; (3) *relative repleteness,* or a "fullness" of construction such that meaning is contained in the physical features of the work beyond its obvious reference to an object or idea; (4) *exemplification,* or "participation" in meaning such that the work is a sample (metaphorically) of what it represents; and (5) *multiple and complex reference,* or "multiplicity" such that a work may be serving many or interacting functions, for example literally representing an object, metaphorically exemplifying an emotion, and at the same time referring to different and interacting meanings (1978). The expressive portrayal of a sad child, created by a great artist out of downturned lines, muted colors, and weighted shapes demands a certain attention not only to what it literally represents, but also to the fine details of presentation and reference—the construction of the image as well as its impact within and beyond that structure. Its reference to objects and ideas is complex. Among its functions, it: (1) literally represents a sad child; (2) refers more generally to the concept of sorrow; and (3) is in itself (metaphorically, not literally) a sad painting.

In reducing Goodman's opaque and provocative symptoms to thickness, complexity, fullness, participation, and multiplicity, I have probably said both more and less than I should. It would suffice to note that these symptoms all suggest a mode of perception, a mandate for making sense, that is rigorous and thoughtful, and apparently far from what we have described as the experientially available emotive perspective. Requiring careful attention to literal, structural, and metaphoric reference, symbols, when they function as art, appeal to the head even when their various objects of reference speak to the heart. It is not the move to tears or sisterhood that is of concern in this perspective; it is the manipulation of symbols in conscious and complex representation.

Figuring out the method, circumstance, and implication of representation seems far from feeling communion through a work of art. The thinking approach speaks to a conversation around ideas that may be represented both in the content and form of a work of art. The feeling approach speaks to communication through art of the unique and universal emotions that join us as human beings. The thinking approach situates artist and perceiver in critical discourse around symbolic structures; the feeling approach situates artist and perceiver in a shared identification with emotive content. A thinking approach frames artistic encounters as learning opportunities for both artists and audiences who make and find meaning in the same artistic productions. An emotive approach frames artistic encounters as personal opportunities for both artists who give shape to unruly experience and audiences who recognize in that shaping their lived lives and personal identities.

From the feeling perspective, intention involves deliberate conveyance of felt experience, perhaps even with the functional objective of effecting social or personal change. From the thinking perspective, meaning is unresolved in the work—fodder for a coconstruction of understanding in which both artist and audience play an active, essential, and unpredictable role. In the feeling perspective, artist and audience engage in a shared personal relationship; in a thinking perspective, artist and audience are engaged in interactive cognitive rapport: experience versus discourse, intuition versus interpretation, bonding versus building. Perhaps addressing both approaches and their respective emphasis on the perceiver of art, 20th-century graffiti artist Keith Haring put it this way: "Art lives through the imagination of the people who are seeing it. Without that contact there is no art" (quoted in Celant, 1992, p. 52).

While the "symptoms" discussion serves to highlight the different tenure and detail of a thinking versus feeling approach, it also serves as important groundwork for more recent considerations of both children's artistic production and adult attitudes toward the role and function of the arts in education. For example, do we already see in Tolstoy's approach the setting of a stage on which art education is viewed as an arena in which children can release and communicate emotion? And do we find in the thinking or cognitive approach ground laying for a view of art education as an intellectual arena in which the skills of careful observation and thoughtful interpretation might be cultivated? At the heart of these perspectives two roles for arts learning abide: that of the maker and that of the perceiver of art. From a feeling perspective in which intention is associated with experience sharing, the role of artist may seem more pivotal than that of audience. From a cognitive perspective in which critical perception is emphasized, the role of perceiver of art may hold more importance. Shall we educate our children as makers, perceivers, or both—and why?

Goodman's distinctions are reflective more broadly of what is known as a "symbol systems" approach to meaning making. For symbol systems philosophers (see Langer, 1942, 1953), different kinds of symbols invite different kinds of responses from perceivers—responses that range, as we have discussed, from right or wrong answers to multiple interpretations. When considering symbols (entities that refer to or represent other entities), we see that various types of symbols (e.g., gestures, words, graphic marks) function in different sets or systems. Accordingly, dance can be thought of as a system or language of gestures (gestural symbolization); poetry of words (verbal symbolization); marks of drawing (graphic symbolization). These systems of symbols, under certain circumstances, can function as what Goodman calls the "languages of art" (1976).

In the various systems of symbols available to the artist in his or her construction of a work of art, a crucial difference lies between what are called "discursive" or "notational" and "non-discursive" or "presentational" symbols (Langer, 1953). Discursive or notational symbols, like numbers or words, are made up of arbitrary details (e.g., dots and lines for musical notes) that have little to do (structurally) with the meanings they convey. Note the line in Goodman's cardiogram. Presentational or non-discursive symbols are those that embody meaning (as with the painted line in the mountain landscape or the graphic rendering of the sorrowful flower) even in their construction.

Extending the notion of the arbitrariness of the physical properties of the cardiogram line to discursive symbols like letters of the alphabet, we learn that the shape "a" designates a sound and can be combined with other letters into a language of words that we use to describe and manipulate objects and ideas. But the mark itself has nothing in its presentation as a curved line with tail that would connect it, for example, to the apple with which it is so often associated in alphabet books (see Sloboda & Rogers, 1983). We can read *a*, we can recognize the word apple, and we know that we are talking about a particular fruit and not another, just as we know the mark "6" for some agreed-upon reason designates six items and not five. But there's nothing about the curved and closed line that comprise the number six that tells us on its own of the "sixness" it represents. The *a* and the "6" are marks, notations like individual musical notes, that *designate* rather than *describe*. Like the data points on Goodman's cardiogram, these marks deliver meaning that can be "read" correctly or not.

A painting of an apple, on the other hand, may be both more direct and more ambiguous. Symbol systems theorists would call the image of the apple a first-order symbol; it refers directly to and bears perceived physical similarities to the apple it represents. The word *apple*, on the other hand, is a second-order symbol. Rather than refer directly to the fruit, it represents the set of sounds we use to name the fruit and the letters of which it is constructed bear no physical likeness to the apple it represents. In spite of its more direct reference, however, the image of the apple provides more questions than answers.

Perhaps the red the artist uses has a lot of yellow in it . . . it might be orange, could the image be an orange? There seem to be shadows around the apple—or are those shadings actually more apples—three or maybe even four more? We need to attend carefully to the details of the construction of the painting not only to identify the subject of the work but also to interpret meaning that may go beyond the apple itself. Is it a warm round shape that embodies a sense of well-being? Is it dark and placed on its own in the center of an empty canvas . . . perhaps an ironic vehicle for unrealized well-being? How does the child dressed in red at the corner of the stage on which she is participating in a "fruit" dance, perceive and represent her "appleness"? We need to look carefully and consider her thinking as it is reflected in the pose she strikes, the shape she gives her body, and perhaps even in the expression she mindfully or in spite of herself displays on her face.

Uncertainty of Interpretation

We attend in a different way to non-notational or presentational symbols whose display itself contains the unclear meaning we must thoughtfully interpret. Our interpretation in itself will have messy edges ("this apple painting may ironically represent unrealized well-being or perhaps speak more to a sense of power and isolation") and no doubt differ from one perceiver to another. But it is out of our attention to the details of presentation of the image that we construct an interpretation. Those aspects or conditions of presentation are what Goodman is calling the "symptoms of the aesthetic." His presentation of these properties (1978) is in itself dense, complex, and open to multiple interpretations, such as mine (from thickness to multiplicity). In this way, Goodman has pushed the limits of conventional clarity and exhibited in his writing about the symptoms of the aesthetic the very attributes he describes.

The symbols or notes that mediate music are less negotiable than the marks that are used in graphic symbolization or the gestures and movements that dancers employ. For example, in the realm of drawing, a wiggly line can mean many things—in music, middle C is middle C. An extended arm can mean many things in dance—middle C is middle C. But musical notes combined and structured into aesthetic works (like crystal-clear words into dreamy poetic language) are interpreted and performed by thoughtful musicians and invite the same sort of exploration of meaning involved in perceiving any complex work of art.

There are those who argue that a technically skilled performance of a piece of music that lacks emotion demonstrates more of a thinking rather than a feeling approach to art. We often hear that a musician is technically skilled but artistically flawed, as if technique were associated with head and artistry with heart. But, from a symbol systems approach, the expression of emotion in the medium of art is a cognitive triumph. The really "thoughtful" performer is the one who goes beyond "reading" and "playing" the notes to "interpreting" and "exploiting" their aesthetic potential, thereby demonstrating to the audience that the music embodies emotion.

Aristotle suggested in the *Poetics* that "even dancing imitates character, emotion, and action" (1951, p. 9). Philosopher Arnold Berleant (1991) takes exception with the "imitative" possibility that gesture or dance movements might constitute a "translatable" vocabulary for expressing emotion. Indeed, he says that "dance does not express; it is" (p. 163). He objects to the confusion in any art between embodiment and communication of emotion, saying that dance "embodies characteristic experiences" and that "this incarnation of feeling, combined with the perceptual unity of perceiver and performer is what gives dance its emotional force" (p. 163).

There is a "when" to dance as well. Aesthetician Frances Sparshott points out, "anything can be done as dance or can be called dance, just as anyone can make random marks and call them poetry; what is at issue is what can be done meaningfully and sustain itself as dance" (1993, p. 230). Poet Kenneth Koch has also made this distinction. Citing the poet Valery, Koch notes the fact that poetry is kind of a "language within a language"—made out of ordinary words put together in such a way that whatever was said in a poem could not adequately be translated into ordinary language (1998, p. 19). For Koch, as for Valery, there is a transformation in poetry through which the language that is used becomes both poetic statement and musical song. The words have been transformed, like Goodman's line from cardiogram to mountain range, so that the listener hears beyond their content (the opposite of attending to driving instructions), attends to the tones and rhythm of the language (as one attends to music without words) as vehicles of the ambiguous meanings that the poem presents.

We may celebrate in this context the notion of ambiguity, of alternative and wonderfully unclear meaning. This notion, however, may at the same time be unsettling and is certainly not rooted in the seeds of specificity associated with subjects fit for school. When the teacher asks the English class, "What was this author trying to say?" she implies: (1) that the work was an attempt (not necessarily successful) at communication on the part of the writer; (2) that something for sure was intended to be said that she knows and you can too; and (3) that meaning is clear and durable and less negotiable than our symbol systems ruminations may suggest. The teacher also implies that works of art are translatable—that we can talk clearly about what art unclearly proposes and that this "talk about" can be measured and evaluated. The voices of our thinking perspective in art (Berleant, 1991; Goodman, 1976, 1978; Koch, 1998) would take issue with these claims.

Do we find ourselves then, even from a thinking perspective in which we focus on the nature and multiplicity of meaning-making through symbolic functioning in art, still in a territory (as we were with the realm of transference of known and felt emotion) that is on uncertain footing on the terrain of school? Is school irrevocably a place where the transmittance of information is valued over the construction of meaning and measurable right or wrong is pursued more earnestly than individually mediated interpretation? While modes of thinking are clearly more valued in schools than feeling skills, is the interpretation of meaning on the part of a thoughtful audience for art driven by or separate from emotion? Do we *recognize* or *feel* sadness and is the distinction as clear as some philosophers would have us believe?

There is something much less personal in the referencing and recognition asserted by Goodman than in the infecting and communication Tolstoy describes. Goodman's artist does more thinking than feeling through the various media or languages of art. But for both, the response of the perceiver (through "re-feeling" or "re-cognizing") determines the status of the work and points to a transience of artistic status, a *when* for art. The ancient tool Chadirji studied in the museum in which through his careful attention he found expressive meaning, might be perceived by another merely as a hammer that had more or less physical value, or by its user as a means to secure a nail. My failed tragic effort in the Saturday classes of the American Academy of Dramatic Arts might have moved another viewer differently or contained symbolic details overlooked by a teacher eager to speak a response and get on with his day.

In both thought- and emotion-driven views of art, active participation of a certain sort on the part of the perceiver can confirm or deny the status of the work as art or as achieving artistic ends. But from an emotive perspective, that viewer or perceiver feels deeply and actively experiences the content of the work; indeed encounters the work with more emotional intensity than ordinary daily life may afford. From a more cognitive perspective, on the other hand, that viewer thinks hard and actively interprets the form and content of the work, and engages in the cognitive activity of interpretation more taxing and engaging than the decoding or reading of meanings through which ordinary daily life is mediated (see Parsons, 1991).

In Tolstoy, representing a view of art as felt or experienced emotion reaching another through the work, we find a sense of constancy or truth in a shared humanity that may communicate through affect across circumstance and time. In Goodman, our touchstone for a more thinking or cognitive view of art, we find a view of transience or negotiability of artistic status that depends on a certain kind of thinking, recognizing, and agreeing that may or may not be present when a work is questioned as art. Goodman, like others who see the languages of art as systems of symbols, recognizes that humans are distinguished from other animals by their need for or interest in symbolizing and therefore there is even in the simple action of decoding or interpreting symbols a shared human capacity that also necessarily crosses the boundaries of circumstance and time.

Symbol system philosophy resonates with the thread of Aristotle's claim that the "instinct of imitation" is implanted in humans from childhood. The imitation of human action in poetry, theater, and visual art, like the imitation of sounds of nature in music or of everyday gestures in dance are transformative. The artist's recreation of what we see, hear, and witness render new constructions of meaning that may change forever or leave no impact on the way we make sense of our lives. Nonetheless, and here is where symbol system philosophers come in, the "wrapping" of experience in the media of the arts provides new encounters that need to be "unpacked" by attentive and most thoughtful meaning-makers: those who are audience to and active purveyors of the products of artistic thinking (Reddy, 1979). Symbol systems provide the various vocabularies that are the media of different art forms. Interpreters of art need to be multilingual to find meaning within and across these cognitively mediated "languages of art."

Historical Context

Necessarily, Goodman's thinking emerges from a different context—a most different backdrop from Tolstoy's. On the art historical front, Goodman was deep into the modernist era and his attention to new modes of reference and artistic expression seems parallel to the new exploration of media and representation that artists such as Rothko were exploring. As a philosopher, Goodman was particularly sensitive to what was called the cognitive revolution that in the second half of the 20th century was being played out in the fields of philosophy, psychology, aesthetics, and education. Experts of the scene have placed the cognitive revolution—a revolution in thinking about thought—in the mid-50s (see Gardner, 1985). The "revolution" was connected to and perhaps most tangibly imprinted on the historic invention of the electronic computer. The electronic computer offered evidence that we knew enough about what transpired in the human mind to recreate it with impressive effect in a machine, a machine that served as a model of human thought and as a metaphor for human thinking (Davis & Gardner, 1992).

Technology would prove to be a resource and a challenge to 20th-century artists. Keith Haring described his interest in chance in his work as a response to the computer age: "Computers and word processors operate only in the world of numbers and rationality. The human experience is basically irrational" (in Celant, 1992, p. 52). While computers generated an interest in issues of planning and organization of thought, Haring insisted that his drawings, even for large murals, were never preplanned. Similarly, Picasso said of his work in progress, not only that it was not planned but also that only after he had made a drawing did he know what he meant (in Arnheim, 1962). Haring felt his spontaneous attitude toward working was "particularly relevant in a world increasingly dominated by purely rational thought" (Celant, 1992, p. 52).

In the early part of the 20th century (1920s to 30s), a behaviorist approach dominated the field of psychology, with necessary implications for other disciplines, including the field of education. Behaviorism focused on outward and visible phenomena such as how individuals act and react in various environments. Turning their lenses inward, cognitivists would focus on how individuals represent and make meaning out of experience. Where behaviorists would look, for example, at how individuals responded to reward or rejection, cognitivists would look at how individuals constructed understandings of those terms. Where behaviorists would study reaction, cognitivists would study interpretation.

Though difficult to quantify, the emotive view of art that we have been considering would not be entirely out of line with a behaviorist perspective. What does art do? Does it make one teary or overtly happy? Does it hold our attention for long periods of time or not? From a behaviorist perspective, outward manifestations would bear the imprint of the effects on the individual of a work of art. Marketing researchers estimating the relative success of exhibits at art museums would count the number of minutes museum-goers stand in front of different works or the number of images observed in one visit. Harder to monitor are activities like problem finding and solving, and manipulating symbols in such structures as language—let alone within and through the languages of art. Art museum educators and curators embracing a cognitive perspective are challenged to find evidence of the understandings and information that museumgoers take from their viewing—regardless of how long they stand in front of a painting.

In braving the study of things harder to measure than the manifest details of human behavior, a number of these cognitive scholars took interest in the thoughtful activity of constructing understanding through art. Some cognitive developmental psychologists turned to children's artistic production as a resource for determining intellectual development with regard to quantifiable aspects of information processing such as memory retention and incidences of complex versus simple representations (see Dennis, 1991). They might see whether Octavia at age 4 could remember the instructions to and put together all at once in her drawing: (1) the lion in its cage; (2) a mouse under the cage; (3) Octavia waving at the lion; and (4) her mother looking on.

Still others were drawn to children's development in the more qualitative aspects: the messy interactive processes of artistic production and perception (Gardner & Perkins, 1989). Advocating the latter approach, the already mentioned psychologist Rudolf Arnheim, a leader in art-related cognitive theory, cautioned that a "compulsive need for quantitative exactness" could obliterate an understanding of what art is all about. He pointed out, "The metronome speed of music can be subjected comfortably to statistics, but it is the rhythm rather than the beat that holds the secret, and we are guilty of neglect of duty if we fail to deal with rhythm because it requires qualitative description" (1966b, pp. 19–20).

In psychology, the leader in representing a cognitive perspective was the legendary and prolific Jean Piaget, an epistemologist, or expert on knowledge, whose close study of his own children's intellectual development provided both a great source of information and new methodological strategies (1985; Piaget & Inhelder, 1948). Piaget saw the child as an active constructor of knowledge moving through a series of hierarchical intellectual stages from birth to adolescence. These stages describe developing ways in which the child learns from: (1) *sensorimotor,* where the child figures things out through manipulating objects; to (2) *preoperational* or *symbolic,* where the child becomes able to represent objects (to him- or herself and to others of whom he or she is becoming increasingly aware) and to anticipate action; to (3) *concrete operations,* where the child builds understanding through the manipulation of symbols that represent actual objects; to (4) *formal* operations, in which thinking, "freed from the concrete," is mediated through abstractions upon which intellectual operations may be performed—entirely in one's head (Gardner, 1982, p. 62).

These stages seem not unrelated to the recent history of Western art, as we have reviewed it from early concrete literal representation of objects in the perceived world to the manipulation of ideas apart from any clear-cut representational link. Did Piaget's stage theory approach suggest a valuing of reason over emotion? Absolutely. Piaget's view of the educational end state for the child's development was as a logician, abstract thinker, perhaps even a scientist.

Cognitive Investigation

In 1968, Nelson Goodman founded Harvard Project Zero, a research center originally dedicated to studying children's development in the different symbol systems or languages of art and the site of many of the research projects in which I have worked and that I describe later on. Perhaps Tolstoy would have recognized as good the intentions of this project that was dedicated to informing general and art education—albeit a new art education based on a view of art as a process of thought. As was true of many cognitive endeavors, the project was interdisciplinary and looked for inspiration not only to the aesthetic philosophy of Goodman but also to the developmental perspectives of epistemologist Jean Piaget and the art perceptual theories of Rudolf Arnheim.

In *Toward a Psychology of Art,* written in the mid-60s, Arnheim clearly rejected the emotive approach to the arts that had informed a view of art education as the education of senses and feelings and counted as absurd the notion that a work of art "expressed" or "transmitted" emotion: "Once it is acknowledged that emotion is nothing but the tension that accompanies practically all psychical processes, the psychologist should be able to show that emotion cannot be the content of a work of art but only a secondary effect of that content, and that art is no more emotional than is any other reasonably interesting human occupation" (1966b, p. 21). Reflecting a cognitivist/modernist perspective, Arnheim proposed that while non-artists clung to the idea that artists created " in order to communicate something to other people," artists themselves either gave no credence to or consciously separated themselves from this notion.

As the senior researcher of his "art as thinking" educational research project, Goodman trained two young graduate student assistants who went on in later years to direct Project Zero and to contribute greatly to the field's thinking on cognition, development, and art: Howard Gardner and David Perkins (1989). And in 1973, 5 years after the start of Harvard Project Zero, psychologist Howard Gardner wrote a ground-breaking book called *The Arts and Human Development* in which, with respect to the venerable Piaget, and the cumulative thinking of cognitivists and aestheticians, he proposed an alternative end-state for the thinking child. Instead of the Piagetian view of the mature individual as logician or scientist, Gardner proposed the artist as a viable end state for development and, by implication, for education.

REVIEWING THE COGNITIVE
APPROACH TO THE ARTISTIC PROCESS

What elements do we take from a view of art as thinking that can inform our journeying forth? Where with the emotive view, we embraced the centrality of emotion, communication, and intention; from the cognitive perspective, we were more concerned with issues of thought, symbolization, and interpretation. Echoing the views of those who see these elements as precarious distinctions, we must ask, What is emotion without thought that fears, embraces, or represents it? And what is thought without feeling that humanizes, confounds, and directs it? How would communication be realized without the vehicle of symbolization? Can fixity of intention ever escape the multiplicity of interpretation? The lines between thinking and feeling I believe, and believe I have shown, are more readily than clearly drawn. Even Goodman saw an active role for emotion in a cognitive approach. He explained, "To some extent, we may feel how a painting looks as we may see how it feels. . . . Emotion in aesthetic experience is a means of discerning what properties a work has and expresses" (1976, p. 248).

A return to the painting of young Octavia may help to exercise and clarify our own thinking about thinking. When we describe the fluid process of Octavia's thoughts of her visit to the zoo, finding form in the expressive image that is her painting, we acknowledge that her thinking process is out of sight, but hear reference to it throughout her endeavor. She speaks of the experience that she is embodying in the work. There is reference to the encounter itself, and arguably to meaning beyond the visit. The animal in the cage is smiling. Is this because it is safe, or because of some other underlying reason? Or is it because Octavia has one symbolic schema at hand, one representational format that is applied to all living creatures in her work—the lids and the smile?

Either explanation applies to a cognitive approach to her activity. In the former possibility, Octavia is thinking through the use of her symbols so that their construction will embody the contentment she associates with the lion. In the second possibility, Octavia has an approach to symbolization or a structured symbolic shorthand that works for her in the representation of living beings. Overall, like any artist engaged in graphic symbolization, she is problem solving around the challenge of representing three-dimensional form in two-dimensional space. All of the above point to the thoughtful construction that cognitivists posit as involved in art making as a process of problem finding and solving—rich thoughtful experience.

The fluid dot dot dotting—the activity I likened to Sondheim's layered representation of Seurat's painting process in music—this too can be interpreted as the thoughtful representation of rains or leaves—or even as the filling of space to create the sort of compositional coherence that a balanced aesthetic statement is thought or intended to have. Octavia can be regarded from an emotive process as so involved in (swept away by) the emotional process of making art that she does not notice the change in color of the paint or the muddiness of the colors she is developing. From a cognitive perspective, Octavia may be thought of as engaged in a process activity that has its own objectives—perhaps the learning involved in mixing colors or of setting one objective for oneself and seeing it change as the tools and media for construction are altered by exploration.

Interpretation is, from a cognitive perspective, what is going on both for Octavia as producer of art and for us as perceivers of the process. We make meaning out of the elements she puts forth just as she chooses lines, colors, and marks to make meaning out of an experience, to give it symbolic form that takes the encounter to another level—one that may even by some viewers and under some circumstances be regarded as art.

In citing their distinctions, we again reveal enormous overlap and interaction between the two perspectives. While a thinking versus feeling approach to art has implications that play out on the stage and in the scenes of art education, the interrelationship of the two is undeniable; indeed, the harder we work to clarify them, the blurrier the distinctions become. Nelson Goodman acknowledged the blur: "The actor or dancer—or the spectator—sometimes notes and remembers the feeling of a movement rather than its pattern, insofar as the two can be distinguished at all" (1976, p. 248). Sondheim's cross-generational muse, Dot, offers irreverent advice: "Darling, don't make such a drama. A little less thinking, a little more feeling . . . I'm just quoting Mama (1991, p. 162)."

2

The Child as Artist

OCTAVIA TWO

Octavia is entering the kindergarten at her local school. The first day is an exciting one filled with unknown expectations, unbounded excitement, and unsurpassed apprehension. An older sibling has warned Octavia that she might not have the "academic skills" to do well in her class. Her mother has spoken enthusiastically of the pleasure of having 23 other children with whom to play. An orientation visit to the school has introduced Octavia to the colorfulness of the room—the many pictures hung on the walls, the calendars of numbers, the bulletin board of children's names—and to the kindness of the head teacher, a seasoned educator who seems truly excited by the thought of another school year.

The school building is large and filled with children ranging in age from Octavia's 5 years to her older brother's 12. Entering the school, Octavia is impressed by two 8-foot-high doormen painted on the wall alongside of each door. Beyond that on the stairs going down is a hippopotamus ridden by a clown. The words painted above them read "to the" and a word Octavia doesn't know: "Gym." Up the stairs, painted trees line the walls, an eagle soars—a man in blue overalls squats under the weight of the wall's radiator, which in the wall painting; it appears he is carrying it. A visiting artist to the school oversaw the wall painting in the entrance, working after school with children from all grades, hard gloss enamel paint, and an explosion of good humor that remains in the work. The unexplained but everywhere resonant refrain in Sondheim's *Sunday in the Park*: "Children and art" (Sondheim & Lapine, 1991, p. 163).

A sixth grader's elephant has two riders sitting back to back, painted respectively by a second and fourth grader on different days. The welcoming walls evoke comfort and creativity even as they set a less organized tone than the space Octavia is to enter. Around the perimeter of the kindergarten room, above the bulletin boards are the letters of the alphabet printed as a border and tacked a little too high for close perusal. But the presence and elevation of these powerful letters is clear.

Tables and chairs rim an arena that is broken into various interest areas, each marked with a clearly written sign, some words of which Octavia knows. "Reading Corner." "Dress Up Corner." "Block Building." "Today's Activity." The space has some of the beckoning to exploration of the children's museum that Octavia visited, and the high noise level and implicit warmth of the room is welcoming and reassuring. A series of easels awaits participation. Children and art.

To Octavia's surprise, on each easel a painting has been started. Each neatly pinned-up piece of newsprint has a vertical painted line flanked by two horizontal green ovals. The sign "Flowers We See" is painted above the easels and the children are clearly invited to paint a flower-head on the top of the provided stems. This framework, like the pile of "color in the lines" printed worksheets on the desktops, is new to Octavia and lets her know that things are done in a particular way in this new place called school.

After the delight of hearing a good story in circle time, the children are invited to sit at their little tables, share boxes of big crayons, and draw for the teacher pictures of their families. Octavia feels particularly excited at the thought of the familiar activity of creating an image in this unfamiliar but energy-filled space. After all, she makes many images at home; a zoo painting she had done last year was framed in oak and set among the other artist images her mother hung on the living room wall. Her crayon drawings were plastered all over the refrigerator door. Many of them were embellished with glue and glitter, or leaves pasted on the paper and transformed into dresses for the figures she drew or into bodies for the various animals.

Octavia jumped into "family drawing" with enthusiasm. She thought she'd begin with herself. A large circle in the center of the page, the tri-angulated dress, and the half-lidded eyes—now with lashes and a bow shape on her head balanced with a sphere (pigtail?) on either side. Her mother appeared largely the same but with longer hair—a radiant smile wrapped her face. Octavia wanted to make her big brother taller than the top of the paper would allow and his somewhat squashed head add-ed interest to the humorous expression that Octavia gave him. As she thought of her brother and drew, her face felt as she perceived his—and a crooked smile found her lips. Father was next and, unfortunately, had to be squeezed into the right edge of the frame. Large shoes gave him a strong foundation and sense of presence even as his necessarily slim body bent to fill in the space left on the paper. All of the family members were drawn with great movement and joy. The image resounded with affection and vitality. The floating figures on the page were reminiscent of the work of artist Marc Chagall—the use of primary colors, the "out in space" arrangement of floating forms, the overall energy of it all. In a way that made sense to her, Octavia added some differing floating lines to fill what empty spaces persisted. She spoke quietly as she finished and with a loving look at the whole—as if she had successfully, accord-ing to Tolstoy's mandate, infected her work with emotion that could be "refelt" by the perceiver—said "my family."

The teacher and her assistant were spending time with every child's drawing. As the teacher leaned over Octavia's shoulder, Octavia felt the intimacy of her new relationship, the pride in her work, and the sheer pleasure of complete attention to her drawing. "Wonderful!" the teacher exclaimed. Octavia was proud of everyone in the room. The teacher had said "wonderful" or "beautiful" in response to everyone's image. "Now tell me about this drawing." Octavia was about to tell her about this and other drawings she had made—how she loved the process, how they were hung at home alongside of the work of other artists whose work her mother admired. But the teacher's intention was clear. She went on to ask Octavia, "Who are these people?"

In response to each naming of the members of Octavia's family, the teacher wrote in neat print sometimes above in a space or even over parts of the drawn image where there was no space: "Mother." "Father." "Brother." "Me." Then at the top of the image a title: "My

Family by Octavia." The image had been crowded before, but now it even seemed a messy backdrop for the neat letters that had been inserted to explain the content of the drawing. Any discussion of color, form, movement—the use of graphic symbols to embody the emotion that poured out from this drawing—was overlooked for the important work of the day: the introduction of these tidy second-order symbols that go beyond depiction to indication and make clear that which images (in other settings "gloriously") make unclear.

The implicit messages were sure: (1) the space of Octavia's drawing was not her own. The teacher had the right to enter a composition of Octavia's making and add to the creation these powerful structures called words; (2) drawings did not say anything on their own—their content was there to be explained and better understood through words; (3) drawings were meant to represent things in the world that we know and can name (like father and mother)—not conceptions or feelings (like the color and energy of relationship) that find particular and untranslatable realization in graphic form; and (4) school was a place where words and specificity were valued and shared. In the context of school, children's drawings were a means to an end. They helped introduce children to a more significant graphic code—the written word and the nature of its connection to meaning. In time, Octavia would learn to write so well that she would not even need to draw anymore. In line with that development, drawing would soon not need to take up precious space in the limits of her day at school.

INTRODUCTION TO THE GENERATIVE TENSION: THE CHILD AS ARTIST—ROMANCE/REASON

Do we value the art making of young children as a process in and of itself? Or do we regard childhood artistic expression as a window into children's minds and a threshold to their acquisition of more precise modes of communication? Are we romanticizing childhood when we compare the playful artistic creations of children to the serious work of adult artists? Or are there rational grounds for the assertion and for empirical investigation of similarities between child and adult art? What are the implications of either possibility—romance or reason—for our cultivation or neglect of young children's artistic predilections and the responsive and relative role of the arts in education?

While the nature of the attention has changed over time, there has been a long and well-documented history of interest in children's drawings—often on the part of artists (see Ricci, 1887). Groups of 20th-century artists (e.g., Blaue Reiter circle and the Russian avant-garde) and individual artists like Paul Klee and Pablo Picasso frequently expressed their longing to see and represent things with the "innocent eye" of childhood (Fineberg, 1997). But even as great artists have celebrated the rule-breaking, fresh, and expressive creations of early childhood, others have discounted child art on the grounds that children lack the skills to draw or paint in any way other than they do. Evoking the salience of artistic intention, doubters argue that the child artist seems *necessarily*, rather than by artistic choice, to violate the conventions and agreed-upon vocabularies of representational form.

While the adult artist *intends*, for example, after Tolstoy or Goodman to "infect" a work with emotion—the child may do it "unconsciously." Octavia smiles and, by continuous instantaneous gesture, so does the figure of her brother—this is immediate, not preplanned. The professional artist, on the other hand, can "decide" to give her family drawing a joyful cast and consciously vest the lines and structure with that emotion. Octavia does it without awareness of the possibilities of the medium. Similarly, a child's drawing of a table with legs emerging from top and bottom of a malformed rectangle may capture the essence of "tableness" and be visually intriguing. This distortion might even be a presentation that an adult artist would choose to employ over a standard rendering with three-point perspective. The child's uninformed (she has yet to learn three point perspective) rule-breaking may add a certain charm, vitality, or apparent creativity to her efforts, but it is not the same as the process of the well-trained artist who, knowing them well, chooses to break the rules.

Distinguished arts educator Nancy Smith advised that we not confuse "the going back of an adult purposefully leaving the everyday reality with the constructive effort of the purposeful child seeking to order everyday reality" (1972, p. 349). Smith, who was also a developmental psychologist, explains that children's "capacity to integrate the narrative, emotional, and compositional aspects of a painting surpasses that of most adults since these strands have not yet become separated for them" (1983, p. 11). The young child is employing art (in the same way that children "use" pretend play and other imitative media) to help make sense of and learn how to enter the everyday world.

The adult artist is exploring artistic media as a means to step away from that world and from a distance, "to bring order to the whole" as Sondheim's Seurat said, "through design, composition, balance, light, and harmony" (Sondheim & Lapine, 1991, pp. 17–18).

This distinction can be viewed as a restaging of the debate between thinking and feeling, which was explored in the previous section. On the one hand, we find the experienced artist, as Goodman has suggested he or she might be, thoughtfully pushing the limits of symbolic media. And on the other, we have an "unknowing" image-maker exploring for the first time both the nature of artistic media and the shape of experience and emotion. Lacking awareness of the various modes and stereotypes of expression that adult artists strive to ignore, the child artist seems more directly connected to the artistic content of her work—the "feel" of that emotion or subject. A famous refrain of Picasso's attributed, with slight differences in detail, to his reaction to a display of children's artwork after the Second World War speaks to the point: "Once I drew like Raphael, but it has taken me a whole lifetime to learn to draw like children" (cited in Gardner, 1980, p. 8).

Arts educators, cognitive developmental psychologists, and artists themselves study child art and contemplate with various ends in view the comparison of children's work with that of professional artists. Arts educators and advocates find in the early facility and in the comparison the seeds of an argument that defends the need for art in our schools. For them, if the unrestrained and untrained artistic productions of young children are in any way similar to the important work of experienced artists, child art is a priori valuable and should be cultivated continuously throughout school curricula. A natural affinity between child and professional artist sets the stage for curriculum that features serious artistic training, exposure to professionals working in the field, and respect and encouragement for the early artistic endeavors of young children.

Cognitive developmental psychologists have more interest in what child art in general and in comparison with adult artistry can teach us about children's developing states of knowing and knowledge. Some of these researchers (those interested in information processing) would find in Octavia's drawing of her family ripe examples of her developmental stage (after Piaget) with regard to the cognitive strategy of planning. Ignoring the possibility of "Chagall-like" aesthetics of presentation, these investigators would consider the relative maturity of Octavia's decisions about where to place the members of her family on the page—or her responses to the physical constraints of the paper. Thinking more about thinking than about art, they would consider whether and when Octavia might have thought ahead about the placement of her figures so that she would not have to compensate with, for example, winding her father's shape around the rest (see Golomb, 1991).

Alternatively, cognitivists in the symbol systems tradition are decidedly interested in the aesthetics of the child's artistic presentation. They consider not only the young child's apparently enviable facility with graphic symbolization, but also its developmental trajectory. Is this facility, so ripe for comparison with the expressive prowess of adult artists, an early gift that young children possess and lose throughout their development? (See Davis, 1991a, 1993c, 1997a; Gardner, 1980; Winner, 1983.) It has been said that a 5-year-old's free flowing nonrepresentational drawing, properly framed and matted, could be slipped, without notice, onto the white walls of a museum of modern art. But a 10-year-old's constrained creation would stick out like a sore thumb (see Rosenblatt & Winner, 1988). Is artistry an early and perhaps even universal gift that gets lost in the course of development only to be reclaimed by the very few? In the early 1970s, this question was of interest to Goodman's research project, Harvard Project Zero, in which children's symbolic activities in a number of languages of art were compared with the work and/or examined with the same criteria as that of professional artists (Davis, 1997b).

As for artists like Picasso and others who have tried to recapture the knowing or feeling or doing of child artists, a romantic view of childhood and a reverence for the child's "pure vision" clearly seems to inspire their efforts. Some claim that the study and reclamation of child art is a modernist phenomenon and just an example of one of many modernist strategies for breaking new boundaries and defying traditional expectations for "fine art." Art historian Jonathan Fineberg has studied the collecting of children's art on the part of adult artists and the actual copying or reproduction of some of the images that children employed in their adult productions (1997). Fineberg attributes the "romantics" of the late 18th and early 19th century with "allying" "the naiveté of the child with 'genius'" (p. 3) and the efficiency of the child's modes of expression with a true and direct connection to emotion.

In sum then, in consideration of a view of the child as artist as a romantic or rational perspective, we find those representing a romantic view are adult artists themselves who, with an eye to enriching their own depth of experience and artistic output, closely and purposefully study the child's artistic process. Whether to reclaim or to return to the children they once were, or to defy traditional boundaries of age and experience, these artists embrace and even emulate the alternative and intense artistic expressions of early childhood. Educators and psychologists represent the "reason" side of this generative tension. They are interested in the implications of a comparison between early and adult artistry for our knowledge of and service to the development and education of children. At the heart of either perspective is a recognition of and respect for what very young children can do, and such regard has serious implications for the role and value of the arts in the education.

THE CHILD AS ARTIST—ROMANCE

My grandson and I recently visited a beach in Rockport, Massachusetts. The beach was dotted everywhere with women, apparently in their 70s, wearing large straw hats and seated at folding easels. These were members of a local painting class and they were all painting seaside landscapes. Emerson, now 7 and still a dedicated creator of images, sidled up to one of the painters and peered over her shoulder. "Nice job," he remarked. "Your painting is very realistic." The woman, clearly charmed, turned to the lanky young commentator. "Oh," she said, "are you an artist?" "A beginning artist," Emerson replied with enthusiasm. And he continued, "I'm actually working right now on a sea scene of my own." The woman attended with genuine interest as he explained, "I'm also doing the sea and the rocks, but from underwater, from the perspective of the creatures that live in the sea."

The Artist Decision

When do children decide that they are artists, and perhaps more frequently, decide that they are not? I remember the story of a mother, an art teacher herself, facing the challenge of an unrecognized child artist—her 6-year-old daughter Dana who was a first grader at the local public school. Dana had brought home a lively and dense crayon drawing on the back of which the teacher had written an emphatic *F*. The mother was more aware of the significance of this letter than her daughter and called the teacher for an explanation. "Why is this drawing graded *F*?" she asked, even as she wanted to sputter, "How can you give a grade to a six-year-old's drawing?" The teacher responded that she had asked the children in the class to draw the jungle and that she felt Dana hadn't even tried. The paper was just covered with messy colors and no shapes anywhere. The curious mother ("not trying" wasn't like Dana) brought the drawing to her daughter and asked simply, "You made this in school?"

Dana's reply was buoyant. "Oh yes," she said, "it was great. The teacher asked us to draw the jungle and I thought about it and imagined the jungle. There would be lions and tigers and gorillas, but not like in the zoo. In the jungle they would be running around and you would only see their colors and the leaves and . . . " Her hands moved across the surface of the completely colored drawing and her mother could feel the excitement spilling off the page. "I feel," she said to her daughter who didn't know what *F* meant, "when I look at this drawing that I am with you Dana in this exciting jungle. You are really an artist."

Every year, I asked my graduate students, many of whom are artists, all of whom have an interest in the arts, when they decided they were or were not artists. For most, it was a given when they were young children, a possibility when they were older, and a self-awareness triggered at any point by the recognition and regard of a respected elder or peer. My students have told me repeatedly that it most frequently wasn't a single event or experience and that furthermore, with a nod to Goodman, identification as an artist may be more of a "when" than a "what."

Some of them sometimes feel like artists, or felt like artists when they were in high school, or hope to feel like artists again someday. Others feel so truly artists that they can say they are even if they haven't lifted a brush or touched a piece of clay or been on a stage for years. Some of them feel that all of us are artists anyway and others agree with art historian Ernst Gombrich that it is the being and working of an artist that determines art. Gombrich opens his classic art historical treatise, *The Story of Art* (1950/1995), with the simple statement: "There really is no such thing as Art. There are only artists"(p. 4).

But who are these artists that by virtue of what they think, feel, and do, make art happen and define what art is? And what sort of romantic window washing does it take to call the work of an Octavia "art" because it accidentally embraces the compositional novelty of a Chagall, or to call a 7-year-old Emerson an artist because he takes an unexpected approach to a traditional artistic challenge? Is Dana's mother a romantic because she sees the work of an artist in what was deemed unacceptable chaos in the tidy arena of school? What is it that draws artists, presumably experts on who they are, to the vision and work of children?

Artist as Outsider

In the short story "Tonio Kröeger," renowned German author Thomas Mann (1989) provides a portrait of a young artist that is very much in line with the portrait of Seurat that Stephen Sondheim creates. A young writer, Tonio, like Sondheim's Seurat, is the quintessential outsider. Notably, both these portrayals of artists are by artists themselves. Mann's story of Tonio, the young writer coming of age, discovering himself and his difference from the mainstream of society ("the blonde blue-eyed people") is often thought to be autobiographical. Sondheim has mentioned that his shows are his "children" and it seems certain that the nature of the creative talent he ascribes to Seurat is imprinted with his view of his own. In any case, the vision of the "outsider" artist that both these creators provide is layered with the music and lyrics of a show, the lyrical writing of a master author, and the particularly personal views of artists displaying their knowledge of what it is to be an artist and/or to be themselves.

"Tonio Kröeger" was written in 1903, 2 years after Mann's novel *Buddenbrooks* had been released, through which he gained acclaim as a major artist/writer. He would go on to win the Nobel Prize in 1929. Sondheim won the Pulitzer Prize in 1984 for *Sunday in the Park with George* and also earned many other awards in his long career. So we have behind these two portrayals the vision of very successful and seasoned artists—artists who have gained the recognition of the respective fields to which they both ascribe and the apparent authority to decide who among us is and isn't an artist.

Sondheim's field of others on stage deride the artist outsider: "Artists are so crazy; artists are so peculiar . . . "(Sondheim & Lapine, 1991, p. 43) and elsewhere: "Condescending artists observing, perceiving . . . well, screw them!" (p. 44). But Sondheim's Seurat sees the distance that the artist must maintain in order to gain perspective as necessary: "It's the only way to see" (p. 66). Of course in the world of everyday living, beyond the world of those who live to see—those who are artists through their vision—the artist's need to remain outside of the circle isolates him or her from what Mann calls "the dance." Tonio tells us, "The artist must be unhuman, extra-human; he must stand in a queer aloof relationship to our humanity; only so is he in a position, I ought to say only so would he be tempted, to represent it, to present it, to portray it to good effect" (Mann, 1989, p. 96).

In *Sunday*, George loses his lover because he cannot leave his painting of a hat long enough to take her to the Follies. Mann's Tonio stands on the edge of the dance longing to be "regular," feeling as a boy even disdainful for his artistry: "he himself felt his verse-making extravagant and out of place and to a certain extent agreed with those who considered it an unpleasing occupation. But that did not enable him to leave off" (p. 78). In Tonio's not being able to "leave off," we see another facet of the artist that many imagine as a prerequisite: the mandate to make art. "If I were an artist I would be driven to make art all the time." "I am an artist when I make art but not when I don't." "I am what I do." George is driven to make a hat where there never was a hat . . . in spite of personal loss. Tonio is driven to make art even though he (if you can believe him) disdains the isolation that his poetry making requires. Expressing the relationship between outsider artists who will not, or possibly cannot, participate in the dance, Tonio suggests that their art making may even be compensatory. He describes them as, "people who are always falling down in the dance . . . the kind to whom poetry serves as a sort of mild revenge on life" (p. 103).

Child as Outsider

Many young child artist actors who are deep in pretend play, either on their own or collaboratively with others, fluidly change roles and costumes to recreate the world they are exploring. As a point in hand, young Frannie opened a classroom in her basement after her first day in kindergarten (she kept her playschool open for several years). In her play in that setting, she often was the teacher, demanding "perfect work," bemoaning the "diseases" that some children's writing exhibited, and rewriting the wrongs of the school day—for example, disallowing children to play in groups of three to keep the third child from being left out. Frannie's classroom, a lush and useful alternative world, demonstrated the point made by researchers who study the activity of playing school—that it can serve a compensatory function (see Heron & Sutton-Smith, 1971). Like Tonio's poetry, the action of playing school allows a child who feels diminished or marginalized by the classroom to experience the power of being at the center and being in charge.

The notion of the artist as an outsider resonating throughout these portrayals certainly evokes comparison with the romantic vision of childhood as beyond or outside the adult world of conventions and rules. Mann's Tonio describes his self-discovery as a writer: "It begins by your feeling yourself set apart, in a curious sort of opposition to the nice regular, people . . . " (Mann, 1989, p. 97). Sondheim's George similarly sacrifices or rejects participation in the regular world to produce for that world original art. "How you watch the rest of the world from a window while you finish the hat" (p. 65). Tonio sees isolation as a prerequisite: "good work only comes out under pressure of a bad life . . . he who lives does not work . . . one must die in life in order to be utterly a creator (p. 93)

Nonetheless, Tonio decries his outsider status: "I tell you I am sick to death of depicting humanity without having any part or lot in it" (Mann, 1989, p. 97). He longs to be on the inside: "how regular and comfortable they must feel" (p. 79). Ultimately, he explains "there is a way of being an artist that goes so deep and is so much a matter of origins and destinies that no longing seems to it sweeter and more worth knowing than longing after the bliss of the commonplace"(p. 79). This statement again reminds us of that quintessential outsider, the young child longing to acquire the conventions of the adult world. The child struggles to make sense of the world through play, visual art, and any other available imitative media that will allow her to come to understand the "bliss of the commonplace" and to avoid falling down in the "dance."

But we should not align Tonio with the unfettered attachment to emotion that we have cited as a possible attribute of the artistic process of the child artist. Indeed, Tonio's stand on our thinking/feeling tension is clear. He comments, "Spring is a bad time for work and why? Because we are feeling too much. Nobody but a beginner imagines that he who creates must feel. Every real and genuine artist smiles at such naïve blunders as that" (Mann, 1989, p. 96).

Challenging the Comparison

Mann's light and perhaps loving touch as he describes Tonio is every-where edged with a sort of irony. We sense and believe Tonio's pain, but we feel somehow, as it is for Sondheim's George, that the artist respects more than derides his outsider status and understands that it allows him or her an otherwise unattainable vision of the whole. Marking the difference, Sondheim's Seurat describes his non-artist lover as "seeing all of the parts and none of the whole" (Sondheim & Lapine, 1991, p. 39). Agreeing with Sondheim's image of the artist as having a "mission to see," art historian Ernst Gombrich says that art-ists teach us all how to see: "If we follow them and learn from them, even a glance out of our own window may become a thrilling adven-ture" (1950/1995, p. 8).

Gombrich gives new insight into the distinction that, unlike chil-dren, artists know the rules and consciously break them. He describes the artist's process as more "removed" from the rules than in interac-tion with them. Rather than following "fixed rules," Gombrich says, the artist's process of striving to achieve balance—structural unity achieved through the careful arrangement of aesthetic elements in a work of art—is like the familiar activity of putting flowers in a vase and rearranging them responsively in relationship to one another, the red here, the blue there . . . until it all makes visual sense. While ad-mitting that throughout different artistic periods, laws have been for-mulated, Gombrich maintains, "It always turned out that poor artists did not achieve anything when trying to apply these laws, while great masters could break them and yet achieve a new kind of harmony no one had thought of before" (1950/1995, p. 11).

Gombrich's observation that the working artist, in spite of all his knowledge, is "feeling his way" as he achieves balance in his com-position resonates with the identification and admiration that many artists espouse for the seamless processes of young child artists. Is feeling one's way more authentic if one does it without knowledge rather than in spite of conventions? Children feel their way through their work unencumbered, for example, by an awareness of the rules and conventions of representing three-dimensional reality in the two-dimensional space of the paper. Is the genuine feeling of one's way the really "innocent" eye that children have and artists seek to reclaim?

Reclaiming Childhood

It is interesting that artists not only seem to celebrate their child-hood activities but even to return to them or seek to reconcile them in their most mature art. The painter Philip Guston offers an apt example. Guston began his artistic training in the Cleveland Cartoon Correspondence School and he ended his career painting works that look somewhat like cartoons. His early drawings were of Klansman and he returns to that subject again, in his late work, but with a different angle. Guston reflected that when he was a teenager of 17 or 18 he drew the Klansmen to document history; at the end of his life he says, "They are self-portraits. I perceive myself as being behind a hood. In the new series of hoods my attempt was really not to illustrate, to do pictures of the KKK . . . the idea of evil fascinated me . . . What would it be like to be evil?" (In Stiles & Selz, 1996, p. 252) Playing roles, exploring ideas and the space between the person in time and the person in idea—is this function of play not only the work of children but also perhaps of the most mature artist?

On the subject of returning to his youthful activities, Guston has said, "I wanted to be complete again . . . as I was when I was a kid" (Corbett, 1994, p. 89) and his dear friend and collaborator poet William Corbett expands on this: "The late drawings combine this desire and its fulfillment. The best are as effortless as an athlete's flawless play. Fifty years of practice become innate grace. They have the child's total concentration that we lose, remember ardently, and must struggle to regain . . . It takes years of doing to earn the confidence Guston displays here and to draw so that the mark is the thought" (p. 89).

Corbett's comment is reminiscent of the distinction made by 19th-century author and illustrator Rodolphe Topffer in 1847 with regard to the child's intention (or lack thereof) in drawing. Topffer suggested that the child's intention was not less, but "different" from that of the adult artist: rather than "imitative," it was an "intention of thought." Substituting "confidence" with "ignorance," Topffer sounds like Corbett when he notes that in child art, "thought is all the more evident because of the graphic ignorance of the designer" (in Leeds, 1989, p. 98). Guston described his own realization: "So to know and how not to know is the greatest puzzle of all, finally . . . It's a long long preparation for a few moments of innocence" (In Stiles & Selz, 1996, p. 250).

REVIEWING THE ROMANTIC VIEW OF THE CHILD AS ARTIST

What, at this juncture, have our reflections contributed toward an understanding of a romantic view of the child as artist? With an eye to the artist's overarching mission to see—and I would argue that this mission applies across artistic domains—three aspects of the young child's process motivate reclamation on the part of the adult artist: (1) *connection*: an unfettered attachment to the idea or feeling being expressed in a work of art; (2) *freedom*: a lack of awareness (a condition of not knowing) of the conventions or rules of artistic expression; and (3) *distance*: that quality of being an outsider removed from the world of which both adult and child artist (albeit with different intentions) strive to make sense.

When we see Octavia's face literally assume the attributes of her brother's whimsy, we recognize the child's connection to the thought that will be imprinted on the mark she makes. But this activity is what the great drawing teacher Nicolaides explicitly asks his student artists to do—to assume the position of the model they draw, to internalize the external (1941). For the young child the boundaries between internal and external are thin and the expression of thought and feeling are contiguous and direct. Dana's jungle of colors racing across the page may have been hard for the teacher to apprehend because of their attachment to a whole thought instead of to the details of differentiated form.

As Octavia creates and responds to her developing drawing, making choices that present even as they limit alternatives (like the crowding of her composition), she is not bothered by an awareness of more standard family portraits or the convention of presenting figures of equal size in a row. She is free to respond both to her developing ideas about what to draw and to the developing composition that she has drawn. Emerson's move in perspective from on the shore to under water may seem innovative to the artist on the beach. But as a child, he may just be expressing a freedom from knowledge of the expectations of seascapes and an admirable ability therefore to move from beach to water to the creatures therein.

As Octavia naively considers her kindergarten classroom, the fixed stems of flowers on the easels, the canned responses of teacher to the children's drawings, and the new expectations for drawing, she presents a clear example of her status as an outsider to the culture of school as well as to the range of adult constructions of culture that await her. The child plays school to understand better what it is; the child draws an experience to relive and know it better. While distance is the shared marker, the child strives to enter the world she seeks to understand even as the artist strives to separate himself from it. Whether entering or leaving, distance enables the viewer to see the whole and not be distracted by its parts.

The vision of the artist connected to ideas, freely expressing emotion and sitting on the edges of society differs greatly from the attribute of social responsibility that art critic Suzi Gablik attributes to the work of many postmodern artists. Gablik posits a divide between "aesthetic art" and what she calls the new "ecological paradigm": value-based art attached to relationships and social reconciliation (1991). While a relational aspect may be another face of "connection," the traditional idea of the "self-indulgent" artist outsider may have outlived its usefulness.

Writer Virginia Woolf refused invitations to speak at academies of higher learning because she feared that entering institutional structures would threaten her otherness, that "outsider vision" that she cherished so dearly and that allowed her the distance to see and write (Caws, 2001, p. 25). But Carol Becker, Dean of the Art Institute of Chicago, challenges the relevance of the traditional view of the outsider artist for whom "freedom of expression consistently has been the central concern" and who "has always lived in a marginalized or antagonistic relationship to society" (1994, p. xv). Becker offers an alternative view that honors the socially ameliorative contributions of art and reconsiders "responsibility not so much as a constraint but rather as a condition for freedom and as a mark of the culture's maturity" (p. xvi).

Just as the comparison between child and artist may celebrate a romantic view of children, it may be edged with a dismissive view of artists as the "children" of society—those who do not have to live up to the same hard expectations as the non-artist population. Although throughout the musical *Sunday*, we hear the respectful refrain "Art isn't easy," the subjects in the painting speak to their disdain: "Work is what you do for others . . . art is what you do for yourself" (Sondheim & Lapine, 1991, p. 55).

Artists may appreciate and seek out the freedom to play with which so many children are equipped; but artists' respect for and entitlement to play can present a threat to others or invite an attitude of disrespect. Nonetheless, as will be discussed later on in greater detail, throughout history, artists have repeatedly self-selected themselves to serve communities abandoned by others and to assume the role of educator when others would not. A visiting artist helped children create the vibrant entrance to Octavia's school. Beyond social and political action—just through making art—artists present to the rest of us a sense of the world that allows us to see what is and to imagine what is possible. After the destruction of New York City's World Trade Center on September 11, 2001, a devastated population looked to artists to make sense of it all through image and word, and on numerous socially conscious Web sites a viewer could find, and find comfort in the drawings of young children.

The romantic perspective of the outsider artist as both looking on from the edge of the dance and creating the music that is the dance informs the first verse of the classic Ode by 19th-century poet Arthur O'Shaughnessy. The implications for child artist will become clearer as we move on.

> We are the music-makers,
> And we are the dreamers of dreams,
> Wandering by lone sea-breakers,
> And sitting by desolate streams;
> World-losers and world-forsakers;
> On whom the pale moon gleams:
> Yet we are the movers and shakers
> Of the world forever, it seems.
> (O'Shaughnessy, quoted in Quiller-Couch, 1900/1931, p. 1,006)

THE CHILD AS ARTIST—REASON

The image of the artist or poet as simultaneously a world mover and forsaker works well in this climate of generative tensions in which neither pole of the tension (whether thinking or feeling or romance or reason) holds a sufficient alternative and each pole of the tension is enlarged or made better by the other. Does the artist choose to forsake worlds in order to move them? And what worlds does she forsake and move? The worlds of non-artists, or of the commonplace as represented by Tonio's dance or George's follies? The broader historical/political worlds of O'Shaughnessy's empires? The worlds that artists create for themselves like those of expressionism or modernism that are abandoned for new movements or worlds of art? And what are worlds made of if not our various understandings and representations of experience, all guided by our varying and shared ways of seeing?

The Shadow of Intention

From a thinking/rational/cognitive approach, the developing child is taking in and making sense of experience as part of the development of his or her individual worldview (Weltanschauung). The symbol systems of art give the child media both for the internal construction of representations or understandings (meaning-making) and for the external representation of those understandings to others (communication). The arts, as O'Shaughnessy puts forth, give shape to history and frame a vision for the future. On an individual basis, they provide the tools for a child to build her own culture or worldview, make sense of her own past and present, and imagine/dream a "what if" for the future.

As part of a fourth grade's visit to Harvard University's Fogg Art Museum, a young boy who called himself Teriyaki came across his first Miro. Incredulous that such an "easy" drawing was framed and featured in this august setting, Teriyaki sat down and immediately reproduced what he saw. When one of the museum's curators came along to welcome the children, Teriyaki rushed up to her and asked, "Who decides what art belongs in the museum?" She explained that the art that was displayed was the work of great artists. "I know," Teriyaki responded, "and I can do what they do." As evidence, he proudly showed her his rendering of the apparently simple drawing by Miro. Teriyaki's reproduction looked quite close to the original.

"Yes," the curator agreed, "but the difference is that a great artist like Miro can make many different images and *chooses* to make this painting look as if someone your age had made it." Momentarily silenced, Teriyaki piped up, "I see what you mean. But I can do lots of other things too. Can I bring in some of my other drawings to show you?" Again, we see the weighty shadow of intention. Art is art because artists intended to make it so and artists can have intentions for art because they are artists. Children cannot. Even while we hear from artists that in the process one always needs to make room for what is not on purpose, for the surprising turn of a phrase or the moment when one's hands play the piano as if motored by some source beyond one's self—even in this climate of artistic "magic" or reaching for lack of control, we turn to the criterion of intention to distinguish adult from child art.

In a documentary entitled "Feast of Reason" (Sutherland, 1986), the painter Jack Levine describes his daily return to a work in progress. Paraphrasing loosely, his words are something to the effect: "You have to look at what's wrong with the work. That's a place to begin. What's right—you have to work around." Out of such descriptions of the artistic process come notions of the generative mistake—the opportunity to build and learn in one's work. I remember gratefully apprenticing for a master art teacher in the 60s, Charles Taylor. "Charlie," as the children called him, dressed in a coatlike smock that looked like a painting by Jackson Pollock, and would stomp around the art barn calling out, "Every mistake is on purpose! Figure it out!"

Still, when a young child's painting reaches some expressive height, psychologists who study the development of thought will call the moment of artistry a "happy accident" and point to the fact that skill in a medium gives the artist real choices that children do not have (see Winner, 1983). From the romantic perspective, we have the child unencumbered by the self that artists strive to forget in the artistic process—that disembodied "flow"—that reverie of finishing the hat. From a rational perspective, we say this child needs to acquire techné or mastery before we can think of her as an artist. And if she turns out to be a really fine artist, she will be able to forget the techné and move beyond it. As mentioned with regard to music, there are some who suggest that the techné is the thinking and the rest is feeling. Are we saying then that child artists feel, and adult artists think and long to feel again? When Guston says he wants to return to that time when he was a child and complete—is it the reconciliation of or lack of differentiation between emotion and thought to which he alludes? That seamless moment that Corbett, writing about Guston, describes: "The mark is the thought" (1994, p. 89).

Cognizing Romance

In the late 1980s, I set out to explore, through a large-scale empirical study, the similarities and differences between the work of professional artists and the playful productions of young children. I did this by asking children of various ages as well as adolescent and adult artists and self-acclaimed non-artists to "draw" three emotions: happy, sad, and angry (See Plate 3). I was interested, from a cognitive perspective, in the extent to which young children and adult artists might actually employ some of the same strategies of symbolic reference in constructing graphic representations of the three emotions.

I used for the comparison criteria derived from work that has been previously discussed by Goodman (1976, 1978), Arnheim (1966a, 1966b, 1969), and other students of art making as a cognitive endeavor, that is, as a thoughtful construction of meaning through symbols rather than a visceral Tolstoy-like infection of emotion. I also based my protocol and framed my developmental expectations around the prodigious work of other cognitive developmental psychologists, many of whom worked at Harvard Project Zero, and who explored the artistry and expressivity of young children's drawings (see Davis, 1989). These researchers included Howard Gardner (1973, 1980), William Ives (1984), Diana Korzenik (1973), David Pariser (1979), Ellen Winner (1983; and see Winner & Gardner, 1981), and Dennis Palmer Wolf (Wolf & Gardner, 1980; Wolf & Perry, 1988).

In my study, I was exploring the reconciliation of emotion and thought—this notion that it is thinking that vests art with emotion. I investigated the conscious construction of emotion through various strategies of symbol use with an eye to changes that might be associated with development. Specifically, I considered: (1) the choice of a *symbolic vehicle* or subject of the drawing (representational or non-representational); for example, would a participant use a chair to represent sadness or a series of heavy undefined forms? (2) the use of *line* (as relatively replete or not); for example, to what if any extent were the lines in a drawing vested with meaning in their own construction, for example, droopy and curved down for sad? (3) *composition* (with an eye to the relative use of balance to embody meaning) as perhaps in a solid well-balanced composition to express the security of happy, and an asymmetrically balanced drawing to represent the "off" feeling of sorrow. (4) *overall expressivity*—the metaphoric exemplification that Goodman had described in which a drawing actually embodied or *was* (metaphorically of course) the emotion it represented (1976/1978).

Two well-trained judges (an artist/art teacher and art collector/gallery dealer) examined, "scored" (in terms of the relevant aesthetic criteria described above), and tried to determine the depicted emotion in more than 500 drawings from 140 subjects in seven age groups (see Davis, 1991a, 1993c, 1997a). That is, after considering the criteria listed above, the judges were asked what emotion the drawer had intended to express and in those cases where the judges' "reading " of the depicted emotion in a drawing was off (e.g., a sad drawing was thought to be happy), they were asked in a final session to revisit their scoring of the aesthetic criteria with an eye to the artist's actual intention.

In this way, I could consider that slippery issue of intention in terms of the drawer's relative success in using the aesthetic elements of line and composition both in terms of the construction of expressivity (i.e., the extent to which the drawing was seen as embodying *any* emotion) and in the communication of intention (i.e., that the viewer recognized the *particular* emotion embodied in the image). I mention this because from a perspective in which meaning is thought to be coconstructed by the producer and perceiver of art, the effective use of aesthetic elements to construct complex aesthetic wholes takes priority over the simple delivery of clear-cut meanings. A stick-figure depiction of a sad story (i.e., one of the stick figures is lying dead) may not embody, through its thoughtful use of line and composition, the emotion of sadness (it is not in and of itself a sad drawing); but a "reader" can easily determine the drawer's intention. Such a rendering does not ask of the viewer the sort of attention described by Nelson Goodman as associated with/demanded by symptoms of the aesthetic. This distinction should become clearer.

Loss of the Gift

In my research, I was especially interested in the imprint and occurrence of a reported loss of interest and proficiency in drawing. Picasso (quoted in Fineberg) has called the gift of early artistry the "'genius of childhood' . . . 'a period of marvelous vision' that 'disappears without a trace' when children grow up" (1997, p. 122). Researchers in the late 1970s at Goodman's Project Zero had been interested in what they were calling "U-shaped" development. The U was configured such that the envied expressive work of the very young child was situated on one high end of the U, the flourishing deliberate work of the professional artist on the other. In the center at the bottom were situated the less expressive drawings of children in middle childhood (e.g., the stick-figured narratives). Researchers designated as the "literal stage" middle childhood's apparent loss of what they identified as a "flavor-fulness" in drawing and understood the phenomenon as a giving in to (or giving up in the face of) a perceived mandate for photographic realism (Gardner & Winner, 1982; Rosenblatt & Winner, 1988).

This apparent loss was a phenomenon I had experienced firsthand in my college summers teaching art in New York City to 200 children aged 5 through 12. Where the youngest children drew with a freedom that seemed to be what my night-school teachers at the Art Students League were asking me and other adult students to achieve, the 8- to 10-year-olds seemed almost scripted in their renderings. The boys at that age were dedicated to drawing airplanes and battleships and copying from one another the strategies for representation that seemed to them most convincing: for example, outwardly radiating lines to represent the blast off of a rocket, or the fire of a gun off a ship. The girls had an agreed-upon rendering of a rainbow that appeared in many of their drawings and a schema for the garden (horizontal green base line with vertical flowers like the ones Octavia's teachers had painted in for the children in her kindergarten classroom).

These gender-associated drawing codes were of interest in them-selves but also could definitely identify a given drawing as the work of a 10-year-old girl or boy. Delores Dunning, an innovative art teacher and graduate student at Harvard, did a study in which she asked boys of that age to draw as if they were girls and girls as if they were boys. She found that the participating children knew exactly how to render the expected gender-related stereotypical output. Where, she asked, were the children learning these unspoken but clearly heard guide-lines for what and how to draw (Dunning, 1999)? How and when, she wondered, might the advent of feminism and redefined gender roles make a difference in the content and choice of stereotype in drawing?

In my art barn in the 1960s, I had seen the wildly expressive and moving humanoid figures of the 5-year-old children turn in a few years into constrained stiff figure drawings. In the older children's drawings, carefully rendered details such as belt buckles and hats re-placed the vision of a cohesive whole so present in the well-balanced compositions of the youngest children. As introduced earlier, a bal-anced composition is one in which all the forms on the page are placed in such a way that they seem to make sense in terms of one another. It has been said that in a balanced composition, the disruption or re-moval of any part of the whole would destroy the unity or cohesion of the visual construction (see Aristotle, 1951; Arnheim, 1966a). The youngest children in my classes seemed naturally to attend to balance, while the older ones were more concerned with details often randomly placed on the page.

The move from a concern for overall unity to a distraction with part, mirroring the developing child's growing awareness of her own differentiated self, is reminiscent of Sondheim's Seurat's view of the non-artist stance: "Seeing the parts and not the whole." Must the developmental acquisition of differentiation undo the cohesion of early vision and understanding? What were the reasons for and relative necessity of this development from artist to non-artist sensibility? Regardless of the reason and implication of this change, what I found of most concern was that the change also seemed to mark a falling off of interest for the children. By the time they were 12, only those students who identified themselves as artists were really eager to draw (see also Winner, 1983)—the others insisted they "couldn't" and preferred to master the skills of potholder and lariat weaving than take the risk of expressing themselves through painting or drawing. It seemed a shame that so many children entering adolescence, with its profound emotions and awareness of perplexing issues, were apparently reluctant to explore this intensity through artistic media.

Nancy Smith has noted that adolescence is the time at which young people are developmentally "ready" consciously to explore and employ symbols in their art (1983). Why then did so few seem confident and engaged with the challenge? Why is the vocabulary of art not regularly taught to youth at this stage? Adolescents—junior high and high school aged children—have the cognitive equipment to make great use of the media, but we hold it aside at this level of education for those who self-select the arts as electives—presumably the same young adolescents who would be exploring it on their own in any case. In out-of-school ateliers (often in garages or basements) young comic book art makers learn on their own from the masters (like famed Spiderman artist John Romita) whom they select and study themselves. In community art centers in urban and rural areas, adolescents can find alternative arenas for development in visual and performing arts. But in most schools, the provision of arts education decreases in inverse proportion to children's readiness to explore media with maturity and purpose.

As I was studying painting after teaching hours, I often gave to my young art students the exercises my instructors at the Art Students

League were giving to me. I noted that when children at the "part over whole" stage drew as I was asked to with the wrong hand, their drawings became freer. When they sat across from one another at a long table and drew each other's faces without looking at the paper, their drawings had the sophistication and piquancy of drawings from *The New Yorker* magazine. Indeed, when I mounted these sketches on simple black mats for exhibit, their parents could not believe what they saw. Where were the schema-driven flowers and boats?

I carried from that period of teaching into my work as a researcher decades later a persistent suspicion of the notion of a "fixity" in artistic development (from early height to ultimate decline and dissolution) and a belief in the possibility that teachers could help reverse the perceived cycle of loss. The artist Vasily Kandinsky wrote that "Adults, especially teachers, try to force the practical meaning upon the child." Their criticism at the superficial level of appearance or functionality (e.g., whether the person in the child's drawing can walk with one leg) devalues what the child has accomplished: "The artist whose whole life is similar in many ways to that of a child, can often realize the inner sound of things more easily than anyone else (in Fineberg, 1997, p. 47).

Challenging Loss

Teachers, like parents, get blamed for much. But teachers, like parents, do have great power in contributing to the child's world making— great power in providing children with what they need to construct their worldviews: from introducing children to a range of constructive symbolic media to providing them with the faith that both their vision and their ability to give it form are worthy. Studies of teachers' responses to children's art indicate that classroom teachers celebrate the push toward realistic portrayal in the drawings of middle childhood. The 9-year-old who has mastered the perfect schema for a popular icon like Mickey Mouse or Pokémon is likely to find greater recognition in the classroom than the child who is covered with charcoal as he explores light and dark or laughs at the distortion of his drawing of his favorite cat.

What if, instead of asking Octavia to tell her about her drawing (with an interest really only in who the individuals represented therein might be), her teacher looked carefully at the drawing—allowed herself to be an adult artist attending to what adult artists seem moved by in the work of children. Might she not have responded to the vitality, the color, the interest in the composition, the joyfulness she might experience in looking closely at what Octavia had done? How might that have let Octavia know that the teacher valued what she did and appreciated that what she did was not necessarily translatable (nor need it be) to the words they used to talk about the drawing?

What if, instead of decreasing art instruction as children develop in school, we taught it every day along with other subjects and responsively met children's interests and desires for their artistic growth? Would it be possible to help children in middle childhood attain the techniques required for the kind of representation to which they are inclined? If we could keep them producing through their various stages of artistic development, could we avoid sacrificing the joy of creation and gift for pure vision of the essence of feeling and things with which they began. Artists, perhaps because of their great talent and passion, seem to survive, persevere, and even enjoy a "literal" stage in their own development (Pariser, 1989). It is only when we keep producing art on the other side of the trough of the "u" that we can consider the period one of expanding repertoire. Should not all children have the chance to continue their growth as meaning-makers in the various media of art?

U-shaped development in cognitive and behavioral functions is not uncommon. Think of the way that a young baby may seem to "stand-up" on your lap months before he has figured out how to sit or crawl. U-shaped development is usually marked by three phases, in which: (1) the behavior appears, (2) it apparently disappears, and (3) it reappears (Bever, 1982; Strauss, 1982). For the majority of us, it would seem, u-shaped development in drawing is not completed. That early gift or penchant for powerful mark making disappears, as Picasso suggested, "without a trace," only to be reclaimed by the very few of us who decide or discover that we are artists.

Researchers who challenge the claim for a u-shaped trajectory of development in drawing often attribute the celebration of early mark making to a modernist ethic in which non-representational expression is valued over realism. Arguably in a context in which realism was the governing artistic ethic, or psychologists counted faithful representation as a "higher" stage of artistic development than distorted or nonrepresentational renderings (see Stern, 1924), the attempts at realism on the part of children in middle childhood would seem more advanced. Researchers like Dennis Palmer Wolf have celebrated that stage that has been called "literal" because of its preference for visual recount over interpretation. Wolf sees the acquisition of the skills of negotiating stereotypical representative schemas as a building of repertoire for the young artist, an activity that should be associated more with gain than with loss (Wolf & Perry, 1988; see also Duncum, 1986).

Certainly we can note, just from the description of activity in my summer art room, features of the drawings of middle childhood that are associated with personal development. The 5-year-old artist is thought to be egocentric (Piaget, 1962) with a view of self that is almost "undifferentiated" from the surrounding world. That perspective is reflected in the "me-ness" of the drawings of that age. When children at that age are asked to draw an emotion like happy, as they were in my research, they will render it in terms of themselves. Five-year-old Tyler spoke as he drew, "When I am happy, my eyelashes go up." Smiling at the self-rendering of a full-figured happy solidly composed round person, 5-year-old Michael noted, "See the round belly and my muscley arms. See the smile . . . that's happy."

In a television interview, Stephen Sondheim reported that in his study of Seurat's painting of La Grande Jatte for *Sunday in the Park with George*, he noted that none of the figures in the painting were looking at each other. It became apparent to Sondheim that the painting wasn't about them after all—it was about Seurat. And that became Sondheim's point of entry into the creation of his show. This achievement of ownership or central presence of the artist in a work is apparent as well in reports of professional artists. Philip Guston says of his late work, "I am the subject" and Mark Rothko claimed he liked to paint large pictures because "to paint a small picture is to place yourself outside your experience . . . however you paint the larger picture, you are in it" (quoted in Stiles & Selz, 1996, p. 26)

The lack of distance between the artist and the youngest children and their artistic output resounds through stories, such as the one in which a 5-year-old child who was asked to draw a scary house simply drew a house and growled at the researcher as she drew (Winner & Gardner, 1981). This centrality of self in children's artistic output no doubt crosses the boundaries of artistic domains. In the domain of language, young children are thought to be natural metaphor makers even before they have learned the concept of a simile, or the grammatical rules for drawing likenesses between two entities (Winner, 1988). It is a 5-year-old's voice in a crowded office building elevator descending quickly from the 35th floor: "We're melting!"

The drawings of the older children in my art barn reflect an awareness of other individuals (see Korzenik, 1973) not just as sources for the acquisition of a vocabulary of forms or as traffickers of cultural conventions and stereotypes, but also as perceiving others who will want to make sense of the content of their drawing and may decide whether it is good or bad. In the drawings of the older children in my study, this developing awareness of others and the parts they played in the older children's emotional lives was apparent. Where a 5-year-old would draw a picture of himself as happy or sad, an 8-year-old would draw a scene (e.g., a sleep-over at a friend's house) in which she was made to feel happy or sad.

Unpacking the U

From the perspective of overall expressivity and compositional unity, the 5-year-olds' drawings scored with the judges in my study a great deal higher than the drawings of older children and were equaled only by the scores of adolescent study participants who were self-declared artists. But the judges could more consistently and accurately decipher the specific intended emotion in the older children's drawings. Where the aesthetic aspects of the older children's drawings may have been lacking (e.g., a birthday party representing happy was stiffly rendered with little sign that the lines and forms embodied emotion), their communicative rendering or representational content (e.g., judges could "read" a birthday party as happy regardless of how it was drawn) was clearer. Awareness of a "reader" of the image presumably motivated the older children to reach for clear communicative content.

From a process perspective, this awareness of others was also apparent. For the 5-year-old, I could see the beauty of the opportunity-rich mistake. Five-year-old Nicky began his sad drawing by making a smile. He looked at it and exclaimed, "Oh no, you said to draw sad." Without pausing for a moment he turned his paper over so that the smile was now down-turned and built his sad face around it. The face had a wonderful length to it that added to the quality of sadness even though it began with an unintentional placement of the frown. Five-year-old Gabby's hand would suddenly produce a line that seemed to surprise her. Considering it a moment, she would giggle, "Now, I don't know why I did that," and then she would responsively develop whatever addition had occurred almost of its own accord. She spoke as she drew and seemed in dialogue with a drawing that was clearly in all aspects an extension of her self.

This wonderful freewheeling rapport with the drawing seemed to disappear with age. The 8- to 11-year-olds encountering unexpected turns in the drawing would ask if they could work in pencil instead (so they could erase) or request a new paper to begin again. Mistakes had moved from opportunities to embarrassments and there was a clear awareness of a right and wrongness to drawing that seemed to inhibit more than to inspire. This new ethic and set of standards may be the result of a growing awareness of the culture of school to which the children, like Octavia, were just being introduced. Teachers, parents, and the broader context let children know the values and expectations of school. The new codes that are becoming familiar to children in this setting offer a preciseness that they may begin to crave for their drawing.

The intrusion or infusion of written words was very apparent in the drawings of children in my study between the ages of 8 and 11. Indeed, the children in this age group added words to their drawings more often than any other group. An angry face would have a comic book bubble that said, "I'm angry at you!" The words "Boo hoo" accompany the scene in which a sad event is encountered by an 8-year-old. There is the expectation that the drawing will not in itself tell the story (shades of a teacher adding words and/or saying, "Tell me about it."). Notably, the self, so front and center in the 5-year-old's drawing is still at the center, albeit of the scene, that the older child depicts.

"This is the family having ice cream together and my brother stole the cherry off my ice cream and I am telling him off!" Eleven-year-old Rachel explained to me that the people in her drawing were angry about what was happening and what was happening in the drawing was something that also makes her angry. "It makes sense, "she explained to me, "to draw things that happen to me." This is a change from the attitude of the 5-year-old artist who seems to think, "It makes sense to draw me."

A change in process reflects the new distance that has been achieved between child and image. I watched closely as another 11-year-old girl drew carefully, and paused to consider thoughtfully each shape that she put on the page. Her earnest behavior was reminiscent of the collaboration (between child and drawing) that 5-year-old Gabby had demonstrated so cheerfully. When I asked the 11-year-old what she was up to, she explained, "I know what I want to draw, but I never draw it as I planned. So I look at what has been drawn and decide what I can do from there." There was a joylessness in her account—a clear shift from reveling in process to monitoring product; from spirited collaboration to steadfast compromise.

Across all the dimensions of my study there were few differences in the scores of adolescents and adults who had self-identified as "non-artists" and the 8- to 11-year-old age groups. There was evidence, however, of a developing understanding of the symbolic and aesthetic potential of the drawing, even if realizing that potential seemed beyond reach. For example, while the 11-year-olds would draw a scene in which someone was made angry to represent the emotion of anger, the 14-year-olds would draw a token of the scene. An 11-year-old drew an angry scene in which someone raised a gun at someone else (including the bubble that says "I'm going to kill you"). A 14-year-old artist drew with expressive use of line an exploding gun to represent angry. A professional artist employed the expressive explosion lines with no need for a representational component to imbue the drawing with the powerful emotion of anger. A non-artist adult drew a portrayal of sadness with a series of lines of which the judges could make no sense. The use of a nonrepresentational subject for the drawing, however, indicated sophistication on the part of the drawer (who kept protesting, "I know nothing about art"). Although she did not have the graphic skills to realize it, she clearly understood as a possibility for a drawing the artist's abstract expression of emotion.

The modernist penchant for nonrepresentation or abstract representation has been thought to be a prerequisite for my study (see Pariser & van den Berg, 1997). But in my study, drawings that were representative (e.g., the sorrowful scene of a child weeping on his bed) as frequently scored high in terms of overall expressivity as those that were not (e.g., the drooping diagonal lines of what might be tears). What was apparent was that only professional artists used nonrepresentational subjects as frequently as representational and only professional artists demonstrated a consistent and conscious control over the construction of the drawing.

While 5-year-old Gabby and professional artist Linda both drew anger as a series of tightly and endlessly scribbled lines, and both of them maintained a furious facial expression as they pounded their pens into the paper, Gabby was lost in the adventure . . . embodying anger quite visibly as she pressed herself into the image. "Angry," she explained as she handed the drawing to me. "If I'd had more time, there would be no white showing through." Professional artist Linda, on the other hand, skillfully and self-consciously provoked herself to elicit the same attitude toward her drawing. Deliberately thinking of the policeman who gave her a ticket and other assaults on her well-being, she playfully conjured the emotive attitude that was at such ready disposal to the 5-year-old (See Plate 3).

My study demonstrated that, with significant difference from the other groups, adult artists and 5-year-old children performed comparably with regard to the attribute of overall expressivity in their drawing. Unlike the other participants in the study, both artists and young children employed Goodman's repleteness in the embodiment of feeling through the graphic strategies of line use and composition. In the use of symbols, professional artists exhibited a range of choices, from the extensions of self so prevalent in the youngest children's drawings to the nonrepresentational vehicles that only they seemed able to control well.

Similarities were also observed in the way the youngest children and the artists created their drawings. Unlike the other participants in my study, the 5-year-olds and the professional artists maintained a positive and productive rapport with their developing drawings. The youngest child reacted playfully to unexpected new developments; the adult artist seemed to actively seek them out. These differences in perspective reflect the difference in distance between a drawer whose drawing is an extension of self and a drawer whose drawing is an invention of self. The distinctions then are found in distance, process, and understanding of symbolic reference. The similarities reside in the emotive content of the drawings themselves. The 5-year-old perhaps unconsciously possesses a gift that is lost to most of us. In the artist's conscious repossession of that gift, she also redefines it (Davis, 1997a).

Using aesthetic criteria derived from the cognitive framework for perceiving art proposed by Nelson Goodman, I was able to derive a more "rational" or "thinking" analysis of the comparison between child and adult than personal anecdote would allow. But without my own observations as a teacher and student of art, I doubt my interest in the topic would have been so strong. In fact, were it not for my experiences as an artist and teacher and my own admittedly romantic views of childhood, I think I would neither have been able to orchestrate nor have enjoyed so greatly the collection of drawings from children and artists in studios, living rooms, day care centers, and schools.

REVIEWING THE RATIONAL VIEW OF THE CHILD AS ARTIST

An empirical study of drawings in which artists and children were engaged in the same drawing tasks (as opposed to more haphazard comparisons) helps us to identify aspects of the child's artistry that can be reasonably likened to the process of the adult artist. Perhaps unsurprisingly, with different content and context, these attributes can be aligned to and expand our thinking on those features derived from the previous discussion of the romantic perspective. The question here, as it is with all the tensions, is not so much, "What does this perspective allow that the other will not?" More accurately, the question is, "What else (and surely more) do we learn when looking at the same phenomenon through apparently dichotomous lenses?" And especially, as it was with thinking and feeling, what is there to learn from the interaction of romance and reason? Resisting the "either/or" and now considering the "if both, then what" perspective, our three romantic aspects of the similarities between the work of child and adult artist are expanded by our considerations in a rational or cognitive mode:

1. Connection. Where from a romantic perspective this direct connection was considered as a personal one between child or artist and the emotion or vision expressed; from the rational perspective, the connection is seen in the expression of the image—the drawing itself in which, for artist and child, self is imprinted and with which child and artist are in continuous and active rapport. Whether turning the paper round and round to reencounter the image from new perspectives as artists do in order to consciously discover new possibilities or responding flexibly to an unanticipated turn of the crayon as young children do with freedom and invention, the artist and child are connected and have an active relationship with the works of art that they are creating. There is, also, in both these examples (the reencountering of the image from new perspectives and the active response to unexpected mark making) a fluid connection between the roles of producer and perceiver with the child and adult artist shifting as seamlessly between them as children involved in pretend play. The result of these various connections is palpable. The expressive work of both these groups of individuals is thought to embody or *be* the emotion expressed.

2. Freedom. From the romantic perspective, the notion of freedom was considered in terms of the conventional expectations for drawing. For the child, freedom was an uninformed breaking of rules—for the artist, a conscious attempt to break expectations or rules. From the cognitive/rational perspective, again attending here to the construction of the product, freedom is seen as a variety of choices on the part of professional artists to use, for example, representational or nonrepresentational symbolic vehicles or to select alternatives for the application of line or composition. Young children's images appeared to be free from the constraints that development and knowledge placed on the older children. Free from the awareness that someone else needed to make sense of or "read" the image, free from a fear of judgment of quality of the drawing, the youngest children created images that had expressive quality comparable to that of artists, even as a lack of knowledge of the media made the children's drawings less reflective of choice (almost all 5-year-olds used representational or self-images in their drawings).

3. Distance. From a romantic perspective, this distance was construed as a sort of "outsiderism." For the young child, standing by virtue of age and experience on the skirts of the world of convention and expectation, drawing is a vital means for making sense of an unknown world. For the professional artist, removed or self-removing from the mainstream, the distance may allow a purview for making sense of the world that preoccupied central involvement would obscure. From a cognitive perspective, a lack of distance can be seen in the relationship between the symbolic representation that is the drawing and its reference to meaning. Where lines and form are embodied with meaning, there is a fusion between idea and mark that enables the metaphoric exemplification that is demonstrated by the youngest and most advanced artists. This lack of distance between symbol and referent, like the connection between artist and work, enables the work to *be* the emotion it expresses and the artist to *be* the subject of her work whether she is literally represented therein or not.

Returning to Octavia's experience in class, we see that in school the translatable symbol systems of writing and reading are prioritized over that of aesthetic expression through the untranslatable language of art. A teacher interested in the cognitive strategies involved in Octavia's construction of her family image might ask questions such as, "How did you decide to make your father's shoes so big?" "How did you make your brother's face look so real?" "What are these lines you've drawn here and how did you think to make them?" Questions such as these help the child to know that she is involved in the thoughtful construction of an image that is valued for the very properties it contains. The teacher would be showing the respect that she has for the child's thoughtful process, the decisions she makes along the way, the whole she has constructed out of various parts.

A question can be more honoring than one of 24 "Wonderfuls." A question speaks of the attention the teacher has paid a work, the landscape for not knowing that is contained in the image, and the possibility for multiple interpretations. If the teacher had shared with the class a collection of family portraits done by artists of differing styles, the children might see in those images the connection between their work and those that are sufficiently valued to be reproduced in books or hung in museums. What did "other" artists include or leave out of these images of family? What have you included and why? Comments like these honor the child's ability to represent his or her world through graphic symbolization. Language, as it is used in the world of critics and students of art, accompanies but does not outweigh that which we "do" say in drawing and "try" to say again in words.

The curator at the Fogg Art Museum might have taken a minute to look hard at Teriyaki's reproduction of the Miro. Knowing, as Fineberg has shown us, that Miro took such interest in children's work, she might have shared with Teriyaki how the process had come full cycle: Miro capturing a child's style, a child capturing Miro's. Where would Teriyaki think it should go from here? Could he draw other things in the style of Miro? Might he, like Miro, try to capture the style of another child's in his work? What had Teriyaki learned from recreating the Miro image?

When we level the playing field between artist and child, between producer and perceiver, between meaning-maker through image and meaning-maker through words, we make real and tangible the conversation through art that artists and viewers of art have perpetuated across time and circumstance and culture. If we value this conversation in and of itself, we need to be sure that all our children at every juncture in their development have sufficient art instruction to learn and use the vocabularies of art. Only then will the conversation be perpetuated and extended across more voices than those of the talented and specially trained.

The differences in the content of the terms *connection, freedom,* and *distance,* from a romantic versus a rational perspective, are fine-tuned and important only if the activity of making art is taken seriously and the model provided by the professional artist regarded as an important paradigm for thinking and feeling through art. Respect for an early gift of artistry would require that 5-year-old children's facility with art be cultivated in its own right rather than "used" in the introduction of more valued symbolic codes. Respect for what artists see as the pure vision and unfettered understandings of the young child demands a recapitulation of school structures such that children can better frame the direction of their learning (no more "fill in the flowers on top of ready-made stems"). The gifts of artistry that children bear must be cultivated throughout the course of their education (arts education every day so that developing awareness in perception can be realized in artistic production). The comparison between child and artist, productive as it may be for our broader considerations is not, as we will see, ever at the heart of discussions of general curriculum or often in discussions as to whether and why the arts should be included in mainstream education in the United States.

3

The Arts in Education in School

OCTAVIA THREE

Ten-year-old Octavia's mother, Lucille, at 45, had begun to paint again after more than 25 years of careful self-distancing from the visual arts. Granted a scholarship to art school when she graduated from high school in New York, her parents decided to test the viability of her plan. A neighbor on her block reportedly had gone to art school and Lucille's parents agreed that if the neighbor thought Lucille's work had promise—that it looked as if she might "make it" and be able to support herself as a professional artist—she could accept the scholarship and go to art school. Otherwise Lucille was obliged to study in a professional school that would prepare her for a secure job.

Lucille put together her collection of favorite works, and with her parents went to visit the erudite neighbor. The neighbor politely looked through the pieces, many of them highly abstract—explorations, it seemed to him, that were more of color than of form, and scratched his chin. "Well," he said. "This work shows that Lucille loves what she does. But I can't think that anyone would buy any of this." The parents thanked the neighbor; Lucille remembers shaking his hand even though her face was too red and her head too bowed to see the look in his eyes. When she got home, she threw away her art supplies and vowed never to expose a child of her own to such criticism. Two decades later, she has decided it is not only time for her to work again; it is time for her to teach art to young adults. In her classes, she encourages students to paint for themselves and not for the approval of others. The daughter of Sondheim's Seurat says of the inventor of pointillism: "He never sold a painting in his lifetime" (Sondheim & Lapine, 1991, p. 136).

Thanks to her mother's lifelong relationship with the visual arts, Octavia has always had art supplies at home. From the days before school when she had muffin tins filled with poster paint to her after-school hours at home as a fourth grader, she has always had the media and encouragement to create. But Octavia no longer has art as a regular activity in her classroom. Once a week a teacher comes around with an "art cart." The art cart is filled with pencils, crayons, markers, and papers—all sized to fit within the edges of the desktops in Octavia's classroom. The half hour on Friday (a day Octavia might otherwise be tempted to stay home) is a weekly event that she eagerly anticipates. She enjoys the sound of the wheels on the floor in the hall and the enthusiasm of the art teacher bringing the tools of creativity into this stage set of tests, quizzes, and right or wrong answers.

Octavia's school is one of five the art teacher visits weekly, and Octavia is one of nearly 1,000 elementary school children the teacher meets each week. The teacher is weary; she longs for a permanent art room in which she can oversee sustained projects. But these trials go unnoticed by the children in Octavia's room. For Octavia, the classroom is wonderfully transformed by the opportunity to draw or paint, or to discuss the ideas in a Van Gogh print that the teacher has brought in for the day. When the art teacher takes over, the children are permitted to talk aloud to one another as they work, to collaborate on particular projects, and to explore different media each week.

This particular Friday, Octavia's classroom teacher has hard news. She reports to the class that, on account of the need to study for a series of state competency tests, the children will not have time for "extra" activities, which means no art for 2 months. "These tests are very important," the teacher explains, "and we want you to have every chance to do the very best you can. Art is fun, but we have some serious work to do." And from the perspective of external measures versus internal pleasures, we see in a new light the comments of the non-artists in Sondheim's *Sunday in the Park with George*: "Work is what you do for others . . . art is what you do for yourself" (Sondheim & Lapine, 1991, p. 55).

Octavia's mother is incensed by the school's decision and pays an angry visit to the principal. "How do you expect our children to be well rounded," she implores, "if they do not even have half an hour a week to learn about art?" "How will they develop as whole people capable of expressing their emotions if they don't even have half an hour a week to experiment with visual media?" The principal is sympathetic, explaining that he agrees the arts are important, but *not*, he explains respectfully, "instead of something else." "If we had time in the school day for all these great extras, I'd be the first to include arts education and more frequently than once a week. But between budget cuts and the demands for our students to do well on these tests, the school day isn't long enough even for the subjects that really matter. If you could prove to me that those children would do better on their tests because of the visits from the art teacher, I'd have her come every day. I'd even find a place for her to have a room in the building. But the truth is that art is not about what these children need now that they're moving on to the upper grades in school. Art is about feeling—important, but not the stuff of school. School is about thinking and knowledge and, quite frankly, knowing a right answer when you see one. If you think Octavia needs a real education in the arts, maybe you had better look beyond school walls."

INTRODUCTION TO THE GENERATIVE TENSION: THE ARTS IN EDUCATION IN SCHOOL— JUSTIFICATION/CELEBRATION

There are no subjects as frequently eliminated from the daily fare of school learning as the arts. Surveys indicate that, where the arts are included, visual arts and music are the art forms most regularly offered; dance and theater are the least (Persky, Sandene, & Askew, 1998). Some say that dance presents the most pressing need for a specialist. The English teacher should be able to oversee drama; any classroom teacher can play a musical CD in class, and students can explore "independently" and without skilled instruction the visual arts. But gym teachers are not necessarily dance teachers, and it is possible that the art of movement is hard to justify in a setting in which sitting still is still an ideal.

While of course this is a harsh portrayal of the landscape of schools, a vista that includes inspirational examples of artistic and interdisciplinary learning on all levels, the negative stereotype I offer may sadly resonate in more settings than we'd like to admit. Most often, the arts (bastions of human culture) are thought only to be important as extracurricular activities—like basketball or soccer. In fact, extracurricular parity is frequently proposed between athletics and the arts. You will often hear parents say, "When school budget cuts are necessary, the first things to go are sports and the arts."

Comparisons between the function of athletics and the arts abound as well on a broader social or cultural level at which they are often considered as alternative leisure time activities. Statistics show, to some people's surprise, that in the United States in the year 2000, consumers spent more on admissions to performing arts events than on admissions to movie theaters or spectator sports (National Endowment for the Arts [NEA], 2002). Children's involvement in the arts in school has been considered a predictor for adult attendance at performing arts events and cultural institutions (Davis, 1996a). Childhood participation in athletics no doubt has a similar effect on engagement in spectator sports.

From an active rather than consumer perspective, there are those who argue that school sports and arts provide similar personal outlets, such as a positive resource for the release of energy, or as an opportunity for students struggling in school to find success and self-esteem in a nonacademic arena. Others see the arts and athletics as similarly preparing students for effectiveness in the workplace by offering experiences with decision-making and action. But more people, I suggest, would argue for the importance of the nonathlete participating in school sports (whether for physical well-being or purposes of socialization) than for the "less talented" participating in the arts. We can *see* the positive effects of physical exercise; but few would dare to estimate a relative state of being called "artistic fitness." Even as they are similarly relegated to the periphery of the school day, sports do not hold the same edgy pedagogic tenacity as the arts—tottering as the arts do between academic worth and social redemption, either on their own or as agents to interdisciplinary learning. Art history, art appreciation, or integrative arts courses find their way into selected curricula. But the creation of courses in sports history or the use of sports as entry points to all sorts of learning are, at best, explored in isolated scenarios.

The question is singular. Are the arts worthy subjects for study in school? Do we celebrate the arts' claim to our shared and differentiated humanity and feature them in schools as subjects to be learned for their own sake? Or do we justify them in terms of whatever extraneous value they may provide? It is true that before there were schools that focus on the arts in education—like the 65-year-old High School of Music and Art in New York City or the recently established Arts Academy in Boston—there were always enclaves of adventurous educators constructing and celebrating all kinds of arts, arts-related, and/ or arts-centered learning encounters. Nonetheless, in spite of, or alongside of such individual forays, the arts have consistently maintained an uncertain role in the general education of children in the United States, negotiating fluid justifications for inclusion (beyond intrinsic value) that assume various shapes depending on the needs and priorities of different chapters of history.

One "take" on the scene allows that our thinking/feeling dynamic has found its way to the proving grounds of education. Are the arts most clearly about sensory experience and felt reality—hardly areas that need be covered within the overcrowded curricular day at school? Or are they themselves activities of thought that have usefulness to and/or implications for students' intellectual activities in a number of arenas, including those more clearly associated with and valued by the culture of school? On the justification side of this tension, we find a history of rationalization from the turn of the century to modern times, asserting purposes for arts learning that range from the development of an industrial nation to the elevation of individual scores on standardized testing. On the celebration side of the tension, we find examples both of the models for teaching and learning that can be derived from the artist's process and the power of the arts in schools to forge a cohesive and engaged community of learners.

How do we envision the child as artist in the context of school? Is her identity as a Tolstoy-like artist injecting her work with felt emotion to be cultivated and revered? Or should we develop in her the realization that while very few of us will grow up to be professional artists, training in *percipience* (that cognitive perceptual arena in which Goodman's symptoms abound), may make of her a "connoisseur"—a thinking consumer rather than an emotive producer of art. It is, after all, thoughtful audiences who, through their appreciation for artistic work and support of cultural institutions, keep alive for future generations the precious conversation that is perpetuated through art.

In a distinction between the more justifiable intellectual terrain of art appreciation and the chancy celebration of emotional release through artistic production, our thinking/feeling dynamic finds yet another iteration in the arena of school. Moreover, with regard to prior considerations, the tension between justification and/or celebration of school-based arts learning is necessarily imprinted with the extent to which we embrace or reject the notion of our children as artists and of artists in society as bona fide movers of worlds.

THE ARTS IN EDUCATION IN SCHOOL—JUSTIFICATION

Historians of art education (e.g., Efland, 1990, 1992; Eisner, 1997; Kern, 1985; Korzenik, 1985, 1987), almost without exception, describe not only the history but also the relative viability of arts education in terms of the changing priorities and reform interests of general education. The course of the arts in education does not seem, therefore, to move from one sensibly developing juncture to another as a field growing and refining itself in terms of its past. Rather, art education seems to lie in wait for each new broader educational trend as a chance for or obstacle to inclusion in the general curriculum. Where social studies educators may attend to changing political events with an eye to the content of their curriculum, arts educators worry if changing tides in public thought will precipitate the elimination of their curriculum.

Windows of Opportunity

Examples of this reactive malleability can be found throughout history. When the social efficiency movement of the early 20th century sought to make the general curriculum more functional, arts education would be justified as a way to help students make good use of their leisure time (Geahigan, 1992). Two decades later, on the heels of the Great Depression, the objectives of Social Reconstruction would provide a justification for arts education as a means to promote democratic ideas and community life in the classrooms. Mural making, for example, was promoted in this context as a means to teach group cooperation; the study of art and artifacts from many cultures would foster intercultural understanding. Responding to the Sputnik challenge of the 1950s, arts educators would advocate for arts education as a means to promote the sort of creativity that would make more competitive scientists, engineers, and mathematicians—a claim that, art education historian Arthur Efland points out, "never convinced anyone" (1992, p. 2).

The Aesthetic Education Program (created at Central Midwestern Regional Educational Laboratory, CEMREL), "the largest single investment of monies by the federal government for curriculum development in the arts" (Madeja, 2001, p. 118), responded to the interest in developing critical thinking skills around disciplinary "content" that emerged in the early 60s. Arguing for what could be learned from a "broader context" that encompassed *all* the arts, The Aesthetic Education Program alarmed arts educators who thought that individuated knowledge of the various arts would be sacrificed for an interest in the "aesthetic qualities existing in all phenomena" (Madeja, 2001, p. 122). Arts educator and advocate Kathryn Bloom, a major figure in the movement, held that the arts, in their quest for a high-profile presence in general education, "were stronger when bound together in our schools than they were as separate entities" (p. 124).

But how far would the arts go to stretch and conform to new packages designed to appeal to changing priorities? Did the term *aesthetic education* relieve educators from having to think about those controversial entities, *the arts*? Arts educators saw the wave of immigration that started to surge in the 1970s as a "window of opportunity" (a frequent term in arts advocacy) for justifying arts education as a "universal language," essential at a time when children in major cities would come to school speaking a wide array of first languages. Preoccupation with educational testing in the 1980s and to this day has prompted a justification of arts learning as a means to better test scores in a range of nonacademic subjects (Fowler, 1996). Rationales such as these submerge and reemerge through different junctures in history, and prove more or less successful in securing a more central if never permanent place for the arts in education. It is as if the history of art education is punctuated throughout time with the slam and release of the opening and shutting of windows of opportunity.

Plate 1. Georges Seurat, French, 1859–1891, *A Sunday on La Grande Jatte—1884*, 1884–86, oil on canvas, 81¾ x 121¼ in. (207 × 308.1 cm.), Helen Birch Bartlett Memorial Collection, 1926.224. Reproduction, The Art Institute of Chicago.

Plate 2. Rothko, Mark (1903–1970) © Copyright ARS, NY. *Untitled* 1958[?] Oil on canvas, 16¾ × 17⅛ × 2⅛ in. (MAR [?] 8813). Photo: Christopher Burke, New York. Coll. Kate Rothko Prizel. Photo Credit: © Art Resource, NY.

Drawing of "Happy" by 5-year-old child. Note the strong symmetrically balanced figure with out-stretched arms and upward curving lines.

Drawing of "Happy" by professional artist. Note the similar use of symmetry and line and the difference in choice of subject.

Drawing of "Angry" by 5-year-old child. Note the use of unrelenting dark lines completely covering the surface of the drawing.

Drawing of "Angry" by professional artist. Note the similarities in line and composition and shared absence of representational subject (e.g., an angry person or object).

Plate 4. Thayer, Abbott Handerson (1849–1921). *Peacock in the Woods* (study for book, *Concealing Coloration in the Animal Kingdom*), 1907. Oil on canvas, 45¼ × 36⅜ in. (114.9 × 92.4 cm.). Gift of the Heirs of Abbott H. Thayer. Photo credit: National Museum of American Art, Smithsonian Institution, Washington, DC/Art Resource, NY.

Certainly no educational history exists beyond the context of changing times and political and social interests and needs. But the "outsider" field of arts education seems unique in its dependence on the course of general education to welcome it in or close it out of schools. For this reason, the history of art education may more sensibly be outlined as an unfolding of various justifications for *why* we should study art rather than of *how* we should study art. Educational journals, mostly devoted to aesthetic or arts education, regularly contain titles such as "Why Do We Teach Art Today?" (Seigesmund, 1998), "Why Government Cared" (Korzenik, 1987), and "Justifying Music Education" (Aspin, 1991). Regardless of similarities that may abide between arts and non-arts subjects, we would be hard pressed to find an article called "Justifying Science Education," "Why Government Cared About Reading and Writing," or "Why Do We Teach Math Today?" We would more likely find (and we can) contemporary articles on "Why Visual Arts Makes Students Better at Science" or "How Drama Improves Reading" or "Why Dance Can Help Teach Math." The need for justification has been a virulent thread in the history of the field.

Historical Context

At the time when Seurat was manipulating color and light in France and Tolstoy was wrestling with virtue and justice in Russia, justifications for art education were being negotiated in American schools. Prior to that time, thoughts of arts education had mostly to do with the training of professional artists and the tutoring of affluent young women whose mastery of such "feeling" arts as music, dancing, and painting would bring pleasure to the home. In the 18th and 19th centuries, artists were traveling to Europe to receive "sophisticated" tutelage in the arts and returning to America to mentor others. By 1880, art education historian Diana Korzenik reports, the government was wondering whether hardworking and pragmatic Americans were simply "non-artistic" and whether "fine art" was something that only belonged to aristocratic Europeans. Similarly, the new nation found itself exporting raw materials and importing manufactured articles. Couldn't products that were being imported from abroad be fashioned at home? Were Americans ignorant or unskilled? (Korzenik, 1987).

Korzenik tells us that after the Civil War, Americans turned to art with a "passion" in hopes of making the nation more productive in the face of incipient industrialism. "America's material prosperity," Korzenik explains, "depended on all people becoming artistic" (p. 65). By the late 1800s, then, settlement houses and schools were teaching the skills of draftsmanship to help new immigrants find jobs and to foster a developing sense of the aesthetic, not in regard to handmade objects which were losing appeal, but in the construction of marketable and tradeable products and tools. The teaching of music was being justified as useful to worshippers in church. The study of the visual arts (mainly drawing) could help develop more graceful handwriting for the learned and better manual agility for the laborer (Geahigan, 1992).

Americans were also beginning to consider the possibility that fine art that respected the "principles of beauty" could originate from their new nation and frame what might uniquely count as "the American experience." In historical tandem in this climate, American artists John James Audubon (1785–1851) and Abbott Handerson Thayer (1849–1921) worked faithfully to replicate and celebrate nature and the "land" with an American spirit. Audubon was certainly the young country's most prominent and prolific wildlife artist, recreating with exactitude the details of many birds. But it was Abbot Thayer, who is attributed with discovering theories of "protective coloration," that ultimately helped to bring about the extensive use of camouflage in World War II. Thayer's recommendation of this tactic for use in the First World War was disregarded and he did not live to see its implementation in the Second World War.

At the turn of the century, Thayer (who considered his two fields of endeavor to be art and natural history) wrote several articles for scientific journals and the Smithsonian Institution on his theories of animal "mimicry and warning colors." Thayer pointed out that "only an artist can rightly appreciate" the feather patterns, that obscured the contour of the shapes of birds, and the assignment of coloration, dark on the top areas that are hit by the sun and light underneath, that made them invisible in daylight to other animals (Anderson, 1982, p. 116; see Plate 4). Thayer's theories were widely contested in his lifetime, perhaps most notably by Theodore Roosevelt, and were summarized by his son Gerald in his 1909 book *Concealing Coloration in the Animal Kingdom*.

Was it Thayer's use of and attention to diffused light—which like Seurat, he adapted from the Impressionists—that revealed to him the ways in which the arrangement of coloration of birds' feathers would allow them blurrily to disappear into the wild? Was it his life and work as an artist that made his scientific observations so open to suspicion? What would it take for the broader public to understand the natural interaction between art and science that is embodied in the vision and accomplishments of so many artists? Are we so tied to either/or that the bountiful space between always lies out of reach?

Beyond his epic renderings of New England scenes, most frequently featuring New Hampshire's Mount Monadnock, Thayer also painted lofty canvases bearing idealized and graceful larger-than-life images of members of his family adorned with heroic wings and halos. Other more prominent American figurative painters, like Whistler and Eakins (all trained, like Thayer, in Europe) were at about the same time actively refining their realist/romantic styles and even daring to criticize the Europeans. Artists such as these were helping to move the focus of a developing nation beyond the notion of material wealth to an attention to "cultural wealth."

Art Education as Outsider

Reciprocally, on the art education front, there would be need for trained eyes and minds capable of knowing excellence when they saw it. Arthur Wesley Dow was a leading figure in the American Arts and Crafts revival of the late 19th and early 20th centuries. A successful artist in his own right, Dow was a curator of Japanese art at the Museum of Fine Arts in Boston and an art educator who wrote extensively on teaching art. His book on composition (1899) was used in the public schools and emphasized the aim even of experiential art activities as the systematic intellectual development of aesthetic appreciation (see Efland, 1992). Such an approach would justify art education as a means to cultural development for Americans, who at the time were building museums and concert halls designed to equal those in Europe and to help overcome the artistic insecurities of a new nation.

The progressive educators of the 1920s opened a different sort of window of opportunity for the arts in education. In their appreciation of play and its importance to the development of the child's imaginative or creative potential, they turned to the arts as vehicles for framing playful activities that would foster these abilities (Korzenik, 1987). In the context of a child-centered approach to general education, art education was viewed as a means for students to learn to express and interpret experience through various media as well as to think beyond the given in that particularly human realm of the imagination. Progressivism's interest in creative self-expression would provide occasion to justify the arts as media for such expression and to allow for a respectful vision of the child artist. That vision would serve as a viable realization of a child-centered education, the imprint of political and artistic freedom, and the expression of universal truths (Efland, 1990).

Harold Rugg and Ann Shumaker, in their 1928 book *The Child Centered School*, speak to the vision of the artist as world mover (the romantic breaker of rules) so frequently aligned with a vision of the child as artist (unimpaired by the knowledge of rules). They assert that the creative artist, like the undifferentiated child, "is essentially interested in wholes." Seeing life as a unity, the artist goes beyond surface appearances, holds ownership, originality, and the mandate "to see" as his criterion: "It is the feeling, the spirit's intention, not outer details, in which he is interested" (1928, p. 207; as cited in Efland, 1992, p. 3).

While the blurring of "outer details" in Seurat's work may reflect his prioritization of "feeling," his preoccupation with technique was informed by his dedication to science. Close to the end of his life in 1891, Seurat became interested in the new aesthetic theories of Charles Henry who, in his 1885 work, *A Scientific Aesthetic*, "described the emotional qualities of line and form" (West, 1996, p. 798). Indeed this work inspired Seurat to explore the same principles as those operationalized in my child/artist study of expressivity: specifically, that there were predictable directions for lines that corresponded to various emotions (e.g., upturned for happy or downward for sad). The model that Seurat's work provides of the interconnectedness of scientific theory (around color and light) and the expression of emotion (through line and form) is especially well suited to the child-centered view of education that incorporated a broadened view of the child as developing in school in both the arenas of thinking and feeling.

Philosopher John Dewey wrote his inspiring and influential work *Art as Experience* in the early 1930s and in it positioned the "remaking of the material of experience" at the heart of the work of artists and of all of us seeking order and unity in our understandings of the world. Dewey (1934/1958) challenged directly the classic distinctions between heart and mind: "Only the psychology that has separated things which in reality belong together holds that scientists and philosophers think while poets and painters follow their feelings. In both . . . there is emotionalized thinking, and there are feelings whose substance consists of appreciated meanings or ideas . . ." (1934/1958, p. 73). Setting the stage for cognitivists like Goodman writing a few decades later on the subject of symbol systems, Dewey argued that while visual artists think directly in "colors, tones, and image," and "intellectual inquiry" is associated with the less immediate symbols of words, it would be foolish to think that one set of symbols is more connected to thinking than the other: "If all meanings could be adequately expressed by words, the arts of painting and music would not exist" (1934/1958, pp. 73–74).

The Education of Feeling

By the 1940s, arts education curriculum was dedicated to introducing children to (and studying their development in) the visual media through which they might find opportunities to frame experience that words would not allow. Art educator Viktor Lowenfeld in his landmark work with W. Brittain *Creative and Mental Growth* (Lowenfeld & Brittain, 1947/1970), introduced to teachers Piaget-like stages for artistic creation. Where Piaget's stages described growth in the legislation of thought through action, Lowenfeld's would address the challenge of negotiating emotion through art. Lowenfeld's stages, in condensed presentation, move as follows from: (1) *scribbling* (2 to 4 years) or what he saw as uncontrolled almost "sensorimotor" explorations of the media; to (2) a *preschematic* approach (4 to 6 years), in which shapes emerged and a more emotional than logical approach to spatial organization could be seen; (3) a *schematic* stage (7 to 9 years), in which "exaggeration" of size was used to express strong feelings about the various subjects of the drawings; (4) a period of *dawning realism* (9 to 11 years), in which children attempt and feel inadequate at achieving realistic reproduction of what they see; and (5) the *pseudorealistic* stage (11 to 13 years), in which the child consciously negotiates and expresses emotional experience through visual art.

Based on this progression of stages of "feeling in art," Lowenfeld would introduce art teachers to various art experiences or exercises that appropriately appealed to children's developmental interests and skills. The focus was on the doing, the making of art, the opportunity that visual arts education provided to children for expressing their inner views and emotional engagement in it all. Drawing on the modernist quest for freedom from traditional constraints, students in this progressive tradition were only encouraged to create and not to consider, either on their own or in terms of their developing efforts, the work of famous artists of the past and present (Efland, 1992).

This preoccupation with the child's inner life and intentions seemed to arts educators and advocates a couple of decades later as a "soft" if not "anti-intellectual" justification for arts education, and a ticket to extracurricular status in an educational scene that was moving in increments toward a more scientific, "back to basics," thinking-over-feeling position. By the time the Cognitive Revolution came to pass in the 1950s, arts education advocates were beginning to suggest that, beyond helping the child socially and emotionally, art education was and should be justified as an education of thinking, a kind of intellectual conversation between maker and perceiver that deserved a more central place in school. The Sputnik era was here, educational progressivism was falling on hard times, and schools were preparing themselves for the engineering challenges of the Cold War (Ravitch, 1983).

The Education of Thinking

In 1959, at what is now the famous Woods Hole Conference, a group of influential educators discussed fundamental issues in science and humanities education. Psychologist Jerome Bruner, a key figure in the Cognitive Revolution, was the director of the project, and his report on the conference proceedings resulted in his critical treatise *The Process of Education* (1960/1977). In this work, Bruner formally introduced some ideas that were to have a profound effect on the course of educational policy and practice in the United States. These ideas included two concepts that would affect the course of art education: (1) a focus on the structures of learning, rather than the acquisition of numerous and various facts; (2) a view of the child as a problem-solver ready to face (rather than not developmentally equipped for) the same challenges and structures encountered by experts in the various disciplines of knowledge.

This view, so influential in general education, presented to arts educators of that time the idea of framing the disciplines of art in similar fashion, presenting to children the same sort of challenges and concerns as disciplinary experts in the field. Discipline Based Arts Education (DBAE), an approach proposed in 1985 (Dobbs, 1992, 1997; Eisner,

1988) and the most heavily privately funded arts education movement in history, was framed around these principles. DBAE offered a framework for learning about the visual arts that would: (1) demonstrate that the arts had the same substance and structure as other disciplines and therefore should have a more central place in school; (2) move away from the "touchy feely" world of progressive art education that had suggested that arts were more about feeling than about thinking; and (3) (and this ultimately may have been its most controversial element) offer a form of arts education that could be overseen, if necessary, by classroom teachers rather than specially trained arts teachers, whether in permanent classrooms or on the move with transportable art carts.

Framing its content around the work of disciplinary experts (art historians, artists, philosophers, and critics), DBAE offered teachers a structure that would provide a foundation for any lesson in the visual arts: art history, art making, aesthetics, and art criticism. If you were studying neoimpressionism, you might study Seurat's *La Grande Jatte*, with an eye to each of these dimensions. When DBAE had a short stay at my son's school, Benjamin—then a fourth grader—brought home a really beautiful painterly rendition (mostly in mauve and purple) of a still life with guitar. Taking it in with excitement, I exclaimed that it was "really filled with movement and vitality." "Like it?" Ben smiled proudly. "I did it for you in the style of Van Gogh."

Although Ben identified as a maker of art, DBAE was identified with art appreciation, with knowing and talking about art (Smith, 1989, p. xvii). Since most children will not grow up to be artists, it was argued, they need broader opportunities than just making art, an activity now included in rather than comprising the curriculum. This new emphasis enabled classroom teachers, hitherto anxious about entering the "magic" realm of the arts, to develop curriculum adequately monitored through the verbal preparations and measurable outcomes with which they were comfortable. DBAE helped debunk the myth that there were no right or wrong answers in art. Replete with factual information, critical analysis, and field trips to the art museum, DBAE was bringing the arts out of the realm of free play and into the higher regard in which more traditional school subjects are held. Proponents declared that with DBAE, "Art is viewed as a subject with content that can be taught and learned in ways that resemble how other subjects are taught in schools" (Clark, Day, & Greer, 1989, p. 130).

At about the same time in the 1980s in Goodman's cognitive out-post, researchers Howard Gardner and Dennis Palmer Wolf were developing an alternative intellectual initiative, ARTS PROPEL (see Gardner, 1989). Built on a study of the processes artists employ in the making of works of art, rather than on a study of related disciplines, PROPEL sought seamlessly to incorporate the cognitive activities of production (making art, which was at the center of the triad), percep-tion (noting the aesthetic and constructive details of one's own and others' works of art), and reflection (thinking about the implications of details of one's own work and the work of others toward the develop-ment of one's own production). Project Zero researchers decried the move away from production in DBAE and celebrated the centrality of the experiential activity of meaning-making in PROPEL (Zessoules, Wolf, & Gardner, 1988). But, in the end, there were more similarities between these two approaches than there were differences between either and the creative expressionist movement that preceded them.

When it came to assessing student work in either approach, it was the student's ability to "talk about" art that mattered. Certainly the DBAE student would have more to say about artists and periods of art than the PROPEL student whose own development as an artist was documented in a folio—not of best works but of footprints of learning ("process" folio not "port" folio). But in the end, the PROPEL student who could talk her way (either in spoken exchange or in a journal) through the various reflections and decisions imprinted on her devel-oping folio work was the most successful ambassador of the approach. PROPEL curricula was developed in the domains of music and writ-ing as well as visual art, while DBAE provided the model only for the visual arts but with the hope that other disciplines might be able to adapt the structure—even across cultures.

It is hard, in comparing the two approaches, to separate perception from art criticism, and reflection from aesthetics or even art history, even though art making may only be one of four activities in DBAE while it is one of three in PROPEL. The approaches are both primarily thought-based, definitely derived from a cognitive model of the arts as domains of thinking over feeling, and politically positioned to argue for a view of the arts as more like than unlike the more accepted school subjects. But when you take away the alternativeness of the arts, their ability to appeal to the forsakers as well as the movers, their ability to provide an arena for personal expression in an otherwise information-gathering arena, what is gained and what is lost? Would the reformulating of arts curriculum into the same structures of language and measurement that supported other subjects remove the arts of their power to serve essential needs? One could even imagine the day when there would be a standardized test with number two pencils designed to measure students' academic prowess in the arts. That day would come.

Letting the Outsider In

It is 1996 and I am seated at an arts education roundtable in Washington, D.C. The conversation among arts advocates, educators, and researchers seems pretty much the same as always. Arts advocates are decrying the lack of fit between what the arts most importantly do and the preoccupation of administrators with measurable outcomes. "We know the advantage of the arts," my colleagues were saying, "to transform the realities and possibilities for children, to help students put back together, to integrate, the disjointed learning that disciplinary slicing and dicing provides. But 'they' only want figures and numbers to prove the worth of the arts to education."

An educator from an arts-based high school in D.C. is asking for help. Within a year, new students (some of whom had been skipping many more days than they were attending at their old schools) were coming daily to school, staying late in the day, talking about their futures when before they did not seem to envision the possibility of a future. "But," she lamented, "I really can't prove that their board scores on any of the SATs are better than they were before." I gasped. Why weren't "they" at the table hearing what it is that experts know the arts in schools really do? Why were we so sure that "they" would not care about a student's growing sense of agency and increased attendance at school?

But the groundswell became enormous. Parents grew excited at reputable research findings that suggested that listening to Mozart could raise your child's intelligence quotient (Rauscher, Shaw, & Ky, 1993). In 1998, to increase his citizenry's brain power, Governor Zell Miller of Georgia provided babies coming home from the hospital with free Beethoven CDs. *Baby Einstein* music videos featured images of infants in caps and gowns and classical music accompanied by visuals of toys in motion. Dancers in New York were suggesting that their visits to a fourth-grade classroom in the South Bronx had helped raise reading scores from inadequate to just fine (Davis, 1996b). Drama was found to be a factor in developing reading and writing skills and arts education overall was evoked as a means to ensure that students *would* have higher SAT scores. Indeed, the more arts training that students—from all different backgrounds—received, the higher their test scores (Fowler, 1996).

In the last decade, arts advocates have succeeded in having the arts included in what the government deems as necessary for a well-rounded education (for example, in Goals 2000: Educate America Act or The No Child Left Behind Act of 2001). National standards have been developed for the various artistic domains (just as they have been for other subjects) and testing of children in grades 4 and 8 around their ability to think in, make or perform, and discuss artistic disciplines has also been enacted (Consortium of NAEA, 1994). The arts have not only been justified in terms of how they improve student performance in non-arts courses; they have been awarded the same formats of standards and measurement that may or may not have served well those more traditional subjects that have not had to fight for their place in the curriculum (see Persky, Sandene, & Askew, 1998).

At the turn of the 21st century, two researchers at Project Zero, Ellen Winner and Lois Hetland, set out to test the reliability of the various claims for extrinsic values for the arts in education. Specifically, they were interested in value that was measured by an increase in success with non-arts subjects—that entity most familiarly known as "transfer" (see Burton, Horowitz, & Abeles, 2000). Did what you learned in the arts, such as close observation through painting from life, translate into, for example, your performance in science—perhaps in the level of detail you observe in a science experiment? If the problem solving you did looking at a painting and figuring out which shape or figure was the protagonist helps you to solve the problem in writing of identifying a theme, we can say a transfer of learning occurs. While many educators argue for transfer from the arts of specific academic skills in writing or even math, others argue for a transfer of what are called "habits of learning"—attributes like stick-to-itiveness, engagement, or self-discipline.

In a group of studies that arts advocates have found most controversial, Winner and Hetland (2000, 2001) did a series of what are called meta-analyses, quantitative procedures that facilitate an analysis of another analysis (hence the "meta"). Their protocol was designed to estimate the strength of relationships asserted in other studies. For example, in a study that claimed that studying music raised math scores significantly, Winner and Hetland would closely review the work, analyze the methods and findings, and be able to determine how strong the association between music and math might be (at least with regard to a specific variable). Was the study of music correlated or strongly associated with progress in math? Might we be able to determine that it even caused the progress in math? Winner and Hetland's review of hundreds of quantitative studies of transfer, for the most part, disproved the *causal* associations asserted between arts learning in a number of arenas and increased performance in other subjects.

But causal relationships are hard to find in any case. Take the claim for SAT scores and the relationship between increased arts learning and an increase in performance on SAT scores. While there may be (and is) a viable correlation between these two factors, it is almost impossible to control for other factors and isolate the arts as the *causal* variable in the increased scores—the certain reason that the scores improved. Students who have more arts training may have it because they attend better schools overall—better schools may be more likely to provide arts education than less excellent ones. Quality instruction in all subjects, then, may as certainly account for the improved scores as the amount of arts training received. In that case, there is a correlation and not a causal association between arts learning and performance on the tests.

Some critics challenged Winner and Hetland for using the sophisticated quantitative methodology of meta-analysis. They protested the reduction of arts learning and the potential and breadth of its effect to the tight numerical limitations of quantitative measures (Catterall, 2001). How can the arts that foster multiple points of entry and individualized outcomes be reduced to the prosaic counting of IQ or SAT scores? Wasn't it bad enough that funding that could be spent on increasing and improving arts learning in the schools had been dedicated to studies that tried to justify the arts for extraneous reasons beyond the importance of arts learning for its own sake? Was math ever faulted for not raising expressivity in drawing, or history for not increasing one's ability to read music?

Did we need to add insult to injury and spend another million dollars on meta-studies that: (1) disproved results that had already proved helpful to desperate arts advocates arguing for an increase in attention to the arts in education; and (2) perpetuated thinking in the wrong direction, forcing the arts in education into the same limited measures and outcomes that wrongly dominated the broader educational scene? A number of these studies, created under the pressure of justification, were hastily assembled by researchers insufficiently trained in the methods that Winner and Hetland would scrutinize. A section of the chorus was neither surprised by the results of these meta-analyses nor interested in the territory to which they might lead.

Winner and Hetland defended their work, not only because they felt it would bring increased attention to the discourse on arts in education, but also because, like Standards, DBAE, and other achievements throughout the years, it raised the discussion about arts education to the same plateau as that of other more traditionally accepted subjects. Winner and Hetland insisted: "The arts must participate in the process of use and refinements of such methods or be left at the periphery of those phenomena judged important in human cultures" (2001, p. 14). Does the acceptance of modern quantitative measures as the standard for importance betray the truths of human culture that have throughout time been conveyed faithfully if qualitatively through the media of the arts? Are robust associations and anecdotal accounts of benefits associated with arts learning, from improvements in academic performance to the development of self-esteem, all worthless in the face of tests of causality?

It is important to note that positive correlations are not without import. Outcomes like the amount of time spent on arts activities after school (White, 2002) appear to be most clearly and singularly associated with arts learning. Increased attendance at school, traditionally associated with arts activities (e.g., every principal knows to schedule visiting artists on Monday and Friday—the two otherwise most frequently skipped days) can help us know about the engagement in a learning community that inclusion of the arts helps to foster. But again, the school that includes the arts to counter truancy cannot isolate the arts as a causal variable in an increase in attendance. A school that has visiting artists may also be open to other enrichment activities that could as easily contribute to an increase in attendance. Regardless of whether they are causal, measurable outcomes such as these are not irrelevant.

In the final round, Winner and Hetland could not in all cases rule out causal links. They found causal links between music and math, dance and visual spatial skills, as well as strong effects on language skills from drama. While clearly advocating participation in quantitative measurement of non-domain benefits, Winner and Hetland also supported an "arts for arts sake" position, suggesting that better studies with more relevant questions needed to be posed. They said, "We favor arts for the mind's sake, no less than science and math for the mind's sake" (2001, p. 29). Would raising your IQ score be reason to listen to Mozart? When you get a lead in the school play, are you thankful for the help it will be with your reading skills? Rather than accept that the research questions that propelled the work they reviewed were any more worthy than the methods artist advocate researchers had often clumsily employed, Winner and Hetland described the challenge their work presented to previous studies as a call for new and better research around more important and intrinsic effects of arts learning.

Professor James Catterall whose work (see Catterall, Iwanaga, & Chapleau, 2001) has heralded the positive effect of the arts on both academic and social outcomes didn't "buy" the researchers' claim that their critical meta-analyzing would somehow elevate the field. He said plainly that the researchers "seem to believe that . . . People will buy into the art for arts' sake message if academic outcomes research can be shown false . . . Educators, parents, and school boards have grown to believe, correctly, that the arts do more for human development than increasing arts skills—even if we do not yet know the full story" (2001, p. 36).

REVIEWING JUSTIFICATIONS FOR
THE ARTS IN EDUCATION IN SCHOOL

And so the history of justifications both comes full circle and reaches extreme dimensions. We begin with a notion of art education as the education of artists, then we extend it to the education of a society of individuals who will appreciate and value the work of artists; next we move to the notion that all children *are* artists and deserve to be educated as such. More recently we've challenged that view and questioned the need for broad-scale arts training because so few of our children will in fact grow up to be professional artists. We must ask, of course, whether we would want them to anyway. Do we see as a viable end state for children in our schools the life of a Tonio, melancholically hanging out at the edge of the dance? Do we want our children, like Sondheim's Seurat, to be busy "finishing a hat" while the world passes by . . . out the window? Or is our vision for our children at the center of it all, in the dance, wearing the real hat, world moving within the pulse and conventions of society rather than "sitting by some desolate stream"?

Philosophers and educators throughout time, defending the teaching of the arts regardless of whether our children will grow up to be artists, have argued that we might as well not teach science or writing or math to our children since so few of them will grow up to be scientists, professional writers, or mathematicians (see Collingwood, 1938/1958). But while we wrestle in the world of education with the difference among disciplines, in the world of art, the overlap between art and science is inescapable—from the scientific principles of light and form that fascinated Seurat to the function of camouflage in nature explored by Abbott Thayer to the realm of conceptual art and cyberspace—all that color and light.

What is it that makes us fear the arts so greatly? Is it the mythic reveries of emotion, the awesome triumph of thinking—the visionary understandings that the arts deliver? Are we still engaged in the worries that Socrates expressed that the passion-ridden arts would be dangerous to the rational state of his Republic? Do we fear that the arts will corrupt our schools even though we have observed that they keep our children attending and we believe that they offer alternatives that other subjects do not present? How do we justify inclusion of the arts in education?

The justifications for art education are not divorced from the changing views we have of artists or even of our various understandings of art. We suspect and admire the magic; we embrace the idea of play but resist the possibility that it can be academic; and we appreciate and reject the romantic or conservative view of artists as outsiders. If school is about learning one's way *into* society, where do we place an activity that seems albeit seductively to remove? Throughout the history of education, arts advocates have sought to justify the arts as belonging on the inside and at the same time struggled with the danger that bringing them inside will diminish whatever it is that is so special about the arts.

Octavia's mother might have been aided in her pleas to the principal with a broader understanding of the various justifications that have been employed throughout the history of arts education in the United States. She might even have used the most recent struggles over quantifying the "transfer" effects of art education as an example of the extremes that the world of measurement (to which the principal was so bound) might lead. But perhaps, and this has been suggested by researchers and educators throughout the history of the field—she would have been best served by holistic examples of what the arts in themselves provide.

Those who mistrust or lack interest in justification, ask instead how we go about learning more of the particular and intrinsic values of arts learning. Beyond current trends in general education, these skeptics long to celebrate whatever it is about teaching and learning in the arts that is of particular benefit both in terms of its own rewards and perhaps even in providing models from which other subjects might learn (see Eisner, 2002). Justification requires a translation of arts learning into the vocabularies of other priorities. Perhaps, as with the different art forms, the field itself defies translation and requires new sets of lenses for making sense of its educational accomplishments. Contemporary justification has invited us to study the ways in which skills acquired through arts learning "transfer" to non-arts arenas; recent modes of celebration have dared us to consider the ways in which the arts "transform" individual student learning as well as the collective learning communities that they serve.

THE ARTS IN EDUCATION IN SCHOOL—CELEBRATION

There are ways in which the arts are celebrated, and to greater and lesser degrees, throughout general education; but they are *the* cause célèbre for schools that focus on the arts. Consideration of the more general celebratory modes helps to set the stage for a closer look at such schools and to help illuminate what it is the arts in education can and may do. Toward that end, I offer brief descriptions of eight ways in which the arts enter the scene of general K–12 education (seven familiar and one idealized) followed by a review of the special attributes uncovered in a recent study of schools that focus on the arts (Davis et al., 2001).

Eight Celebratory Modes

I call these eight ways in which the arts do and can enter schools, these eight tentacles of the octopus (with deference to our initial metaphor):

(1) arts based, (2) arts infused, (3) arts included, (4) arts expanded, (5) arts professional, (6) arts extra, (7) aesthetic education, and (8) arts cultura. I should note that there is no standard lexicon here. My terms and definitions are intended more to frame the scene than to coincide (and they may) with the many terminologies that abound in the field.

1. Art Based. The arts-based approach to the arts in education is the most clearly celebratory on the part of general education. In this framework, the arts serve as a basis for general education. Students in an arts-based scenario study the arts intensively in their own right in order to gain artistic proficiency, but also in order to be able to appreciate and apply the arts as a lens through which all other subjects can be encountered and learned. A clear implication here is that without sufficient mastery of the arts on the part of students and teachers, any application of the arts to the comprehension of other subjects is at best superficial. Take, as an example, the study of composition in painting and an arts-based assumption that that study can be used to facilitate an understanding of balance in writing or symmetry in science. The more authentic the student's understanding of balance in painting, the more nuanced the lens she can apply from that venue to a developing understanding of cohesion in writing or symmetry in science. Illustrating the approach, the Leonard Bernstein Center for Education through the Arts employs what is called an Artful Learning Model (see Remer, 1996). Artful Learning begins with student engagement in a particular master work of art, moves on to its study in depth, and then to its use as a lens for working in and encountering different subjects ("experience, inquire, create, reflect"). An opera, for example, can inspire on its own, give rise to the consideration of ratios between musical stanzas in math, the narrative of the opera in writing class, and the study of social themes in history.

2. Arts Infused. In the arts-infused model, the arts are invited from the outside into the general education setting in order to enrich student learning. Music of a period, for example, may be played in the history class. Students create collage maps in geography or tribal masks in social studies. Arts-infused celebrations would also include the case of the visiting artist—a poet sharing her work in English class or a theater company performing Shakespeare for the whole school. In the post-Sputnik second half of the 20th century, in response to the elimination of arts education in schools around the country from New York to California (when our justifications were not working), there was a surge of visiting artist arts infusion. Artists in all domains were finding stimulating (and making extra money through) their visits to classrooms around the country. Organizations such as the parent group, Newton Creative Arts Committee in Massachusetts, the national organization Young Audiences, Urban Gateways in Chicago, and the New York–based Studio in the School were formed to help schools find and place appropriate and effective visiting artists.

This infusion of visiting artists, parallel as it was with cutbacks on arts specialists' positions, presented both a great resource and a challenge to arts education in schools. The concern was that these outside resources might become a substitute for rather than a supplement to school-based art programs. For classroom teachers, visiting artists can enrich curriculum. Professional poets like the late Kenneth Koch did wonderful work making poetry come alive for children and publishing in popular venues the work of child poets (1973, 1980, 1998). Alternatively, visiting artists may represent disciplinary expertise that the teacher feels she may not share or come during class time when other curricular issues are pressing. Many structures exist for making the most of a visit to the classroom from a professional artist from pre– and post–class visits to collaborative planning between teacher and artist (see Remer, 1996).

3. Arts Included. In this model the celebratory stance for the arts in education is one of equity. In an arts-included scenario, the arts are included in the roster of courses offered daily, and celebrated or regarded as equal to any other subject taught. In an arts-included elementary school, like the Hoffmann School for Individual Attention in New York City, all of the children from kindergarten through sixth grade study art, music, theater, and dance on as regular a basis as what are more traditionally regarded as core subjects. In the arts-included scenario, the arts are located alongside non-arts courses within the curriculum. Any issue of transfer from arts learning to other learning is left to the student and his or her own ability to make connections across a variety of venues for development and expression. Development within artistic domains is valued here as much as development in other subjects. In an arts-included school, Octavia's mother might find that Octavia's persistent interest and dedication to the visual arts was of as much importance to her teachers as her engagement and performance in math.

4. Arts Expansion. In the arts-expansion scenario, the arts are celebrated as a cause for adventures that take students outside of school into the larger community. For example, student learning may include regular trips to the art museum, scheduled activities at the local community art center, or attendance at musical performances in a live concert hall. Through school-based initiatives, the arts-expansion model enables students to be introduced through example and experience to the breadth of offerings and enrichments presented to society by the arts. Some educators argue that school is an apt arena for learning such important rituals as appropriate audience behavior; for example, how much or little to talk out loud in a cultural institution, how not to touch in art museums, when to clap in concert halls, and whether to tap one's feet in affirmative response to a dance performance. Pre– and post–field trip experiences enrich the arts expansion adventures and meet the challenge of weaving real world arts encounters with school-based learning.

5. Arts Professional. This is the infrequent though romanticized model (note movies and television shows like *Fame,* in which the struggle of teen performers is portrayed) in which the role of the professional artist is literally celebrated as the desired end state for education. In the arts professional scenario, serious artistic training is provided not just so that students can gain authentic and advanced knowledge of the various artistic domains, but in preparation for professional careers in the arts. Most often students with recognized talent and/or persistence find their way into arts professional settings and graduate from high school with portfolios of work to show to art schools, video or audio tapes of dance or music performances for conservatories, and/or audition skills that will help in assuring a role in theater or a musical gig. While serious professional arts training is not the dominant paradigm within traditional school walls, there are opportunities for such learning in community settings and centers such as the Harlem Boys Choir in New York City or Kathryn Dunham's legendary Performing Arts Training Center in East St. Louis.

6. Arts Extras. This category needs little explanation, for it is most frequently found in our schools today and it represents perhaps the least celebratory (except for "no arts") position with regard to the arts in education. In this model, the arts are viewed as extras reserved for in-school spaces outside of the daily curriculum. Whether it is acting in the after school-play or editing the after-school production of the school poetry journal, balancing participation in arts extras can be a challenge to students, especially when these activities are not valued as essential to student learning. With publication deadlines or late rehearsals 5 nights a week, the grades of young after-school artists may decline. When schools do not provide arts extras opportunities, parents can find and often must pay for them on their own. The cost of private piano lessons or membership in the city's children's theater is prohibitive for many families. The message to students from the arts extras model is clear: The arts are nice, but not essential to life and learning. If you have time, interest, and resources, as Octavia's principal suggested, you can probably find what you need and want in the arts after school.

7. Aesthetic Education. In this category, the arts are celebrated as ways of knowing, perceiving, and attending to works of art (across disciplines) and the media they provide for making sense of one's life. The field of aesthetic education is associated with the Aesthetic Education Movement of the 60s and 70s, in which curriculum was developed around "the introduction of aesthetic values into instruction and the development of aesthetic perception and aesthetic ways of knowing" (Madeja, 2001, p. 122). Similarly identified with the study of aesthetic education is the Lincoln Center Institute for the Arts in Education (LCI) in New York. Since the 1980s, LCI has focused on partnerships between teachers and teaching artists, and on acclimating classroom teachers to the breadth of the aesthetic experience and the ways in which the arts afford them. LCI was spearheaded by arts luminary and educational philosopher Maxine Greene, whose essays on the arts as agents to "awakening" our children are imprinted with the sort of arts knowledge she advocates and the belief that "our lives remain the ground against which we experience works of art." With regard to coming in contact with a work, Greene says "if we are open, if we take the time. If we attend from our own centers, if we are present as living, perceiving beings, there is always, always, more" (2001, p. 16). Weaving together threads from classical literature and popular culture, Greene demonstrates in her writing the possibility for works of art to awaken us to experience and to provide us with the inspiration and ammunition to effect change.

Some arts champions challenge the notion of aesthetic education, seeing it as a way to avoid the "a" word (art) and to slip the arts into education without attending to what makes them special: the hands on experiential opportunities that arts provide. Aesthetic education encompasses a more philosophical approach, that Deweyesque "art-as-experience" approach, in which encounters with the arts are seen as transforming the shape and quality of one's own daily living (Dewey, 1934/1958). In this scenario, students acquire skills of interpretation and become familiar with a cadre of aesthetic texts across domains, celebrating the arts as resources for and examples of the height of meaning-making.

In spite of their somewhat porous boundaries, the above seven approaches can exist exclusive of or in concert with one another. Finding a place for the arts inside, from outside in, alongside, outside, as objective, as extras, and as ways of knowing—these seven scenarios represent a variety of levels and modes of celebrating the arts in education. In considering the eighth model, I confront the most idealistic "celebrated everywhere" scenario for the arts in education. Incorporating, as many arts-focused schools do, all of the categories above, the Arts Cultura model is a composite of what is and what might be.

8. Arts Cultura. Underlying this model is a structure I call, for lack of a better name, the wheel of culture (see Davis, cited in Kindler, 1997, p. 56). As illustrated by the wheel (see Figure 3.1), the Arts Cultura model is based on a celebration of the arts as a way to give form to and connect the cultures of individuals with the larger culture of humankind. Inter-, intra-, and multicultural approaches to general education often make use of the arts as a medium for encountering and appreciating different cultures as they are delineated geographically or by virtue of differing religious belief. But in my wheel structure, the view of culture as associated with race and/or nation is just one stop along the way.

The Wheel of Culture

At the start of this wheel is the word culture, representing the culture or unique worldview of every child in the classroom. That worldview informs and is informed by cultures: the worldviews of cultures (e.g., families, communities, schools, local media); and Cultures (e.g., nationalities, races, and ethnicity—the usual focus of multicultural edu-

Figure 3.1. The Wheel of Culture

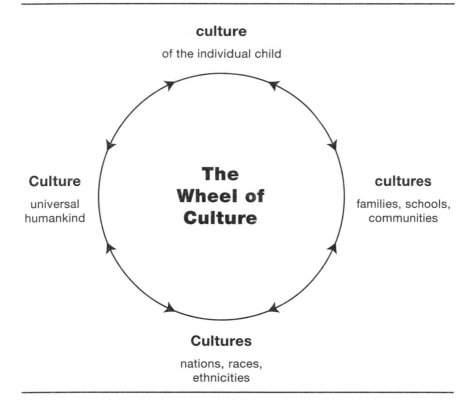

culture

of the individual child

Culture

universal
humankind

**The
Wheel of
Culture**

cultures

families, schools,
communities

Cultures

nations, races,
ethnicities

cation); and ultimately Culture (the common humanity that all of us are thought to share). That universal Culture directly informs and is informed by the culture of the individual child. The wheel that connects these different manifestations of culture is motored by the unique human ability to create meaning through symbols—the source and fruits of artistic thinking—the content and force of art education.

The realm of drawing provides an example of this interconnectedness in terms of specific symbolic constructions. The culture or worldview of the individual child is imprinted on the child's drawing, which has an impact on and is influenced by, for example, the absence, presence, or kind of art displayed at home, on television, in school, or in the neighborhood (cultures). Certainly that art reflects and influences the artistic production of Cultures (e.g., Chicano mural making, North American photography, or Italian Frescos) and ultimately humankind

(Culture)—the universal potential of art to embody our shared humanity. Returning to where we began, perhaps nowhere is that universal undifferentiated expression more evident than in the drawings of the young child (culture)—those expressive structures valued by artists, as we have seen and discussed, throughout time.

This circular continuum embodies the view that the arts give form to a range of understandings and manifestations of culture. In the Arts Cultura model, the arts are celebrated as ways of meaning making that allow us to experience and comprehend the many faces of humanity and the universality of difference. Of importance, in this model as in other recent reconstructions of the notion of culture, the presentation is lateral and continuous, not a hierarchical structure with "high" and "low" cultural levels—determined in relative status by any one canon or tradition. Instead, the wheel admits a broad range of cultural contexts and art forms and an Arts Cultura curriculum would not only honor the art that individual children produce, but equally the art that they value, from cartoon characters to rap music. Images, music, and literature valued by the child (popular culture) would be welcome in the discourse within school walls.

One critique of the DBAE curriculum was that a "connoisseurship" model implied that there were some artists and some works more worth knowing than others. The child was not at the center of this model "mediating" value; instead, disciplinary experts would introduce both the concepts and artifacts of "value" that the child should know—extending the separation from "real lived" world and "school" world, "real and relevant" art and "school" art (see Wilson, 1993). Art educator Peter London, a vocal critic of DBAE, put it succinctly: "Our schools seem to be contained within a bubble of time and space, which is all but indifferent to the actual time and experienced life of both teachers and students" (1988, p. 34).

Educators who implement the Arts Cultura model *begin* by looking to the cultures represented within their own settings (from the small c cultures of individual students across the spectrum to the big C of humankind) for subject matter relevant to a diversified curriculum. By persistently weaving related art works and activities through and across content areas, these educators create curricula that prepare students for participation in the cross-generational, cross-cultural conversation that is perpetuated through art.

In designing interdisciplinary curriculum, "Arts Cultura" educators invite responses to texts in science, math, or history that are not restricted to written format. Armed with the requisite skills, students can, for example, frame responses in movement, visual art, or music. The motion of the blood throughout the body can be articulated in dance or a with pulsing rap; geometric shapes can be given three-dimensional form in a variety of media, including video; and the controversies surrounding war can be expressed in a performance piece, installation, or original musical composition.

Students' individual responses can then be tied to examples of art works from local cultures—from community dance performances to graffiti to familiar local music. "What elements," these educators may ask, "are shared with your work or not?" Further reflection on their productions can be informed by the study of national genres like Mexican folklórico, African sculpture, or American jazz. Finally, these considerations can reach to the broader context of humankind: to issues of dance, sculpture, and music as forms of expression that make sense of phenomena—just as the individual students have attempted in their work. Investigation of the universal as well as of individual implications of a work of art affords students the opportunity to consider similarity and difference all at once: in dynamic interaction. In designing curricula along these lines, educators think beyond the media and technique of Western art forms and equip students with the necessary skills to make sense of works of art from various cultures, from those of different individual children to the aesthetic experience writ large.

Analysis of the artistic productions of young children can inform the study of human development. Investigation of the substance and making of murals or graffiti can illuminate issues of history, value, and collaboration within and across cultures. The study of Chinese calligraphy can afford new understanding of ways to use line and learn tradition. Attention to culturally diverse rituals holds promise for apprehension of universal attempts to make sense of it all. Relating such activities to individual learning, students may ask themselves questions ranging from "What do I learn from shaping a line—about me, about others, about history, tradition?" to " What are my rituals and rites of passage?" to "How am I connected to others who have asked themselves similar questions?" (see Davis, 1999).

The Arts Cultura model would necessarily be implemented differently from child to child, school to school, community to community. Serving a broad range of educators and students, diverse realizations would have only one common denominator: difference. Difference in this context is not a variation but a centrality, not an otherness to be tolerated, but the very thing that we human beings (and therefore the structures of our education) hold in common. Difference, that universal otherness contained in a view of the artist outsider, may be the salient feature of arts education and the thing to celebrate most. In coming to know their difference, students in an Arts Cultura model encounter their humanity—their particular otherness, their shared alienation, their common struggle as artists and as children to make sense of it all. The Arts Cultura model incorporating the other models and perhaps finding realization only in the ideal is fraught with celebratory overtones, honoring the perplexing and vital roles that the arts do and can play in education.

Of importance, the arts are celebrated in such an ideal structure as media for critical examination of self and other that necessarily include challenging confrontations, hard realizations about the limitations and possibilities for the human condition, and the contemplation of the social injustices that have been the subject of artistic expression and agents to the unity and brotherhood that Tolstoy located at the heart of artistic exchange. Questions of what and when is art that include the cultural resources and influences that contribute to individual constructions of understanding reach beyond traditional categories of the aesthetic and include what 21st-century art educators have deemed *visual culture*—the breadth of images that surround us, from McDonald's golden arches to Benetton commercials (see Giroux, 1994).

Contemporary art educators consider the development of a critical consumer of such imagery and the commercial mediation that underlies it as an educational mandate. Moving from the connoisseurship model of Discipline Based Art Education (DBAE), in which children are taught to know the difference between a Van Gogh and a Rothko, Visual Culture Arts Education (VCAE), attributing the roots of its focus on perception/critical analysis (and not just production) to DBAE, advocates the education of a cultural connoisseur who understands that across cultures, interpretation of McDonald's golden arches can range from dead end to capitalist power to national pride (Duncum, 2002). Some argue that the study of visual culture moves students away from works of art as the province of art education to cultural symbols/sites that might as well be the subjects of social studies. But the notion of visual culture, like the study of any of the versions of culture along the stop of my theoretical wheel, expands the idea of art education from being about this and not that (e.g., feeling and not thinking, doing and not knowing, art and not art, culture and not culture) and allows us to celebrate the synthetic nature of the arts—that "place in between," the either and the or—the meeting of psychology, history, math, science, and personal context in a work of art as well as the understanding across domains that artistic vision affords.

Learning from Celebration

A basis of celebration changes the tenure of the discussion around the role of the arts in education. Moving away from narrow to multidimensional understandings, we may appreciate the limitations of reducing the impact of the arts to particular well-defined measurable outcomes. Can we be open to the new, complex, layered, and particularly human understandings to which the arts entitle our children? Might we learn to value and to learn from (rather than suspect) the challenge that arts education presents to standardized educational measurement? Could we ever justify complexity of interpretation as an outcome more valuable than simply answering correctly?

The justifications approach to securing a place for the arts in education has variously effective outcomes. Struggling to keep up with changing general education interests ranging from social reconciliation to spatial or critical thinking, art educators are constantly scrambling to package and repackage the arts in whatever it is about which they think others really care. Some advocates suggest what is unique about the arts is that they *can* be repackaged so easily. Representing a natural synthesis of all disciplines, the arts can be shaped and reshaped to serve whatever needs persist in a given time. Are the justifications then just celebrations of different aspects of what the arts do or can do? Or do the justifications only allow glimpses of what art education is all about? By always settling for whatever part of the pie we can get, do we limit our ability to realize broad potential? What might broader potential look like and how might we attain a vision of the whole?

One approach that educational researchers (myself included) have embraced is the study of arts in arenas in which the worth of the arts is apparently a given. In schools that focus on the arts, as in art museums and community art centers, it is expected that the arts in all their mystery are a priori valued. The challenge in studying such scenarios lies in finding a method that is commensurate with the subject. Where focused studies of individual quantifiable aspects have proved inadequate to the task of capturing the complexities of arts learning, making sense of a whole made up of students, teachers, administrators, and communities presents a daunting challenge. In the face of this challenge, some of us have turned to the arts for paradigms with which to approach these artful subjects. Fashioning rich qualitative inquiries involving detailed descriptive accounts of resonant stories of arts learning leaves room for the inclusion of relevant quantitative data even as it provides a context for viewing the whole, including and beyond the sum of its various parts. The processes of making and interpreting art have informed assessment measures in education (note portfolio- and performance-based approaches) and offer new examples of ways to learn about learning—examples that are layered, contextual, and complex like the understandings that the arts provide.

Borrowing its name from the visual arts, *Portraiture*, is a research methodology that tries not only to provide such detailed accounts of learning (and here, of arts in education in action), but to do so in commensurate form—in artful narratives intended to function themselves as works of art. Accordingly, researchers using this methodology attend in their reporting to issues of style and unity, even as they faithfully subscribe to factual details and close scrutiny of data collected over a period of time. The research reports or narratives are called "portraits," the subjects on the site often thought of as "actors," and the researchers themselves as portraitists (see Davis, 2002; Lawrence-Lightfoot & Davis, 1997).

Portraiture is based on the following assumptions: (1) that all education happens in a *context* and that the portrait of a site of learning must be presented in its particular context, as if it is a work of art situated against a carefully constructed (researched) backdrop or ground; (2) that the researcher has and should acknowledge a *voice* (a particular lens framed by personal experience and the priorities, prior research, and focus of the inquiry) that will resound through the portrayal; (3) that *relationship* between the researcher and the site and the portrait itself needs to be respected and cultivated; (4) that sites of learning, like peoples' lives, are organized around *themes* that emerge from close study and that structure both a researcher's understanding and the presentation of the narrative; and (5) that the narrative itself, in order to be faithful to the understanding it conveys, must fit together and make sense as an *aesthetic whole*, like a work of art so that, as Aristotle suggested, if you rearranged any part, the whole would be rendered unintelligible.

I have worked over the last decade with groups of researchers and individuals implementing and adapting this process, originally developed and applied with enormous impact by Professor Sara Lawrence-Lightfoot (1983, 1988, 1994). With this methodology and an interest in celebration, I worked with several colleagues to produce "portraits" of sites in which the arts were valued—specifically, three schools that focus on the arts (Davis et al., 2001). Portraiture relies on the triangulation of three different sources of data collection: (1) careful review of printed materials that help contextualize and provide specific information about a site; (2) extended on-site observation of the educational site in action; and (3) open-ended interviews that are framed around the particular focus of the research.

The researchers with whom I worked approached our portrait writing with what we called "group voice": a coconstructed and shared perspective made up of agreed-upon relevant dimensions, research priorities, or designated areas of interest. The closely linked and mutually informative dimensions that guided our group view and collaborative study of educational practice had been determined as central to overall educational effectiveness in prior work (Davis, 1993a; Davis, Solomon, Eppel, & Dameshek, 1996; Davis et al., 1993, 1996). They were: (1) Teaching and Learning (the philosophy and pedagogy of a site); (2) Community (served by and surrounding); (3) Administration (its governance and organization); and (4) Journey (a site's history and vision for the future).

Within and across these dimensions at each school that we studied, themes emerged from the data collected—from the language used by constituents, the stories they told, the written materials and the repeated refrains, and the actions we observed that illustrated the metaphors and narratives that constituents shared. Comparing the themes from each site in a "cross-portrait" analysis, we were able to identify particular features that, in their consonance, seemed to distinguish arts learning in these settings. In delimiting celebration, I present an abbreviated overview of this work, providing background on the schools (in terms of the four dimensions cited above), and the results of the cross-portrait analysis, with reference to emergent themes and summary statements about the salient features that we found identifying schools that focus on the arts. Our sites were three arts focused schools in the metropolitan Boston area: the Conservatory Lab Charter School (CLCS), the Boston Arts Academy (BAA), and the Walnut Hill School (WHS). I use the past tense in speaking of these schools, to indicate "at the time" of our research.

Although to some extent all of the schools participated in some way in all of the eight celebratory models that I outlined, in terms of Teaching and Learning, the Conservatory Lab Charter School (CLCS) was most closely, according to our taxonomy, an arts-based school, employing a learning through music model through which music (and to a lesser extent other arts), was being explored as a lens through which all subjects could be learned. In terms of Community, CLCS served children in the elementary grades K–3 in an urban setting. The school maintained a close relationship with the New England Conservatory (NEC), engaging NEC researchers and teaching interns who studied the activities of the school. Administratively, working on its own as a charter school (deregulated by the public school system), then in an "adequate" rented space, CLCS was co-directed by an administrative director and a director of research, assessment, and curriculum. With an eye to its Journey, in its second year of operation, CLCS was looking forward to securing a permanent location, realizing greater recognition and respect for its arts focus and increasing growth in its numbers (of students) and scope (of art forms engaged).

The Boston Arts Academy (BAA), an urban public pilot school (part of the public school system), employed an arts-included model, providing a mutually informative two-track educational high school experience in the separate curricula of arts and academics in which students strived to balance academic and artistic demands. BAA maintained a strong relationship with six local arts institutions of higher learning (Berklee College of Music, Boston Architectural Center, Boston Conservatory, Emerson College, Massachusetts College of Art, and the Museum of Fine Arts' Museum School) that worked together to found the academy. This association set the tone of high expectations for students after graduation, and increased the reach of the school's "arts-infused" encounters that regularly enriched the school day. The six founding schools (Pro-Arts Consortium) also served as an advisory board to the headmaster of the school, who worked with separate deans for academics and arts. Pro-Arts helped in financing and overseeing the remodeling of the building that is shared with another secondary school. BAA opened its doors in 1998 after 14 years of planning by the Consortium and strives for a permanent place in the Boston Public Schools.

The Walnut Hill School, a suburban independent secondary school, is dedicated to the notion of educating the whole child through its 30-year "arts-included" curriculum with equal arts and academic strands, taught by different faculties at different times. As a boarding school, Walnut Hill was the only school to have international students and a separated relationship with the immediate local community, but with strong instructional bonds with the New England Conservatory. Administratively, the school enjoyed a measure of autonomy (the headmistress called it "freedom" to try new ideas) as an independent school and a 21-building campus for its site, separate academic and arts deans, a supportive fund-raising board, and a dedication to disseminating arts-education research.

Framing Celebration

With these summary backgrounds in mind, I offer below the particular features derived from our comparison of the different themes that emerged and organized our understandings at each of the three sites. Like the three sites, schools that focus on the arts may look at these features and say, "Yes, that's us" even though their individual realization of these salient qualities will differ, as they did among our sites. While the dissonant threads, illuminated in the portrait collection have much to teach us, in a completely celebratory mode, I focus here on what "fits," describing, with selected descriptions and quotations from the portraits, characteristics shared across schools that focus on the arts: *process* and *reflection*; *connection* and *community*; *difference* and *respect*; and *passion* and *industry*.

Process and Reflection. Process and reflection were evident at the Conservatory Lab Charter School in the ways in which, as a very new school, it was constantly, in constituent language, "figuring itself out." With regard to the vision of the school, CLCS constituents reported that they were "trying out an idea and seeing what will happen."

Objectives were not determined with a particular end in view. A researcher in charge of testing describes CLCS as "a laboratory school where we investigate questions about teaching and music and the academic curriculum." The prevalent role of research, demanding as it was on teacher effort and output, made a clear statement that the school itself, as a work in process, was one from which educators would learn. A parent offered as emblematic of the culture of process: "it's okay to make mistakes in art" and a teacher explains: "Every day that we're here, we're sort of beginning to understand what works and what doesn't."

At the Boston Arts Academy, constituents designated as a " huge challenge" the work that was being undertaken and that was clearly exploratory, process driven, and monitored by continuous reflection. From arts-related curriculum development to the discovery of innovative modes of implementation, facing the challenge of a groundbreaking new institution was a process, for all constituents, marked by passion, personal discovery, and hard work. Faculty members were challenged to reflect daily and intensely on the interaction between the arts and academics: "Staying sane is a big item." Students reflected on balancing their passion for their arts majors and their weighty academic responsibilities: "It makes it harder. We have to worry about both of them at the same time." Throughout the portrait, there is the sense of the school itself as a work of art in process, exploring interdisciplinary links, considering the possibilities for arts and academic learning as mutually informative and enlarging endeavors. Headmaster Linda Nathan celebrates the ongoing reflection and process: "I think it's a fascinating conversation we are in. I hope we are never not in it."

At Walnut Hill, Headmaster Stephanie Perrin is also clear on the school's process orientation: "The school will never be 'done.' It's never finished." In what emerged as the theme of the "educated artist," constituents here too were reflecting on the challenge of setting high standards in both arts and academics as well as the uniqueness of a student population that is made up of artists. Ongoing reflection makes the place open to change, "in motion," and eager to address its mistakes. One faculty member explains: "These kids understand revision, they don't expect to get it right the first time. Just like in the artistic process, they model, try, and accept criticism, then revise and try again."

Overall, with regard to *process,* we observed that schools that focus on the arts view themselves as works in progress, seek and explore possibilities, and regard mistakes as generative. They invite and sustain an active climate of performance and revision, welcoming challenge as an opportunity for discovery and growth. And with regard to *reflection,* they cultivate a culture of reflection in which objectives, practices, and outcomes are continuously reviewed and the interrelationships between the arts and academics are continuously explored.

Connection and Community. At the Conservatory Lab Charter School, there was a "sense of assembly" that teachers described as "the community effort" of learners bravely exploring new terrain with a purposeful focus on collaboration. Students worked in groups in classrooms and in performances, teachers collaborated in planning and curricular efforts, and parents formed supportive and challenging advising groups. A CLCS teacher described success in her classroom as "Seeing the kids working with other students." Curricular connections at CLCS ranged from building curriculum on "the child's experience and the child's life" to "using chants to get the kids to learn about dinosaurs." Connections with local artists enriched classroom activity and awakened students to role models beyond school walls; and ongoing contributions to the broader arts in education knowledge base demonstrated a sense of connection to the wide community of others vested in that subject. These threads were reflected in the emergent theme, "Everyone playing together like music."

Headmaster Linda Nathan at the Boston Arts Academy is committed to a web of connections. Through relationships with the founding and advising Pro-Arts Consortium and local arts institutions like the Isabella Stewart Gardner Museum, BAA enjoys and demonstrates its connection to other dedicated sites of arts exhibition, performance, and learning. Throughout the curriculum, the arts are used to make connections with student performance and historical events—whether it's to the Holocaust in theater or to Africa in dance production. Constituents' shared passions for the arts forge a basis for internal community enthusiasm—that feeling that folks "are not ready to leave at the end of the day and are excited to come to school in the morning." The emergent theme, "A Collaborative Spirit," speaks to the aura of an artists' collective: students, teachers, administrators, and parents working together in a unique endeavor. As one parent says, the school is a "team effort": "all of us together making education, creating a positive educational experience for our children and for them to progress to their fullest potential."

In written materials, Headmaster Perrin has described Walnut Hill as "a rich and diverse community of teachers, artists, staff, administrators, and students who come from all over the world and are bound together by their common dreams of intellectual and artistic achievement." Students feel a particular sense of "responsibility" (an emergent theme) as members of a boarding school community entrusted on their own with contributing to the school's artistic and academic community. Like the other portrait sites, Walnut Hill enjoys a self-selected population that feels a particularly keen sense of ownership. At all three schools, parents and students have "found" what they want and believe in. As one student said, "I loved it so I decided to come." As with all of the schools, Walnut Hill teachers and students explore connections across arts and non-arts curricula to help prepare students as lifelong learners who know how to "put" their learning and experiences together across time, location, and circumstance. A Walnut Hill teacher explains, "there is a feeling among the kids . . . that it is a gift to be here."

Overall then, with regard to *Connection,* schools that focus on the arts in education identify, demonstrate, and utilize connections between the arts and other aspects of culture, teaching, and learning. They cultivate a sense of connection among students and their work and artists and artwork on local, global, and historic levels. With regard to *Community,* they engender a strong sense of community within the school by fostering collaborative endeavors among all constituents even as they cultivate the interest and involvement of members of the broader community.

Difference and Respect. A first-grade teacher at the CLCS says, "If you ask any child in this school, there's clearly a difference between this school and another school; she will tell you, 'This is my school.'" From diversity in student population to various ways to solve a problem, CLCS teachers and administrators repeatedly evoked an appreciation for difference. A parent explains it as "allowing children to blossom in their own particular soil. And [knowing] everyone isn't exactly the same." CLCS teachers described appreciation for their individuality: "Letting me be me and feeling I have [a] voice."

Throughout the design and implementation of curriculum, constituents recognize that they are doing something untried and promising. A parent explains, "Not in any other school that I've seen so far . . . can I see this much creativity put into the learning process." The honoring of voices at the school—the opportunity for parents, teachers, and administrators to feel their voices heard ("Having a Very Large Voice" is the emergent theme) speaks to the respect for difference at the CLCS. Children are encouraged to think in different ways, as demonstrated simply in the assignment of rewriting the endings of stories in class, and more broadly in sharing pride for CLCS's multicultural student body.

At Boston Arts Academy as well, students, teachers, and administrators are impressed by the difference in atmosphere at the school—the respect that is shown for the arts as well as for students who come from very different places and have very different aspirations. A student explains, "There is a lot more diversity and a lot more respect." Teachers appreciate that their lives beyond school walls are valued. A board member boasts, "The English teacher is a serious published writer. The science teacher is a horn player; the math teacher is a saxophonist. . . . This rather special faculty . . . gives the students at the school exceptional models for their own development." Headmaster Nathan says she is "very proud of the diversity of this faculty and of the administration."

The community at BAA is aware that the school is different from other schools in many ways. A student explains, "If I was at any regular high school, I'm not sure I would have stayed . . . [here;] they actually care about us." Within the developing curriculum, teachers and administrators are considering "different" pathways to learning, because of their shared respect for the arts and artistic learning. A parent describes the "excitement that is here . . . definitely is a different pulse." A student, offering the language for the emergent theme, called it "respect for who everybody is and who everybody wants to be."

Students at Walnut Hill feel they are "welcome as they are" with all the differences that have alienated them from other settings—from personal idiosyncrasies to avowed passion for the arts. The headmaster explains, "They saw themselves in their old schools as not part of the mainstream culture." A senior posits, "A lot of individualists here—non-conformists." "God knows we're a diverse population," proclaims the dean for the arts. Students are encouraged to "express

their individuality." As it is at BAA, relationships with teachers are celebrated at Walnut Hill: "Like in some schools teachers are very powerful, but here teachers are more like your friend." Respect for students'
lives as artists makes for a different balance in the Walnut Hill classroom even as the difference in curriculum requires ongoing reflection
and revision. At the time of the portrait, administrators were working
to fashion one program "not separate but equal" for arts and academics. Headmaster Perrin called it "a program that ultimately . . . is about
what it is to have different outcomes . . . in the process of learning to
become an artist, a young person learns many transferable skills and
attitudes."

Across all portraits, with regard to *Difference*, schools that focus on
the arts expect, celebrate, and cultivate differences among their students and faculty. They encourage students to adopt individualized
points of view, and to regard themselves as alternative and redefining
education. Furthermore, they *respect*: parent involvement, students' visions for their future, the arts and artists in society, and diversity in all
constituencies.

Passion and Industry. The dean of the arts at Walnut Hill tells us
that "the thing about the arts is, the ones that are going to do it you
can't stop" even though "the price of entry is high." BAA's assistant
headmaster explains, "Art is work," and it is harder still "to be both an
artist and a scholar." Throughout the portraits, it is clear that both students' study of the arts and academics, and teachers' and administrators' designing and negotiating innovative optimal curriculum is very
hard work. But the passion that propels it all, and the industry that
passion generates on the part of so many at these uniquely intense settings may be one of the most salient distinguishing features of schools
that focus on the arts.

At the CLCS, a passionate team of founders finds "starting something from scratch" exhilarating. The exhilaration includes passionate
and dedicated researchers, the teachers who find it "exciting"—the
hard but "thrilling" work of pursuing a new idea and seeing where it
will lead even as you conscientiously strive to hear and to attend to so
many constituent voices. CLCS's development director acknowledges
that "what we're doing is quite complex" as a teacher explains, "I find
the whole, I mean what we're trying to do, I find that fascinating." A

second grader explodes, "I love to draw, I love to do writer's workshop and I love to dance and do our play!"

At Boston Arts Academy, teachers repeatedly speak of their passion for the arts and of the passion of their students. A humanities teacher who is a poet explains: "This was very new to me—this sort of coming together of my professional passions and my personal passions, and recognizing that here is an administration and here is a culture that really values that. " BAA's development director turns to members of the school community to serve as ambassadors to donors and guests: "Most people are naturals here because they are so passionate about what they do and they are so articulate and so thoughtful and they have an understanding of why they are here and what they are doing." A senior writes in her college application that at BAA, "There is a passion passed on from teacher to student for knowledge."

Walnut Hill's promotional materials read, "Passion is a word you hear often at Walnut Hill. It describes what motivates our students in their work. It also describes the Walnut Hill artist/teacher." The director of admissions explains: "There are very few schools where you'd find a nucleus of students that are this committed and passionate . . . Passion is a key word for me." He goes on, "If anything, our issue . . . is getting them to disengage. And with the faculty it's the same way." A student at Walnut Hill expresses a resonant view: "We try to have as much focus on academics as on arts, but, since we're all artists, we're more passionate about the arts." A teacher addresses the link with industry: "Regardless of what the student pursues in the future, learning that it takes a daily commitment to their art, they can then begin to know working in art as a passion." And graduates are told, "You will have learned in all your classes to *think* like an artist, with creativity and imagination, and to *work* like an artist, with passion, commitment, and discipline."

Overall then, with regard to *Passion,* schools that focus on the arts serve students, teachers, and administrators who are passionate about the arts and community members who are passionate about the role of the arts in education. This confluence of passions results in a most intense and *industrious* environment in which constituents understand what they do as difficult and complex and filled with high expectations. Indeed, the school itself in these contexts emerges as a work of art in progress that demands the passion and industry of dedicated educators, working as artists, striving for balance.

REVIEWING CELEBRATIONS
OF THE ARTS IN EDUCATION IN SCHOOL

These "celebration" discussions have been outlined with carefully de-limited frameworks: four relevant dimensions that framed our inter-pretive lens, nine emergent themes for three sites, four pairs or eight identified features/descriptors of what happens in schools that focus on the arts. But the contents of these observations and interpretations cannot be given numerical equivalencies—neither in their resonance in and across schools nor in their relative applicability to each of the very different students and teachers in the different schools we have portrayed. The portraits do include quantitative data such as dropout rates, acceptance rates to college, numbers of applicants per place— these numerical tallies are helpful in piecing together the particulars of our vision. But there is no quantitative measure for features like respect, collaboration, passion, or reflection.

Ours is a discussion that may have messy edges, such as those in an aesthetic statement—that may be open to multiple interpretations, as is a work of art. But in attempting to embrace the blurry edges, beyond the content that we have uncovered and that will serve us in our final reflection, I have hoped to demonstrate that purposeful considerations and useful though open-ended conclusions can be drawn from a more holistic qualitative look at the education provided by schools that fo-cus on the arts.

We have been meeting recently with educators who work in such schools and find the "passion and industry" features as apt descriptors of what they do at their best—their ideals for their work. They also speak of daily frustrations, of the weight of the extras that are expected of them in settings that are self-defining and resistant to comfortable answers, trying always to break new ground. They speak of the limita-tions of time and energy; the pressure of preparing their artist students for standardized tests that will not reveal what is remarkable about them. Indeed, they suggest that the aura of "beyond justification" may be an illusion and that even where the value of the arts is up-held, justification finds its way across disciplines and from outside in. Nonetheless, there is ever the sense that they are where they want to be and that their work, though too often without boundaries, is daily engaging and worthwhile.

From the perspective of justifications, we see the arts being "contained" and "repackaged" in whatever is the latest greatest reform movement in general education. From the perspective of celebration, we see the arts being "opened up" as alternatives for learning in schools and their communities. In the justification scenario, the arts are at the door, struggling to come in. In the celebration scenario, the arts are more safely situated within, opening the windows and doors for everyone in the learning community.

I wonder whether in the passion and industry dynamic, we see yet another face of thinking and feeling coming to school. Here we find emotion and the passionate love for the arts driving or compensating for the hard thoughtful work of academics. Here, too, we may find artists as connected outsiders tucked away ("beyond the pale moonlight") in schools of their own design in which they happily and without negative judgment pursue their work as world movers, both on their own and through their mentoring of their artist students. Our child as artist becomes, in these settings, both the reason for and desired outcome of school, and celebration erases, blurs, or holds at bay—even for the moment—the tenuous rationales of justification.

Schools that focus on the arts may dot the landscape of cities like Boston and New York, and exist here and there in random suburban and rural pockets, but for the most part, they are out of the reach of most of our children. Against the backdrop of such elusive and celebratory alternatives, poor Octavia still finds herself at an elementary school that makes little if any room for the arts, and Octavia's mother, a wounded champion, tries to little avail to convince the principal of the importance of arts learning. Throughout it all, Octavia suffers the loss of an activity for which she holds great passion and which could awaken in her the sort of industry from which great students and artists are born. Perhaps the two nearly fictive protagonists who have been leading our journey through the arts in education should, at this juncture, take the principal's advice and look for examples beyond school walls in their community.

4

Arts in Education in the Community

OCTAVIA FOUR

Discouraged, Octavia's mother has decided to do what she can to provide an alternative art education for Octavia, now a sixth grader and, worse than complaining about it, no longer mentioning the lack of art in her school. After much persuasion, Lucille has convinced Octavia to go with her to an art museum, the Art Institute in Chicago. On Tuesdays there is free admission and Lucille leaves work early to meet Octavia right after school.

The mighty building that is the museum is stately and austere. Built in 1878, it seems steeped in a classical grandeur that makes it in itself a work of art to be regarded with deference and respect. Octavia's reaction is less than awestruck. The building seems so large. Her mother has told her that they will look at art there . . . how long might that take? Octavia is meeting her best friend at 5:00. Buoyed by the enthusiasm radiating from her mother through their held hands, Octavia skips into the grand entrance and looks from right to left with measured excitement. "What to do?" "Where to go?" She and her mother seem so small in comparison to the scale of the building, so quiet as they try not to speak but hear the flap of their leather soled shoes on the pristine marble floors. Octavia looks longingly at the gorgeous museum shop, yearning for the familiar activity of shopping.

"When I was a child just five years old," Lucille shares with her daughter, "my mother took me and my sister to the Metropolitan Museum of Art in New York. It looks a lot like this. I kept my hands in the pocket of my dress coat the whole time. Finally, my mother took them out and, much to her horror, discovered that I had in my pockets a few specimens from my worm collection. I'll never forget what she said"—Octavia's interest was peaked—"'We do not bring earth worms to the Metropolitan Museum of Art.'" Octavia laughed, but she had wondered to herself, *what are we supposed to do here at this museum? How are we supposed to act?* Groups of people swarmed about, leaning into paintings in the galleries, reading, talking quietly, stepping back, knowing, or so it appeared, exactly what they were meant to do in this magical, mysterious, and somewhat scary place.

How did they know how long to look at an image? How did they know which image to study? Why did they sometimes smile, shake their head, or look away somberly? Off to the left, Octavia caught sight of a group of museumgoers wearing headphones and listening to audiotape cassettes. She laughed at the way they moved as a group—this quiet attentive collection of strangers, moving in strange synchrony toward one painting and not others in the beautiful galleries. "What if you don't want to look at the one the acoustic guide tells you to look at?" Octavia asked her mother. "What if you want to look at other paintings in the room?" Lucille explained, "There are experts here who know which paintings are the important ones to study and it's good to listen to them. That way you get the most out of the experience." "But hey," Octavia asked earnestly, "what is this place about? I thought we were supposed to look and see with our eyes. Everyone here is listening to tapes or reading things on the walls. Can't you look at art without the words?" One wonders how Nelson Goodman might respond.

Ambling along, exchanging reflections on the new culture of the art museum, Octavia and her mother find themselves in the European painting gallery in front of one of the museum's greatest masterpieces, "A Sunday on La Grande Jatte" painted by Georges Seurat, 1884–1886. The huge oil on canvas is 207.6 by 308 cm and created completely out of dots. Even the wooden frame around it is covered with dots. Octavia is completely taken by the image. Beautiful colors everywhere, wonderful umbrellas and hats—the figures seem to blend in with the scene as if light and color camouflaged them. So many people looking at what? Not at her. "What do they see?" she asks even as the image asks her to be the one looking and exploring. Lucille is reading the wall text near the image, and first she laughs and then looks still. "Octavia," she remarks, "it says here that when this painting was first exhibited in Paris, people made fun of it—they thought Seurat was crazy."

Lucille remembers at this moment the images she made as a teenager when there was nothing she wanted to do more than paint. She remembers the neighbor telling her parents that there would be no interest in her work. She lost a scholarship over that remark. Looking at *La Grande Jatte,* she thinks *It was probably a compliment.* "How does this painting make you feel?" Lucille asks her daughter who begins to look a bit restless. "I don't know," Octavia answers quickly. "Well, how do you think the artist must have felt when he made this work?" Octavia looked at the moving rhythmic tones, the serene mysterious triumph of science meeting art in the optical achievement of pointillism. "Terrific." She smiled. "The artist must have felt terrific to be able to make something like this!"

Outside a public swimming pool in Octavia's neighborhood, a group of teenagers from the Boulevard Arts Center are working under the direction of a professional muralist to create a public mural depicting a water scene, replete with octopuses and deep-sea divers. Every morning the artists return to their work in progress and find a skull neatly painted in black off to the right side of the undersea action. Every morning the artists dutifully clean up the unwanted addition and paint it out. Finally, exasperated, the artists work the skull into the overall complexity of the mural.

Much to the artists' surprise, the next day an 11-year-old boy comes along to introduce himself. He was the artist who persistently contributed the skull. He is delighted that his work was recognized by this group and is eager to learn more from them about the how and what of painting murals. The young artists bring their new self-selected apprentice back to the center, which is located in a former Catholic church. A fence circling the back of the building encloses a sculpture garden. Where flowers might grow, three-foot limestone carvings are perched on wooden tree stumps—all the work of students from the center's summer Arts Employment Training for Teens Program. On the walls of the otherwise worn from wear center, brilliantly colored murals tell stories of the arts taught at the center, and the Afro-American experience, breaking the chains of slavery with the tools of making art. A poem written by a student at the center amplifies the image of an opening eye, portrayed in stages across the walls: "Those that are asleep must awaken, Those that are awake must see, those that see must understand, Those that understand must teach others . . . AWAKE."

From programs for schoolchildren after school to venues for high school dropouts interested in the arts and/or self-development, Boulevard Arts Center works to identify and meet the needs of its community. Embracing an entrepreneurial spirit and the desire to explore the intersection between community development and art, the center struggles for its own financial survival as it works to improve the resources of others. The young mural painters enter the center. It is for them and their families a haven of color, warmth, and support. In a new windowless gallery, "An Exhibition of Various Women Artists' Views from Within" is on display. Student volunteers walk among the centers' regulars serving apple juice, pretzels, pickles, and cheese and crackers. Soft jazz fills the air as laughter and conversation fill the room.

One of the artists stands next to her work, ready to discuss it with passersby; visitors peruse the work and float in and out of the adjoining Children's Gallery, in which a range of work is on display; parents and children stop by the adjacent gift shop to purchase note cards made by student artists. Our young painter of skulls feels oddly at home, excited at the possibilities that surround him, rightly thinking, "My paintings could be on display here. I could do this." The center's writing teacher is explaining his pedagogy to a visiting student from the Art Institute. He explains, "My goal is to get them to understand that, through writing, you can . . . create a whole new way of expression and also a way to unleash some of the anxieties or fears that you have. You can discover a way to create possibilities that may not have existed before." A visiting artist walks around the room, taking it all in with apparent approval. "In our communities especially," she says, "they need a place like this every twelve blocks." And we hear the promise of Tolstoy that art can have something to do with social reconciliation, something to do with feelings shared, unity experienced, and a vision of the good explored.

INTRODUCTION TO THE GENERATIVE TENSION: ARTS IN EDUCATION IN THE COMMUNITY— MIGHTY MUSE/SAFE HAVEN

Beyond school walls, arts education abides in expected and unexpected locations. In art museums, those fortresses of culture, repositories for art and artifacts that shape and communicate our histories and cultures, education exists both as a given and a goal. A traditional argument has persisted that merely by collecting and preserving those works of art deemed precious throughout the ages, art museums are a priori educational. The objects are there, laden with disciplinary and cross-disciplinary content and contextualized within and for the collective knowledge of art historians. But over the last 2 decades, the cry has been loud and clear for more deliberate and structured educational practices in art museums. Findings from a set of critical research studies in the late 1980s precipitated action on the part of the American Association of Museums (AAM) that called for museums to clearly articulate education as part of their mission. At what would prove an historic juncture, the AAM's document *Excellence and Equity* (Hirzy, 1992), proposed a set of recommendations for the reconstruction and implementation of museum education as a means to increase the accessibility of works of art and the diversity of the audiences of the art museum.

Are art museums the seats of authority and information that Octavia's mother believes they are? Are they there for the use and edification of those whose elite upbringing and/or art historical background enable them to value and make sense of the museum's holdings? Or does the museum hold untold possibilities for exploration and self-definition by many individuals who have yet to enter the scene? Is the art museum a place to quietly listen, look, and absorb information? Or is the art museum a place to actively explore individual questions and forge personal journeys based on the experience and background of any museumgoer? Do works of art educate and are the artists that made them therefore the in absentia museum educators? Are the curators in museums building educational curricula as they mount shows and/or affecting public opinion (as in new genre public art)? Or must there be a separate staff of educators within the museum dedicated to the challenge of helping works and displays of art to teach? Is the museum in any case a passive or active force in society's ongoing quest for direction and understanding? Questions regarding the place and/or function of education abound in these august treasure chests of art.

Alternatively, centers of art abide in most urban settings in which arts education is without a doubt the mission of the organization. In community art centers that focus on education, we find artists actively and in person (not just through the works and presentation of art that they produce) framing art education beyond the limits and resources of public education. "Out there" in the community, artists are the administrators and mentors, educators and counselors, working against all odds to provide art education when others will not. In the past 2 decades, these centers have received recognition for the services that they afford to students whose needs may not be met by schools.

Like the American Association of Museums, the President's Committee on the Arts and Humanities also produced an early 90s document, *Coming Up Taller* (Weitz, 1996), which acknowledged and subsequently awarded the impressive variety and extensive reach of these artist-driven sites of learning. The title *Coming Up Taller* refers to the rising of a child's self-image every time she or he bows to applause on stage. Do these community-based centers attend to the mission and objectives for art education that prevail in general education and in schools that focus on the arts? Or do these safe havens, struggling themselves to survive in struggling communities, rewrite the purposes of art education—working not for improvement in test or IQ scores, but for the survival and spirit of youth who have been placed at risk?

Created in the late 19th century to help establish and secure a national sense of taste and aesthetics, American art museums not only exhibited collections of European art, but also emulated the formality (and often the architecture) of their European counterparts. Community art centers also emerged at the turn of the century in the Settlement Movement's efforts to provide immigrants and women with marketable "artful" skills. Another surge in the development of these centers occurred in the 1960s when art education was being marginalized in schools and the use of drugs was rising and/or receiving greater attention in urban communities. In both periods of history, community art centers were created by artists and other concerned individuals to respond, through arts activity and learning, to the needs and interests of the time. In storefronts, abandoned public buildings, and church meeting rooms, community art centers continue to evolve, often in response to community need or interest, wherever they can.

From elitist and populist roots, both art museums and community art centers support and display the work of artists. Dedicated in various degrees and in various ways to education through the arts, these institutions offer examples of a new realization of the thinking and feeling tension inherent in the production of and potential for works of art. Art museums, with their erudite language and study of art, surely fall in on the thinking side of the tension just as community art centers, through personal action and relationship, align with the more feeling functions of art. While art museums are often critiqued as not being truly vested in the social/educational spirit to which they avow, community art centers are criticized for being unqualified for the social work to which they seem dedicated.

In one setting the art perceiver finds a rich and stimulating environment. In the other, the maker of art finds a way to experience the human impact of her work. These are both settings in which the parts of this journey come together, places in which children meet and interact (more or less directly) with both works of art and the individuals who make them. These are both settings in which education, directly or indirectly, is being considered and revised through and because of the eye and hand of the artist.

ARTS IN EDUCATION IN THE COMMUNITY—MIGHTY MUSE

Who goes to art museums? Studies have shown that those who regularly attend as adults remember being taken to art museums when they were very young, either by a parent or by a teacher on a school trip. Excitement, familiarity, and ownership of the experience remain for these veterans as positive associations beyond any worrisome responses to a new and potentially forbidding culture. How do individuals feel in that generalized place that we call the "art museum"? In response to that question in a recent study, more individuals who worked *within* the museum, such as directors and museum educators, expected visitors to have negative reactions (including a sense of lack of welcome) to the museum setting than did outsiders to the scene, such as non-arts classroom teachers (Davis, 1996a).

Prioritizing Education

Although the range of presentations is broad and diverse, we do tend to speak of art museums as if they were all alike—all 19th-century palaces filled with treasures and formality. Most often we think of those marble mammoths that look like the Victoria and Albert Museum in London—such as the Art Institute that Octavia visited in Chicago, the Metropolitan Museum of Art in New York, the National Gallery in

Washington, DC, and so many other venerable stone citadels in major cities around the United States. These stately structures stand as tributes to European culture and to American recapitulation thereof.

The Victoria and Albert Museum (given that name in 1899) was originally established in 1852 with the founding principle of "making works of art available to all, to educate working people and to inspire British designers and manufacturers" (Victoria and Albert Museum Web site, n.d.). These were objectives that were also of great importance to a developing nation on the other side of the ocean, eager to cultivate its own artistic sensibilities, its own sense of good taste, and its own nation of designers and producers of marketable goods. Henry Cole, first director of the Victoria and Albert wanted the museum to be a "schoolroom for everyone" (Victoria and Albert Museum Web site).

About 75 years later in New York City, the Regent Charter of the Museum of Modern Art (1929) stated its purpose as "encouraging and developing the study of modern arts and the appreciation of such arts to manufacture and practical life, and furnishing popular instruction" (Hunter, 1984 cited in Kim, 2001). The objective of *education* and *instruction* seems never to have been in question in the mission statements of museums. But the content of those activities—what and how visitors to art museums would learn from the objects that they viewed—remains a hotly debated topic.

The 1991 mission statement of the Museum of Fine Arts in Boston states: "The museum is a place in which to see and learn. It stimulates in its visitors a sense of pleasure . . . and leads to a greater cultural awareness and discernment . . . The Museum's ultimate aim is to encourage inquiry and to heighten public understanding and appreciation of the visual world" (Museum of Fine Arts, n.d.). "Encourage inquiry . . . " In that one word, "inquiry," lies a central dilemma in the field of museum education. Wherefore inquiry? In these text-bound, information-rich "exploratoriums," what does inquiry look like and who gets to ask the questions? Do we speak of the inquiries that comprise academic research? Or do we envision brave visitors inspired to find and pose their own questions as they make their way through the galleries? A museum educator in a recent study on inquiry in the art museum reported that adults in the art museum are so "intimidated by the art historian; the labels; the big money spent; the other so-called knowledgeable people strolling about" that "they are terrified to talk." She explains that, "Most people have been taught through passive lecture rather than through finding out for themselves and problem solving" (Davis, 1996a, p. 157).

The 1991 creation and approval of the Museum of Fine Art's education-rich mission statement is not without moment. In 1978, the field encountered a landmark publication, *The Art Museum as Educator* (Newsom & Silver, 1978), which lent credence to a view of museum education—actual educational practices rather than the mere presentation of art objects—as a developing field. A decade later, Stanford art education professor Eliot Eisner and his associate Stephen Dobbs (both proponents and developers of DBAE) produced challenging if not scathing reviews of the explicit and implicit state of this "supposed" field of museum education. On the basis of extensive interviews with museum directors and educators, they found uncertainty about the objectives of museum education and inconsistencies about the training and qualifications of museum educators. On the basis of this work, they deemed the practice of museum-based educators in this burgeoning hopeful field: "the uncertain profession" (Dobbs & Eisner, 1987; Eisner & Dobbs, 1988).

Did museum directors actually think that there was no need for trained educators and dedicated learning tools with which visitors might be acclimated to and informed by the works they were encountering? Eisner and Dobbs coined the term "silent pedagogy" to designate those aspects of the art museum experience from which viewers learned whether anyone meant them to or not—aspects such as the explicit signage or implicit lay-out of exhibitions. But even with regard to these inherently didactic rituals, art museums appeared to assume rather than help establish visitors' interest in and/or knowledge of art history (1988). There was at the time a dearth of dedicated programming and educational structure within the culture of the art museum.

Furthermore, these researchers charged that what education was in place was being legislated by volunteer docents or paid coordinators, sometimes with art historical backgrounds, but consistently with little, if any, formal training in education. The word *education* under such substanceless conditions was in itself a misnomer. These harsh and inflammatory reviews were catalytic in the self-reflection that art museums would do with regard to their definition of and position on "museum education."

In 1989, the American Association of Museums created a task force on museum education and convened the 1991 conference out of which the already mentioned and widely celebrated document *Excellence and Equity* (Hirzy, 1992) emerged. The document proposed a set of recommendations that, if met, would assure that the art museum was fully dedicated to the objective of museum education as an active process engaging and enlarging diversified audiences, including collaborative educational endeavors, and increasing educational training for all constituents. The push for diversity as an objective of education would increase the museum educator's responsibilities for "audience development" and promote such outcomes as attendance (from number of return visits to profiles of first-time visitors) as viable measures of educational effectiveness. From a museum educational perspective, the cultivation of "lifelong" museumgoing was a cultural goal; from the institutional development perspective, encouraging more people to attend and support museums was a means of self-perpetuation.

Responsibility for Education

Post *Excellence and Equity*, there was no doubt that an incentive for including education in a museum's mission statement was the promise of expanded amounts of financial support. And this incentive went beyond the public even to the sacred realm of the academic art museum. Professor James Cuno, former head of the Harvard University Museums, protested the mandate "to tailor our grant applications— applications made to both public and private foundations—to emphasize the degree to which our exhibitions and publications are intended for a wide and diverse audience" and resisted the need "to build into our exhibitions budgets expensive multimedia presentations, teacher training programs, and extensive outreach efforts." Realizing the far reach of the incentive, he sympathized, "imagine the pressure on our municipal art museum colleagues!" (1994, pp. 14–15).

Cuno was greatly concerned that art museums were "responding frantically to political pressures for increased access, appearing defensive and reactionary and not at all confident in the greatness that has marked their many decades of service to culture and scholarship" (Cuno, 1994, p. 3). While the mandate was clear for an education-based rewriting of museum missions, Cuno accused current demands of lacking reasoned measure and bearing complete disregard for the dangers of modifying functioning long-term past missions in response to what he saw as "short-term present needs." Perhaps most harsh but to the point, Cuno expressed his belief that public schools had withdrawn from their responsibility "of preparing our children for subtle and sustained inquiry into the complexities of art." Municipal art museums were being called into service because reduced government support had "resulted in the total elimination of art classes in our elementary and even in our secondary schools" (1994, p. 14). Museums, Cuno regretted, were wildly fashioning educational programs for a public uneducated about art and art history.

Harvard University has been the seat of training for many influential 20th-century art historians, like Cuno, who have assumed leadership positions in American academic and municipal art museums. These academicians helped move the direction of the philosophy of museums from a focus on aesthetics and cultural history to a connoisseurship model that situated art history as the mediator and objective of learning in the museum. In this model, academic training in art history became the requirement for positions that had the authority to decide *which* objects would "teach," and *what* those objects would teach museum visitors.

The "lemmings" that amused Octavia at the Art Institute, attending as a group to those paintings pointed out in the Acoustic Guide, were heeding the direction of art historical knowledge, and most surely with a Western bent. The directors of art museums establish the content, tone, and focus of the institution. Their curatorial presence is felt throughout the museum. Indeed, some museum directors designate a series of paintings (usually world famous) throughout the museum as "the director's choice." Gestures such as these remind naïve museumgoers that there are knowledgeable figures of authority who know what matters here and can lead the way for you.

The museum educator of the 21st century, on the other hand, often has a less audible presence on the scene. Nonetheless, her job is formidable. She is responsible for educational programming in the museum (both for adults and schoolchildren) and often for the supervision and dissemination of learning on the museum's Web site. The museum educator is also expected to increase audience diversification, direct docent training, and oversee education-related fund-raising. Typically, she will come to this work with experience both in art history and education, the latter gained from general education programs or those dedicated either to museum studies and/or museum education.

The existence of university-based programs that specifically train museum educators was found greatly lacking in the 1980s when Eisner and Dobbs toured the scene; but such programs are plentiful today. While these newly trained educators are coming to the job with master's and doctorate degrees dedicated to museum-education-related issues, they often find their positions relegated to a low rung on the hierarchical ladder of art museum professionals. Within the world of art museums, education is often primarily associated with the administration of school collaborations and the scheduling of school bus tours full of children. Schoolchildren come to the art museum for many educational purposes alternatively defined by the various teachers in their school.

The art teacher may be introducing works of art as icons of the field. The classroom teacher may be introducing the art museum as one of many resources of the community. The history teacher may be looking for the treatment of famous events or concepts by artists of historical periods. The English teacher may be exploring the "stories" in paintings or hoping to inspire a new way into writing through the careful viewing and consideration of works of art. The museum educator, with little recognition, strives to serve these various incoming school-related objectives while at the same time trying to create a museum-based educational program that reaches out and makes the resources of the art museum accessible to broad and diverse audiences.

A recent job posting by the city of Sacramento makes the distinction clear. The posting is for a "curator of education," a term used in many art museums with the apparent intention of elevating the status of the museum educator from that of museum "educator"—a term apparently invented to elevate the status of the museum educator from that of "teacher" (D. Simon, personal communication, 1996). The curator of education position at Sacramento's Crocker Art Museum calls for qualifications such as "three years of experience in the interpretation and presentation of materials for Art Museum exhibits" (City of Sacramento, Crocker Art Museum, 2002). Nonetheless, the museum takes the time to point out: "The Curator of Education is distinguished from the Curator of Art in that the duties of the former center on development, coordination, and direction of art museum educational and public programs, while the Curator of Art focuses on the selection, care, and presentation of the art work itself" (City of Sacramento, Crocker Art Museum). The curator of art attends to the objects, the overt objective of conservation and interpretation; the curator of education attends to the subjects, the individuals within the museum whose learning is somehow separated out from the selection and presentation of works of art.

In the current context, museum educators are striving to bridge this divide. They are helping to reconceptualize the art museum as an active force in social discourse, and to rewrite the active art of interpretation as an objective in the education of critical viewers who will make better sense and greater difference within and across disciplines and cultures in postmodern society. But still the museum educator in many settings struggles to be included in the planning of exhibits (rather than in the after fact "reinterpretation" of them) and even in decisions on such crucial elements to diversity and education as the choice of new acquisitions for the museums (Benton, 2001). If the art museum really and ever fulfills the controversial intentions promoted at the end of the last century and holds education as a primary objective, the museum educator will *necessarily* be at the center of its function, and not at its periphery.

A Stage for Learning

A dutiful parental museumgoer, I took two of my children when they were 4 and 7 years old to the Fogg Art Museum at Harvard University. Now the Fogg, as an academic art museum that holds the public as the last group served on a list that begins with university scholars (Cuno, 1994), may not have been the best choice for a first experience at the art museum. In later years of visits there with schoolchildren, I would see fourth-grade Teriyaki's interest in an exhibition of child art (his own) dismissed by a curator, and many young teens offended and even angered by the Fogg's insistence that they "check" their book bags at the front desk.

"My lunch is in there" one first-time museumgoer from a local high school protested. "We'll take good care of it," the guard replied. When these teens leaned in to look closely at paintings, a sonic alert brought a guard to their side to ask them to stand back. When they sat on the railing overlooking the courtyard, a reasonable distance from the paintings, a guard would remind them they couldn't sit on the rail. "The art's okay," a 15-year-old first-time visitor told me at the end of our stay, "but I've never gotten in so much trouble in such a short time before in my life!"

Four-year-old Alexander must have sensed the aura of concern as we walked into the glorious central stone courtyard of the Fogg. By the time I had decided in which direction we should go (I hadn't thought to ask the boys), Alex's eyes were closed. As he walked beside me respectfully holding my hand, but with his eyes tightly shut, he said simply, "You can make me come. But you can't make me look." His older brother Joshua felt my distress and stepped closer to one of the paintings. "Mom," he said with apparent enthusiasm, "I believe this is an original work of art. How much do you think something like this sells for?" I could feel the color come to my cheeks. Could I, veteran museumgoer that I was, still be embarrassed by something someone said a little too loud in the museum?

If I could take back the moment, I'd have asked Alex what he heard in the museum as he walked through it with his eyes closed (the sound of those stone floors helps mark the uniqueness of the space) and I'd have allowed that Josh asked a good question. "How much do these paintings sell for?" "Did the museum buy them or were the works given to them?" "Where do museums get their money anyway and who are these people whose names are listed on the signage?" "How much did they pay for these works of art?" At the Philadelphia Art Museum, museum educator Danielle Rice found that one of the five questions visitors most frequently asked about modern art was: "How much is it worth?" and, echoing fourth grader Teriyaki, "Who decides what art belongs in the museum?" (1993, p. 41). If it is true that museums want diversified audiences (and it may not be true that academic art museums particularly care), they—and we as parents and teachers—will need to honor and respect the many ways that different visitors will find their ways into the "visual world."

The other stereotypical image that seems to come to mind when we are asked about art museums are those "white cubes" (O'Doherty, 1999), those "modern museums" where the architecture in itself appears to be a work of modern art. In these settings, the galleries are stark and bare, not distracting the visitor through decoration or color from the splashes of paint on the canvases, the stones arranged on the floor, or the live person who lies motionless in a hammock in the center of an installation. While the art in more classical settings often tells more obvious stories, depicts bloody historical scenes, or brings fruit and china into still-life perspective, the works in contemporary museums seem very obviously to ask more questions than they answer.

"Do I walk around or through this mirrored cube?" "Do I speak to the person in the hammock or is she to be seen and not heard?" "Why is there a person in the hammock?" "Why is this art?" A recent display of kayaks was featured at a museum of contemporary art. Surprised, a visitor asked the guard, "Why kayaks?" "Exactly" was the sage reply. In the wide-open world of contemporary art, it is sure that "inquiry" abounds.

The work in museums of modern and contemporary art addresses a range of current topics from sorting out personal identity through and in spite of media stereotyping to exploring freedom and oppression in different political and personal contexts. In terms of the poignancy of topics and the breadth of media, these museums offer exciting opportunities for collaborations with schools and the stimulation of thinking across disciplines. At the Museum of Contemporary Art in Chicago, for example, a teacher advisory committee works with the staff to create curriculum materials based on the artworks in the collection. A math and art exploration of "a cube is a cube is a cube," using the work of contemporary sculptor Sol LeWitt, asks students to create architecturally sound models and to consider concepts through the process that address state learning goals for Chicago in both Math and Fine Arts (Museum of Contemporary Art, n.d.). Furthermore, through the museum's Web site, these educational exercises, means to assess them, and a display of the work of participating children are available to many more students and teachers than may otherwise have the opportunity to visit the museum.

The world of museums on the Internet offers a range of experiences for countless individuals who may not ever have in person attended an art museum. The number-one reason that teachers in a recent study gave for not taking their students to art museums was the geographic lack of accessibility (Davis, 1996a). Now individuals who live in remote areas can encounter on their own the culture of museums, the works of art they contain, and the educational opportunities that surround them. The effect of these resources is still unknown. The amount of scaffolding required by viewers of all ages and educators seeking to exploit Web museum resources is being assessed.

Will Web visits to museums eventually supplant actual museum visiting? Or will they inspire and empower a generation of museumgoers who might heretofore have felt uncomfortable or unskilled at negotiating their way through actual museums? Will the array of spectacular enlargeable Web-generated images ultimately call into question the value of the traditionally prized actual encounter with an original work of art? This is the fear of many arts educators. What will become of that moment when, through the close contact with a turn of a brush on a canvas or a nick on an ancient tool, we feel connected to a maker of objects whose life preceded ours by hundreds of years? Time will tell what the impact of these resources will be both on museum attendance and on the teaching and learning that happens within and because of them. Of interest to cognitive developmental psychologists may be the impact of repeated online explorations of works of art on the aesthetic development of perceivers.

Stages of Aesthetic Development

Just as there have been stages of development observed and documented in the artistic production of the child as artist/maker of art, there have been stages determined for the development of artistic perception—the nature of responses to art that change with time, development, and experience. In her 1983 doctoral thesis, *Eye of the Beholder*, arts educator and cognitive developmental psychologist Abigail Housen studied the "stream of consciousness" responses to works of art by adults with a range of different experiential backgrounds. Housen posited, after Piaget, five hierarchical (from novice to expert) stages of aesthetic response: (1) the accountive, (2) constructive, (3) classifying, (4) interpretive, and (5) re-creative.

In corroboration with Housen's findings and in a different study involving children as well as adults and a scaffolding rather than free flow of responses, Professor Michael Parsons came up with a very similar pattern of development. He published his findings a few years later in the book *How We Understand Art* (1987). The timing of these studies—right around the critiques of Eisner and Dobbs and the educational ruminations of the American Association of Museums—was ripe. Their timely allure, as theory emerging from academia with particular usefulness to museum education, helped to make this work and the curriculum that would emerge from it of particular interest. Great excitement surrounded the introduction of directed theory that could infuse and lend credibility to the work of educators in the museum. More than a decade later, interest persists and application of stage theory in museum education curricula abounds.

A very brief overview of these stages, conflating the different findings of Housens and Parsons (who had slight differences in their respective articulation of stages 4 and 5) presents the following picture of development in aesthetic response—the ways in which developing individuals attend to works of art. At stage 1, naïve viewers apparently respond to the most obvious aspects of a work of art—for example, the subject of the work or its colors and texture. What they see may prompt associations with their own experience that help them "tell the story" of the work of art (what's happening in it) or a story that the work evokes. At stage 2, viewers may think beyond their own personal associations with the work to consider how it was made (the medium used), obtained by the museum (that contextual piece), or how beautiful or realistic (aspects that are both valued at this stage) it may be. Stage 3 viewers have some knowledge of historic "schools" or "styles" of art and they may strive to "place" the work in one of these contexts. They may also consider the purpose of art to be the expression and stimulation of emotion, rather than just the portrayal of reality. Stage 4 viewers find and interpret symbols in the work and structure an understanding of the symbolism through their own emotional memories.

At stage 5, the highest stage at which we might find veteran museumgoers who have backgrounds in or knowledge of art history, individuals "playfully" encounter the work and re-create the problem solving that the artist experienced as the work was being made. Stage 5 viewers may judge the meaning of the work through very personal values based on individual and broad analytic experience and leading to a kind of reinterpretation of self. Where we considered a "u" in development of artistic production, there is also the suggestion of a sort of "u" in this sequence. For the most advanced viewer, there is an application but also an "overcoming" of all the knowledge reflected in the middle stages in order to "interact" with the work in a very personal and individual way. Housen quotes a Stage 5 viewer commenting on a reproduction of Picasso: "The elements come back to what I felt in my first childlike impression" (1987, p. 32). Another face, perhaps, of what we saw in the realm of art making as learning the rules in order to break them.

Housen and former Museum of Modern Art educator Philip Yenawine developed an inquiry-based curriculum, Visual Thinking Strategies (VTS), around this stage theory approach for use by museum educators, docents, and teachers in the museum setting. Many museums, including Boston's Museum of Fine Arts, have structured their museum educational strategies around this curriculum, which basically asks viewers to share their perceptions of the work ("What do you see?") and defend their perceptions in terms of actual elements in the work ("Why do you say that?"). Both these questions rely equitably on the thoughtfulness and perseverance of the viewer in a way that "What do you know about this work?" does not.

A Web site and numerous publications make VTS widely accessible (see http://www.vue.org/). These resources inform the visitor that Housen has staged her interviews (Aesthetic Understanding Interviews/AUIs) with thousands of individuals and found that virtually all of them provide responses that fall into one or another of the different stages. Additionally, Housen and Yenawine have found that almost all "beginners," whether children or adults, fall into the Accountive Stage (Stage 1). Based on this assumption, in his highly skilled back-and-forth with groups of museum visitors of all ages, Yenawine focuses on helping viewers discover the *stories* of a work or art—sort of meeting them where they are expected to be in their thinking. Additionally, from this approach, works of art that most obviously tell stories are considered the most appropriate for naïve viewers and are thought to reap the most benefit in their ruminations, which Housen and Yenawine assert definitely transfer into critical thinking and problem-solving skills across the curriculum.

A storytelling approach to making sense of works of art proceeds by more than half a century the considerations of cognitive developmentalists. The first American conference of art museum instructors was held in 1915 at the Metropolitan Museum of Art, and on the table was the topic of storytelling. Anna Curtis Chandler was a "preeminent" and often costumed storyteller at the Metropolitan. Her career in museum education, which began in the early 1920s, resulted in several books and radio presentations on the stories associated with works of art. Chandler also taught courses such as "The Humanizing of Art through Stories," "Illustrated Talks," and "Simple Plays" at Hunter College. As early as 1924, she advocated for better resources and "gallery training" for classroom teachers bringing children to the museum (Zucker, 2001).

As the stage theory approach was being developed at the Museum of Modern Art, it was noted that within the galleries, classroom teachers seemed to interact with more success with their very young students than did the docents who were implementing the visual thinking strategies. The reason for this success given by proponents of the approach was that the teacher was most likely closer in aesthetic stage to the children than was the docent who was an experienced viewer of art. The idea that a teacher would be, even if it were hers as well as the children's first visit to an art museum, at the same developmental stage as her children brings into question the sensitivity of the structure of stages. Parsons—the other parent of stages in aesthetic response—was clear: "I do not believe that most of us are consistent in thinking about art, and therefore are not 'at' a stage . . . people are not stages, nor are stages labels for people. Rather, people use stages, one or more of them, to understand paintings" (1987, p. 11).

Alternative Views

Parsons advances the same "repertoire" approach to aesthetic perception that other researchers have offered in response to the u-curve in artistic production (see Duncum, 1986; Wolf & Perry, 1988). Thinking less in terms of the stages as invariant hierarchical structures, they are viewed instead as repertoires of skills for making and perceiving art that are acquired and transformed with maturity and experience. When looking at a nonrepresentational painting that is filled with color and texture, for example, a stage 1 attention to those sensual aspects serves the viewer well—no matter what the range of available interpretive skills.

Differences in works of art, personal biases, and interests, and the nature of the presentation of works in galleries may all have an impact on the character of individual responses to works of art. Accordingly, stage theory in aesthetic response may hold more interest as a collection of aspects of and reactions to works of art than as a way to classify an individual's commentary on what he or she sees. Responsively, rather than frame curriculum around an expected level of interpretation (telling stories for folks whom you think care about stories), why not use this research to help construct curriculum that supports multiple ways into works of art without presuming to know from the age or frequency of museum visitation what an individual will notice in those messy-edged unpredictably human creations that we call "art."

In response to challenges such as these, in the early 1990s, a small and dedicated team of researchers at Harvard Project Zero organized a national collaboration on museum education that ultimately engaged nearly 600 educators. Our collaborators included classroom teachers, museum educators and school principals from the United States and abroad (Australia, Canada, Colombia, England, Israel, Italy, Japan, Mexico, and Spain). Together and through snail-mail circulation of drafts of learning tools, we worked to develop curriculum that would provide wide access to a range of different learners encountering a range of different works of art in the setting of the museum.

In our preliminary review of existing museum education curricula, we noted that most connections between learning in schools and learning in art museums were based around the *topic* being learned. Connections would be made, for example, between classical Greek statues in the museum and the study of heroes in English class, or between paintings of the American Revolution and the study of that period in history class. Alternatively, we were interested in tools that were what we called "learner based," based on the learner's acquisition of a variety of skills that might be useful in the wide realm of academic and other cognitive challenges. The specific object of interest to us in the museum was the visitor, and most especially as visitor, the student.

The tool we developed that has the longest history, having originally been drafted in the late 80s in response to Parsons' and Housen's studies, was The Generic Game (Davis, 1990, 1993b). This "game" is comprised of a set of ten questions that *any* viewers of art can ask themselves in the consideration of *any* works of art. Novices were meant to be able to play the game as easily with arts aficionados as with other novices. Because the game was designed to be used with any population, any rather than specific works of art and art forms, and in museums or other educational settings, it was originally named "Generic,"a term as unpleasant in its medicinal overtones as Goodman's "symptoms" of the aesthetic. The game was *learner* versus *subject* based and embodied the features that seemed most likely to facilitate that perspective. These were: (1) *Inquiry*: the posing of open-ended questions—questions that do not have right or wrong answers; (2) *Access*: accommodating a range of differences that obtain among learners; and (3) *Reflection*: providing a structure for students to think about their own thinking.

In the construction of the game, the developmental stages of aesthetic response were considered not as rungs on a ladder of personal development, but as layered points of entry into the experience of a work of art. Stage 1 attention to surface features of the work informed the structure of the early questions and was considered the outermost layer. Stage 5's connection between perceiver and maker, addressed in the game's last questions, was seen as closest to the core. Through the sequence of questions, informed selectively by the schema of the stages, the learner was poised to enjoy a journey in which the information gathered from early responses (e.g., regarding color and physical content) informed the understandings (e.g., symbolism) addressed in later questions.

The structuring of the game also therefore incorporates the techniques of inquiry-based processes of learning through which one idea and perception builds upon preceding ideas and perceptions. Along these lines, these insights are elicited through open-ended questions that simultaneously rely on what the learner already knows and encourage the learner to develop and use that knowledge independently (see Duckworth, 1987). The hope was that the move from question one to ten would feel as if the viewer were peeling the layers of skin off an onion and entering ever deeper into the work of art.

The "game," summarized below, is a tangible and tested example of a learning tool that asks rather than tells the learner. The question of what artistic movement a work represents not only has a specific answer; it relies on art historical knowledge on the part of the respondent. The questions in this learning structure rely only on personal experience and the immediate encounter with a work of art. The game begins with the question, "Do you like this work of art or not?" This question was originally selected as a starting point because many individuals who feel they do not have art historical backgrounds attest to having some comfort with deciding what they like: "I may not know much about art, but I do know what I like." The thought was that this opening question would start the respondent off with a level of comfort that would encourage him or her to play on. Collaborators have suggested that the question might as easily or preferably be, "Does this work interest you or not?" to assure that liking need not be interpreted as an objective or necessary result of close observation (Davis, 1996a). The questions have been printed on a set of cards or in a small booklet that viewers can carry around the art museum and use, responding quietly to themselves or out loud with other players, with whatever work they select.

The Generic Game. The first card tells "players" that the game can be played alone or with others and that depending on how one plays, the questions can be asked to one's self or taking turns with others. The viewer is asked to select a work of art to consider and urged not to read anything about it before playing the game. Viewers are reminded that not only do they not need an art historical background to play the game; there are no right or wrong answers.

After the pre-game question of whether the viewer likes the work or not, the game moves to studying the work from outside in:

1. Colors: "Look carefully at the work of art in front of you. What colors do you see in it? Take turns listing the specific colors that you see (e.g., 'I see red.' 'I see purple')"
2. Objects: "What do you see in the work of art in front of you? Take turns listing the objects that you see (e.g., 'I see an apple.' 'I see a triangle')"
3. Action: "What is going on in this work of art? Take turns mentioning whatever you see happening, no matter how small"
4. Association: "Does anything you have noticed in this work of art so far (e.g., colors, objects, or events) remind you of something in your own life?"
5. Realism: "Is this work of art true to life? How real has the artist made things look?"
6. Content: "What ideas and/or emotions do you think this work of art expresses?"
7. Expressivity: "Do you have a sense of how the artist might have felt when he or she made this work of art? Does it make you feel one way or another?"
8. Art history: "Take a look at the other works of art displayed around this one. Do they look alike? What is similar about the way they look (e.g., objects, events, feelings, the way they are made)? What is different?"
9. Identification with the artist: "What would you have called this work of art if you had made it yourself? Does the title of the work, if there is one, make sense to you?"

The last and post-game questions ask the learner to reflect on her learning:

10. Metacognition: "Think back on your previous observations.
    What have you discovered from looking at this work of art?
    Have you learned anything about yourself or others?"
Post-Game Question: "Do you like this work of art? Why or why
    not? You may notice that this is the same question that you
    were asked before you played the game. Has your reaction to
    the work changed? Do you like it more or less than you did in
    the beginning? Why?" (Davis, 1996a, pp. 82–88)

At the end, viewers are asked to note that the questions could all be
answered from their own observation and urged to explore questions
of their own that might have arisen through the resources of the museums, such as labels, wall text, and resident experts. The return to the
same question at the end of the game ultimately gives the respondent
the opportunity to consider what he or she has learned throughout the
playing of the game. Certainly the question of what one has learned
is addressed directly in question number 10. Nonetheless, a return to
the first question at the very end offers respondents the opportunity to
think about their own thinking and to see how differently they might
answer that question—how the journey through the questions has
changed (hopefully deepened) response.

In numerous trials of the "Generic Game" with individuals and
combinations of players of different ages and backgrounds, we found
that, in response to this post-game question, players often offered
more complex reasons for why they did or did not like the painting
they had considered. Take a hypothetical example. On first consideration of Seurat's landmark pointillist achievement, *La Grande Jatte*, a
respondent might say, "I don't like it because it's blurry and hard to
see what's happening." After playing the game, the respondent might
explain: "I still don't like it, but not just because it's blurry and hard
to see what's happening—that's actually kind of cool when you spend
a little time taking it in. And there are other paintings in the museum
that have that look. I don't like the way the people all look away and
seem sort of disinterested, sad—stuck in their places not doing anything. It reminds me of the way I feel about certain things that don't
interest me. I don't like parks anyway. The painting is well done, I
guess. It must have been hard to make the whole thing just out of tiny
dots. And I agree with what the artist thinks of his subject—all those
unaware people just soaking in the light. But I still don't like it."

Less frequently, respondents changed their minds about their feelings (liking or not) about the work. But we infrequently saw in response to this last question comments that were representative of just one stage or another (e.g., just talking about the story of the image). We did often see increases in the number of representative stage aspects contained in the responses. For example, in the earlier sample responses to the Seurat painting, the viewer's response to the pre-game question bears aspects of stage 1 (attending to surface features—the blurriness). The response to the post-game question, however, bears aspects of all five stages (from surface features to identifying with the artist and the challenges that he faced).

Inquiry versus Information

Perhaps of greatest interest, the game, like the many other inquiry-based structures employed in art museums (see, e.g., Broudy's aesthetic scanning, 1987), did seem to give individuals with little or no background in looking at art within the formal structure of the museum a level of comfort and confidence that was often surprising to them. Individuals who had never looked at a work of art before were spending upwards of half an hour interacting with an individual painting. This strength of the game was also its weakness. In a one-time visit to an art museum, does a visitor want to take the grand tour, having a superficial but broad awareness of the many different works contained in the galleries? Or is the best use of time a deep encounter with a single work? Veteran and frequent museumgoers do seem to visit and revisit a few favorite works. But novices are often "paraded" by school groups or parents through the whole museum, barely glimpsing the many works that abound.

We have come to know that frequent short visits that include careful viewing of selected works, combined with preparation and follow-up to visits, make for the most enjoyable and rich encounters. But these discoveries do not benefit as many children as we'd like. Most children who attend art museums through school visits do so no more than once a year. And more children than that do not visit art museums at all. Teachers will explain that with one museum visit allotted per year, a trip to the science museum makes better or more obvious sense, or they will not have a museum visit allotted at all, or their schools' locations will not allow easy access to an art museum.

In the brave world of the Internet, educators are using inquiry-based learning tools alongside of accessible information-based resources. This may resolve a frequent objection to the game and to other tools that build on what the viewer knows rather than regarding her or him as an empty vessel to be filled with the art historical knowledge that abides in the museum. The objection is that with an inquiry-based approach, viewers will "miss out" on all the information that there is to enjoy. Whether attending to an accoustiguide, docent tour, or wall text, museumgoers are surrounded in the art museum with rich historical and art historical information that can enlarge not only their sensibilities and experiential range but most especially their knowledge of the history and content of art.

But a tool like the game is not intended to replace information-based resources. Its objective, rather, is to change the dynamic from passive powerless learner being told what he or she should know, to active powerful learner exploring on her own the questions that she may have or may acquire in the great new sphere of the art museum. The desired change is from unasked-for distant canonized information to self-selected relevant and individually mediated facts. A professor in Texas taught a summer course in which, with her class of advanced education students, she studied the objectives and shape of the game. The group of teachers with which she worked assured her that the most important aspect of the game was not the particular questions that it posed, but the examples of open-ended queries that it provided. It is much easier to come up with a question to which you know the answer than to create real questions that inspire rather than test knowing.

The vast marble halls of the museum are ideal for personal adventure and need not be forbidding to the visitor regardless of his or her prior history with or enculturation into the world of viewing and responding to works of art. Inquiry-based approaches may open the door to classroom teachers who are otherwise intimidated by the particular air of out-of-reach knowing that can prevail in the art museum setting.

REVIEWING ARTS IN EDUCATION IN THE COMMUNITY— MIGHTY MUSE

What is a museum? The accrediting program of the American Association of Museums answers that question as follows. A museum is: "An organized and permanent nonprofit institution, essentially educational or aesthetic in purpose, with professional staff, that owns or uses tangible objects, cares for them and exhibits them to the public on some regular schedule" (American Association of Museums, n.d.). Reading between the lines of this statement, we find a distinction reflected in the classroom teacher's selection of a field trip to a science rather than an art museum. Science, history, and children's museums are clearly about education—about providing information and teaching visitors something they did not know before they arrived, something that is obviously attached to the objectives and content of learning that goes on in schools. But art museums are about the "aesthetic," about what counts as art and issues related to beauty, virtue, and the sublime—hardly at the core of everyday learning in school.

It is the ownership, care, and display of "tangible objects" (whether an ancient tool or a contemporary painting) that makes all museums museums. And ultimately, it is learning from or responding to objects that comprise a museum experience. Objects in the museum are a source and imprint of experience even as they reflect and frame our understandings of culture from the smallest to the biggest C. And the hand of the curator, perhaps more obvious in the context of the art museum than in other museums settings, shapes with impressive authority what and how we will come to understand. Above and beyond the museum educator's decision to ask questions and/or to provide information, the constraints of the exhibit invariably prevail.

In this context, compelling discussions revolve around whose artifact is whose work of art, and what objects do or do not belong in conservation or on display. Against a backdrop in which museums are considering the ethics of, for example, displaying sacred objects that some individuals regard as alive and/or returning objects to cultural groups from which they have been taken, the question of what counts as education may be both at the heart of the matter and held at bay. Some educators argue that the very issues with which museums grapple should be the content of educational activities in the art museum. Others contend that such contextual/relational frames distract art museums from the business of providing exhilarating arts encounters for arts aficionados. In a postmodern frame, art museums wrestle with the decision of how and whether to find ways to serve and educate a diverse and often disenfranchised public.

Whether art museums are about aesthetics, culture, conservation, history, humanity, status, affect, intellect, information, or inquiry, their commitment to education, however ingrained or formulated, is after all to the education of a viewer of art. Those who go to museums for inspiration for their own work are primarily the very small portion of the public that count themselves as visual artists. While many argue for the educational benefit of making art in the museum, the purview of education in that world of display is the cultivation of critical perceptive powers enriched through the visions of the artists and curators that abound in the museum. "Object-based learning" is a term that denotes the contemplation of objects—the use of objects (whether classical paintings or the popular Barbie doll) in museum and school settings to both teach the past and present that is embedded in the object and to awaken the critical perceptual abilities that abide in the student.

The new face of our thinking and feeling dynamic in this context is of the viewer of art as a literate thinking perceiver rather than a passionate feeling producer of art. This thoughtful perceiver is someone who "talks about" art and learns from as he or she contributes to the panoply of words that surround the works on the walls of museums and emerge from the voices of the knowing in the corridors and in the shop. Surely the student who has been educated through DBAE, or any other connoisseurship model, will find in this arena an opportunity to exercise his or her learning. And regardless of the lively interactive rapport that they seek to evoke, tools like the Generic Game or Visual Thinking Strategies also play to the power of words and the possibility of framing irrational artistic response in rational verbal performance.

As a gesture in response to the World Trade Center nightmare of September 11, 2001, the museums in New York City opened their doors and invited devastated New Yorkers to come for free and find comfort in the preservation of objects that resides within these temples of culture. Attendance to museums at that period was the lowest in recent history (Arts Journal, n.d.). Some people say that is because a visit to a museum is seen as a pleasurable encounter and New Yorkers could not think about pleasurable activities at a time of such grieving. But others say the truth is that most people don't regularly go to art museums and don't feel within them the level of comfort and room for expression of emotion that was needed at this difficult time.

Is it true that museums are more about thinking than feeling, about talking and knowing rather than expressing and learning? When Octavia's mother asked Octavia how she thought Seurat must have felt when he made *La Grande Jatte* (question seven in the Generic Game), Octavia said he must have felt great to be able to make such a wonderful painting. That answer was the most frequent response to the game's question (in consideration of many works of art) by first and fourth graders in the MUSE study (Davis, 1996a). Collaborating museum educators had cautioned that children might not feel comfortable with the emotion questions in the game. For that reason, question 7 is the only question that can be dismissed with a yes or no response. Nonetheless, overriding any expectation for responses to that question, from the naïve response that sad paintings were made by artists who were sad to the Goodmanesque response that the artist did not need to feel any way at all to make a painting that was happy or sad, overriding any stage theory expectation that puts identity with the artist at the most mature level of response, these children, like Octavia, shared some version of "the artist must have felt terrific to have been able to make something that good."

Young children who are still making art identify with artists and feel as artists do the challenge and engagement of the work and the hard work and triumph of the doing. As it was for Teriyaki, the austerity of the setting does not seem to be an obstacle to and may even appear as a viable possibility for ultimate display of their work. In the wonderful courtyard of the Isabella Stewart Gardner Museum in Boston, where that eccentric patron of the arts recreated as her home a lush palazzo-style Italian villa, a third grader sat drawing in response to our tour of that ornate "house" museum of art. I looked over her shoulder and commented, "Wow, you're quite an artist!" She lifted her small face in my direction and spoke with confidence, "Well yes I am and when I grow up, I will live in a place just like this. Only difference will be that all the paintings on the wall will be made by me."

The attraction, respect, and connection between artist and child that can flourish in the art museum is at the heart of a very different sort of community institution, unequivocal in its dedication to education and unwavering in its emotive and transformative focus. Moving from the austere and spiritual setting of the mighty muse that is the American art museum, let's consider those works of artists that evade traditional institutional walls and exist as tangible alternative worlds. Rather than being displayed and viewed, these live creations of education and art function as participatory safe havens designed to serve artists and children. Having scratched the reliably luminous surface of the mighty muse, let's turn our attention to the often dull surfaced structures that house those urban community art centers that focus on education.

ARTS IN EDUCATION IN THE COMMUNITY—SAFE HAVEN

We have traveled a distance from our original considerations of an emotive view, selectively represented by Tolstoy and his notion of the "infection" of emotion into works of art, a cognitive view selectively represented by Goodman and his image of "symptoms" of the aesthetic, and a reconciliation of feeling and thinking in the expressive/scientific method, pointillism, selectively presented to us in the fictive portrayal of Seurat by popular guru of musical theater Stephen Sondheim. In this last community-based dynamic, we find institutional realizations of the tension between thinking—as embodied in the privileged discourses of art museums—and feeling, as embodied in the populist contributions of community art centers. Indeed, in this last arena, we discover yet another imprint of the work of that world-moving outsider that is the artist in society and a new iteration of a work of art as agent to social reconciliation and change. In a national study of community art centers that focus on education in economically disadvantaged communities, the artist administrators of these sites repeatedly explained, "I see this place as a work of art in progress" (Davis, 1993a).

Arts Education as Service

These works in progress—community-based arts-educational centers conceived and realized by artists—abound throughout the United States in urban, suburban, and rural settings, crossing all art forms, addressing popular and outsider issues, meeting the needs and preferences of constituents, and struggling for the financial support needed to carry on. The activities of these initiatives include the training and scheduling of visiting artists who bring poetry, theater, dance, or visual arts into schools, prisons, elder centers, and institutions that support individuals with a range of disabilities (see Cleveland, 2000). These centers frequently provide support and work space for local professional artists, maintain performance or gallery shows for the community, and provide short-term arts workshops or long-term sequential arts education experiences for community members of all ages.

Within the last several years, attention from educational researchers, private foundations, and the national government has been given to the nature and quality of the arts education provided in these out of school arenas. Here in environments created and led by artists we find young people for whom school has not been an arena of success and growth: young people who, on the basis of circumstance and performance, have been designated as "at-risk." In a recent study of community centers that provide youth with after-school opportunities in sports and arts activities, Stanford professor and linguist Shirley Bryce Heath and researcher Elisabeth Soep discovered that successful educational and social outcomes for youth at art centers far outweighed the positive effects (which were considerable) of comparable sports programs. Furthermore, across a number of relevant variables, including "violent schools and unstable economic support for their families," the students that self-selected the arts programs were at considerably higher risk than those who chose to participate in sports (Heath, Soep, & Roach, 1998).

Alienated from mainstream culture by virtue of the trials of adolescence and/or other personal challenges, young people may be well positioned to identify with the outsider image of the artist. Perhaps they are attracted to the daring edginess of the mysterious weaver of magic who dresses in black and challenges conservative values and conventions. Perhaps they are inspired by the example that artists set of embracing risk and sharing from the fringe-celebrated visions of the whole. Cleaving to the "world mover" ethos, these young people see in the professional artists with whom they work in community settings, heroic images of individuals who have great skill and achieve enviable accomplishments. Like Octavia's friend who painted the skull in the community artists' mural, children choose artists to be their mentors—sometimes without the artists needing to reach out in any other way than to demonstrate their deft art making.

Reportedly, among directors at these community art centers, the top criterion for teaching artists is the quality of their portfolio (Davis, 1998). While experience with teaching was cited as important for working with the preschoolers, quality of artistic output was cited as most important for working with older students. The children will find the way, directors explained, to communicate and learn from an artist who is demonstrating something that they would like to do (Davis, 1993a). Arguably, students who select their own mentors and find ways to learn from them "own" their learning in ways similar to those of museumgoers who explore their own questions as they peruse the rich sources of information and learning available in the art museum.

Another story of "inreach" makes the point. At a high-intensity arts collective in the Midwest, where artists working in metal and glass had pooled their resources to secure and develop gallery space in an old warehouse, there was a daily problem with break-ins. The center was located midway between an elementary school and a housing project and every day after school a group of about 15 children between the ages of 8 and 10 would break into the center and disperse. It would take the artists about an hour and a half to collect all the children and see them out. In order to address the problem, the artists met and considered their options. They decided that they could get a security system and/or better locks to be sure the break-ins did not continue, or they could meet with the children to see why they kept doing it. The artists chose the latter alternative and learned from the children that they wanted to see what the artists were up to "in there" and to learn how to do "it" themselves. The artists agreed to give classes two afternoons a week; the 15 children brought 50 of their friends. And that was the start of an educational arts program that now annually serves 600 school children from all over the city.

At the turn of the century in settlement houses like the famous Hull House in Chicago, Karamu House in Cleveland, and the Henry Street Settlement in New York, instruction in music and art was helping a burgeoning population of immigrants acclimate to America and contribute to the incipient manufacturing and cultural wealth of the nation. What were known as Community Music Schools, nonprofit seats of quality music education, were organized in 1940 in a guild dedicated to collective activity around "enriching the lives of individuals, less privileged financially, through participation in the performance, understanding and appreciation of music" (National Guild of Community Music Schools Quarterly). In the late 19th century, YMCAs and YMHAs began a tradition that continues today, of providing quality arts performance and education.

Well-known artists such as dancer Katherine Dunham, jazz musician Jackie McLean, poet Kenneth Koch, and visual artist Keith Haring have long been associated with community efforts in arts education. Dunham, who is attributed with putting "Black dance on the map" of the United States (Haskins, 1990, p. 93), created community-based dance schools in New York City, Chicago, and East Saint Louis. Over the last several decades, Dunham trained a generation of dancers of color who shared her belief in the essentiality of studying African history and tradition in order to understand the movement of Black dance. These students, many of them now community arts artist educators, also followed Dunham's example of offering the discipline of dance to young people who might otherwise be drawn to life on the street.

After more than three-quarters of a century of creativity and service, Dunham still champions the cause of the wronged or underserved. She sees social service as a part of the artist's journey and, in a 1991 interview, explained to me that even beyond demonstrable talent, artist teachers in the community must be able to demonstrate the joy of teaching their craft to others. She said, "They must be very sensitive to other people and they must *feel they need to give* and try to teach the children, and not just with words, but with their own 'comportment' try to show that you can be happy in doing things for other people" (Davis, 1991b).

A young artist from Maine who has dedicated his life and work to often-forgotten youth in the South Bronx perhaps exemplifies Dunham's charge. Tim Rollins, an artist and former special education teacher in the New York Public Schools, created an atelier, The Art and Knowledge Workshop, in which participating youth came to be known as artists in the art world. For more than 2 decades, Rollins has mentored young artists, the Kids of Survival (KOS)—almost all young men—and, in a mentorship/collective spirit, created works of art that sold in galleries and are on display in major museums around the world. The young men with whom Rollins worked all had difficulty reading and Rollins led them in an alternative journey into the heart of some of the major works of Western culture. Under Rollins guidance, the youth painted "wounds" as at the core of Hawthorne's *The Scarlett Letter* or made collages out of selected pages from the work of Twain and Faulkner (see Paley, 1995).

The youth who stayed with Rollins and weren't lost to drugs, pregnancy, or drive-by shootings "broke into" the gallery scene at places like New York's Boone Gallery, defying at such gatherings the crowd's expectations for disenfranchised urban youth (see Geller & Goldfine, 1996). Indeed many of Rollins's students went on to college. Rollins paid his apprentices, put the money they made aside for their college education, and played "tough" with his expectations that they show up, work, do well in school, and plan to go to college.

But Rollins was widely criticized for his work. It was noted that his students might be having meaningful encounters with literature through their work with Rollins, but their ability to read words was not improving. His choice of literature—Western classics—was challenged as not being appropriate for or relevant to the children of color with whom he worked, and his missionary spirit was chastised as being fanatic (Rothstein, 1996). The students were seen as Rollins's opus and the high stakes "playing" with human lives—whether he was "saving them" in any respect or not—was as harshly criticized as it was reverently applauded.

The model that Rollins exemplifies is one of relationship and dedication. A young man from Maine going into the heart of the South Bronx to do good merges the image of world mover and world forsaker even as it challenges contemporary resistance to the idea of a white middle-class man leading children of color out of their neighborhoods. Artists working in the community have faced the disapproval and suspicion of insiders and outsiders for as long as they have been working there.

In Englewood, Chicago, at the Boulevard Art Center described at the start of this chapter, Patricia Devine-Reed began as a white woman director of an all-Black center in an all-Black community. When asked about resistance she may have faced, Devine-Reed was candid in sharing that while she needed to gain trust, she had been a 25-year resident of the community and "back in the late 70s and 80s when discussions began about a new way to organize and develop the community . . . the arts were always central to those discussions and I have a background as a visual artist and a community organizer, and a teacher. So, people sort of looked to me to start the center." (Davis, Eppel et al., 1996, p. 47).

This was true as well of the tiny center MollyOlga Neighborhood Art Classes, located in the fruit belt section of Buffalo, New York (renamed the Neighborhood Art Center), when a decade before Boulevard was created in Chicago, children in Buffalo were starting to come to artist Molly Bethol's house for painting parties. Bethol explains, "Pretty soon there were too many kids to fit in my kitchen and my porch and my living room" (Davis, Soep, et al., 1993, p. 56). Responsively, in 1960, she moved her community art-making activities to the parish hall of her church. In 1971, with the help of fellow artist and teacher Olga Aleksiewicz (hence the name MollyOlga) the by then bustling endeavor moved to a neighborhood convent which was purchased in 1980 with money raised solely through community donations ranging from $.25 to $50.

It was the executive director of the Connecticut Commission on the Arts who asked world-renowned alto saxophonist Jackie McLean to start a community art center in the North End of Hartford in 1970 as an effort to fight the rise in substance abuse that was wracking the neighborhood. McLean reports that the drug/youth scene had been "happening in New York in the 60s," but "Hartford always gets things later" (Davis, Soep, et al., 1993, p. 18). Based on his own 18-year battle with heroin (including imprisonment and the cancellation of his club card), McLean knew volumes both about what there was to lose from drug addiction and the positive role the arts could play in making recovery possible and worthwhile. He and his collaborators planned an oasis within the community. Their original mission statement for their community-based cultural program read: "It is important that ways are found to involve and stimulate our youngsters and adults who have been clicked off by traditional institutions" (p. 20) The Collective, now in its third decade has moved from an abandoned schoolhouse on Clark Street to a new several multi-million-dollar building that provides easy access to the African and Caribbean American population in the greater Hartford area.

Like Boulevard, the Collective is dedicated to that same spirit of art education espoused by Katherine Dunham, specifically to "use the arts as a means of healing and developing the community" (Davis, Eppel, et al., 1996, p. 30). Among Dunham's many mentees was Dollie McLean, Jackie's wife and executive director of the Artists Collective, and Aca Lee Thompson, Master Choreographer and Disciplinarian at the Collective. Thompson's "Yaboo" or Rite of Passage curriculum reflects Dunham's priorities by featuring the study of African history, tradition, music, and dance as a means for young people to develop a sense of self-awareness and competency.

The McLeans' move from New York brought to Hartford (from the start and in the present) first-rate New York artists who interspersed their professional lives in the big city with educational lives in the North End of Hartford. The "New York" aura created an outsider element and thread of community resentment for McLean and his group of teaching artists, musicians, and dancers. Who were these out-of-towners coming into Hartford and working to persuade the community's youth of alternatives to street life and drug use? McLean reported that the New York versus Hartford tension also slowed the progress of funding the center on account of "the funding power elite's ability to overlook an effort that does not seem to be 'coming out of the community'"(Davis, Soep et al., 1993, p. 48). McLean voices the community's sentiment: "Who do they think they are coming in here to help us? We coulda done it!" He goes on, "When I get them all together, I say 'Why didn't you do it? You didn't do it so stop talking about it. We did it'" (p. 48).

Learning from Exemplars

The origins of urban community art centers, like their perpetuation, depend on the virulence of self-selection. The artist directors have made themselves and their leadership available to communities looking for alternatives and advancement, and the parents and students who participate in these oases of art and education vote with their feet. Unlike schools that focus on the arts, community art centers that focus on education work "out there" beyond the constraints and without the benefit of school budgets or oversight. Directed by artists taking on administrative and pedagogical roles, these centers are free to ignore or align themselves with academic objectives or standards deemed appropriate to arts and academic learning.

Far from the pressures of justifying the arts in terms of non-arts subjects, these centers set out to address human problems, embrace troubled youth, and heal aching communities. Far from the austerity of marble floors and elite traditions, these centers find locations that need them and usually "make due" with whatever physical setting will affordably house their work. With brave and "human" goals, egalitarian values, and a dedication to serve the underserved, community art centers offer a unique opportunity to study the arts as and in education. As part of the 1993 study of community art centers that I have already been citing, a small group of researchers set out to see what we could learn from these artist inventions of education and to consider the implications of that learning for art education in schools. A collection of six research portraits represented the culmination of a large national study, including the review of hundreds of centers around the country, with methods ranging from material review, phone and live interview, and long and short site visits.

Our criteria for including centers in our study was that they: (1) *focused on education* (as opposed to primarily presenting performances or gallery exhibitions with occasional adjacent educational experiences); (2) offered *sustained learning* (this is, learning over time—weeks or month-long time periods as opposed to or in addition to day or weekend workshops); (3) operated primarily *out-of-school* (as opposed to primarily scheduling arts-in-schools residences and/or classes); (4) had been around a *long time*, usually no less than a decade (in a field in which most centers last less than 3 years); and (5) operated in *economically disadvantaged* communities.

Aware of the various educational objectives at play in school and museum settings, we set out to explore in depth the educational objectives that might prevail in this unregulated terrain beyond the institutional constraints that perpetually open or shut the door to the arts. We discovered that in this field of artist educators—artists educating, a *range* of goals were prioritized. Furthermore, from center to center, we heard different descriptions of the relationship of those goals to the educational practice and philosophy of the site. For example, some community art center directors told us that if we interviewed all the teaching artists at their center, they'd all know and agree on the educational goals of the center. A shared view of what they were accomplishing was their strength. But as many center directors assured us that if we asked the objectives of the teaching artists at their centers, there would be as many different responses as there were faculty members. In diversity of objectives lay their strength.

We had clearly discovered a field of arts education in which diversity was a given. Beyond that, we quickly learned from these artist educators that the realization of stated goals—a standard formula for educational and organizational effectiveness—did not describe the locus in which their educational effectiveness lay. Indeed, they explained that goals change over time, and unanticipated outcomes may prove more interesting than what one sets out to do. When that happens, responsively the goals and practices change continually over time.

Where educational effectiveness resided in such a context of change was in a close attention to process and a positive regard for and response to mistakes. Mistakes were seen as generative. Like the painter Jack Levine's description early on of coming to a work-in-process every day to look for what was wrong as a place to begin, these artist educators focused on the challenges and let the successes be. Like the schools that focus on the arts description in the preceding chapter, these centers were regarded by the artists who nurtured them as developing works of art in process. And the administrative/educational acumen of their leadership lay in a comfort with the artistic process, specifically and as above: (1) an attention to and flexibility around process; and (2) a view of mistakes as open and generative opportunities rather than closed and decided failures.

Educational Objectives

The range of goals for arts learning that was presented to us by community arts educators was varied and often overlapping. Overall, our various sources of data pointed to five categories of educational goals that were articulated and prioritized (ranked 1–5 in terms of importance) by the many contributors to our research (Davis, 1993a). Listed below, they offer a mosaic of possibilities for arts learning that defies measurement in the best (in that they are beyond measure) and most frustrating (in that most of them cannot be quantified) ways. They are especially interesting to consider in relation to/contrast with the limited range of justifications for arts learning that school educators have grappled with throughout the history of the field.

1. *Personal and Interpersonal Goals.* Experience with personal success, a sense of mattering, self-awareness, self-esteem, self-confidence, and self-expression; sensitivity to and respect for others and the acquisition of skills of cooperation and communication. The acquisition of requisite skills for making aesthetic choices, giving and receiving constructive criticism, setting and meeting standards of excellence, and learning from and providing examples of positive role models in the arts and in the community.
2. *Cognitive Goals.* The acquisition of "habits of learning" (like self-discipline, problem solving, and the ability to concentrate and train diligently and over time); the development of artistic skills (production) and knowledge (appreciation); creativ-

ity; the understanding that there are multiple approaches to a single idea. Notably, while these goals did not include performance in specific non-arts academic areas, satisfactory school grades are often a prerequisite for participation.

3. *Multicultural/Culture Specific Goals.* On a culture specific level: increasing awareness of heritage and art forms within cultures such as African-American, Latino, Chinese, Caribbean, Southeast Asian, and Alaskan; sharing and preserving values, knowledge, and traditions; building personal culture-related identities. On a multicultural level, developing an interest and respect for other cultures as well as cross-cultural sensitivity and the understanding that culture and multiculturalism relate directly to the individual's intimate reality.

4. *Community Goals.* The cultivation of a positive nonviolent environment for youth; social reconciliation; producing useful members of society who through their own efforts and examples contribute to community development; the improvement of the community's daily life through arts performances and festivals; the establishment of the center as a meeting place and source of community pride; the literal beautification of community buildings and the installation of positive collaborations among community organizations.

5. *Professional Goals.* The provision of quality training from professional faculty members and visiting artists and the provision of summer workshop and internship opportunities designed to help students acquire the artistic skills and entrepreneurial acumen to earn careers in the arts. In terms of already established artists, meeting needs for studio and gallery space as well as providing performance and mentorship opportunities.

These goals, realized to relative extent and throughout the teaching and learning of a range of art forms and educational vehicles, share two important features with "works of art." First, they are complex, multi- and interdisciplinary. They describe and include learning that links students to culture as it is most recently variously defined, personal and community development, and the acquisition of skills and discipline associated with professional performance. Secondly, they are achieved through making or doing—learning through mentorship, making something that was not there before the hand or tap shoe or voice of the student created it. A teacher researcher in a local high school tried out the Generic Game with her weekly art class and reported that while her students thought it was "interesting," they resented giving up that once-a-week opportunity "to make things." Building on that understanding of the power of creating, of the sense of agency that making art affords, community art centers focus on the "doing it" of art and the triumph of hard work and mastery.

Portraits of Effectiveness

Out of the many centers that we reviewed throughout our research, we selected six centers for our final research portraits. We selected these centers as representative of the range of factors associated with educational effectiveness in the field considering variables such as goals, facilities, budgets, art forms, student populations, and locations. For purposes of our discussion here, I will focus on three of these centers, two of which I have already introduced: the Artists Collective in Hartford, Connecticut; the MollyOlga Neighborhood Art Classes in Buffalo, New York; and the Manchester Craftsman's Guild in Pittsburgh, Pennsylvania.

As I did in my earlier discussion of schools that focus on the arts, I present each of these exemplars in terms of the four dimensions deemed in our research as central to educational effectiveness (Teaching and Learning, Community, Journey, and Administration) and cite the themes that emerged as relevant. Against the backdrop of these overviews, I conclude this section with descriptors of the overall features of educational effectiveness derived from a cross-portrait analysis of emergent themes at each of these institutional "works of art" (see section 3 for an overview of portraiture).

The Artists Collective has as its educational focus both personal/interpersonal and cultural/multicultural objectives. The Collective provides training in the performance arts with a focus on the African and Carribean-American experience. Featured in the curriculum are the seven virtuous principles of KWANZAA, a major African-American holiday since 1965: unity, self-determination, collective work and responsibility, cooperative economics, purpose, creativity, and faith.

Pedagogical practices (Teaching and Learning) include the provision of positive role models, guidelines for personal maintenance and behavior, and multiple opportunities for success and expression. In an arena of acceptance and high expectation (often in contrast with the low expectations for children of color in the local schools), children as young as 3 study tap dance, musical instruments, and an in-depth curriculum built around African culture and history. As mentioned earlier, that course of study results in what is called a rite of passage ("Yaboo") ceremony in which, with wonderful displays of drumming and dance, in glorious costumes of white billowing trousers and wrapped tunics, these accomplished young people are presented to the community. The student population (Community) for the center is clearly targeted as individuals of color from the metropolitan Hartford area as well as other students interested in African traditions and art forms (including Jazz).

Originated by jazz great Jackie McLean, the center is skillfully directed by his wife Dollie McLean, who believes in and largely maintains a balanced budget. Members of the original family of founders include dance director Cheryl Smith and master choreographer, disciplinarian, and creator of the Yaboo ceremony Aca Lee Thompson. Its board includes this founding group and others in the community dedicated to the center's educational and cultural services (Administration).The center was originally housed in a church basement, moved to an old schoolhouse, and now is housed in a state-of-the-art modern facility. But the growth has been balanced from the start by the center's founding objective to provide alternatives to drugs and life on the street for youth in the community (Journey).

Dollie McLean explains the education provided at the Collective: "I think there are some very simple rules here: 1) we care about those kids, 2) we have something to give to them, and 3) we have certain expectations of them, and it's really that simple" (p. 38; all quotes in this section are from Davis, Soep et al., 1993). Describing the thrill of performance, she points out: "that's how our kids need to get high—off that adrenaline that's so natural . . . when you're getting ready to do something and all of your parents are sitting outside and your friends, and the boys from the hood; they've all come. I hear a few of them [in the audience]—I was sitting behind some of them. They said, 'I can do that.' I leaned over and said, 'Yes, you could.'"(p. 42).

McLean describes the recurrent phenomenon of having a schoolteacher come to the center for a performance and see a student who is a problem in the school collecting money at the door. "Don't you know," the teacher will confide in McLean, "that Raymond is a terror in the classroom. How can you trust him with the money?" "Oh," Ms. McLean will reply. "Raymond organized this whole dance recital. And by the way, have you seen him dance?" (p. 21). The themes that emerged from this center were those of "safe haven," the way in which the center functions as an oasis of art and promise, often for disenfranchised members of the community; "family," on account of the familial connections among center constituents from faculty to administrators to parents and children; and last, "the process of being somebody"— the way in which the center supports in hopeful and positive development its students, many of whom attend for more than 10 years and return to teach when they are grown.

MollyOlga Neighborhood Art classes (now called Locust Street Neighborhood Art Classes) in Buffalo, New York, at the time of our study was considered as primarily dedicated to cognitive goals. One of its themes, "the model of the professional artist," reflected the educational priorities of the center, which focused on the very structured teaching and learning of visual arts, from color theory to oil painting, literally rising from beginner (classes on the first level) to expert (studios on the top floor) with each floor of the brightly colored convent building. A nonnegotiable policy of free classes at the center as well as the context-appropriate opportunity for children to sign up for classes without parental involvement created a sense of "realistic accessibility," another emergent theme.

An open-door policy in which "Even a 4-year-old can register without a parent" is responsible in part for how members of the financially challenged surrounding community understood the dedication and openness of the center to its needs and interests. Olga Aleksiewiez Lownie, then the center's treasurer and a teacher, offered an example of realistic accessibility as she told the story of a preschooler who several years before our study lived down the street and came almost every day to painting classes. "Her mother never knew where she would go with the other kids around 3:00." This little girl died in a house fire and for that year's art show, an entire wall of art in the exhibit was dedicated to her memory and displayed her work. "Somebody told her mother, and her mother came . . . [she] had never known"(p. 74).

The administrative challenges of the center were substantial. MollyOlga operated on the smallest budget of all the centers we studied (in 1992, $75,000). The director and founder, Molly Bethol, was supported by a board made up primarily of family members, most of whom worked at the center. Bethol would invent time to write grant proposals by waking in the middle of the night. Working hours that go way beyond the limits of a standard day, community arts educators like Bethol to this day provide services that become invaluable to the community but do not receive long-term sustaining financial support. Indeed, Bethol thought that the government should support the service that the center provided to the community. While police and firefighters were awarded "legal government contracts" to perform their services, in Buffalo, funding for the arts was considered "unearned income" and from the government "grants-in-aid." Molly Bethol expressed her distress: "I don't see why we should have to lose our self-respect to do the jobs we want to do and that we're good at, and that's what it makes me feel . . . Plumbers have government contracts; why with the arts is it 'grants-in-aid'? A lot of it boils down to a lack of respect for the work that artists do" (p. 61).

The struggle for survival of the center, now in its fifth decade, gave rise to the portrait theme "constant survivor." A student who came from outside of the community to take classes there found the struggle to be an inspiration: "The fact that it's a struggling art school in an inner city—I respect that they're here and that it's free" (p. 61). The center's growth from Molly's kitchen to convent home gives testimony to the center's value to the community.

MollyOlga's vision for the future at the time of our study was for survival, not further growth. Just as Boulevard Art Center's murals seem to be guarded by gang members in the community (they simply are not vandalized) and the McLeans report a circle of safety that youth maintain around the Artists Collective, Bethol describes as "unspoken" the sanctity of the center. She says, "nobody in the neighborhood . . . bothers the building [or] anybody who comes to the building." This is because of shared ownership: "The head of the gang now used to come here . . . Everybody who grew up in the neighborhood has probably been here at least once" (p. 57).

In a center in which students report that the instructors really listen and "meet them where they are," you won't find a teacher as Octavia did, walking around the room calling every effort "beautiful." At MollyOlga, "I'm finished" may not even satisfy their dedicated teachers. "Look out the window." "Attend to the in-between spaces." "You went fast again." A hardworking preschooler brings her piece over to

Molly, "I'm done, but I know you're gonna say 'not quite done'" (p. 69). With an eye to the "talking about" art that we see in school arts approaches like DBAE or Arts PROPEL, we can consider Molly's description of a 6-year-old boy doing a drawing called "Watching a Drive-by Shooting." No one expected him to talk about the piece. "It was just better to let him paint it and put it out," Molly explains, "rather than to feel like he's gonna get quizzed and have to make explanations . . . They won't do it then" (p. 72).

At the Manchester Craftsman's Guild in Pittsburgh, Pennsylvania, "talking about" your artistic constructions is an important part of the teaching and learning objectives of the center. At the Guild, where cognitive and personal/interpersonal objectives prevail, teenagers identified as "at risk for failure" in school become skilled in photography and ceramics (more recently, jazz has been introduced) and learn to break the codes of their neighborhoods to talk to others about the work that they've done. Assistant Executive Director Nancy Brown explained to us that Guild students "are expected to exhibit their work, to be at openings of the exhibits, and to be able to talk with the public . . . As they learn discipline, they are expected to be able to talk about what it is they have created . . . they're learning the technical skills but they're also learning how to speak very openly about how they felt about what they were doing" (p. 102). This alternative form of verbal expression has the very focused objective of preparing students for a conversation that is highly valued at the Guild, with someone called a college admissions officer.

The Manchester Craftsman's Guild is located in a light-filled modern brick structure designed by a famous architect (who also designed the Pittsburgh airport) who was commissioned for the work by the Guild's executive director Bill Strickland. In the beauty of the building, adorned with priceless quilts and other objets d'art that Strickland has collected, the students find what Strickland calls and what emerged as a theme: a "place in the sun." This emergent theme is reflected metaphorically in the bright opportunities students earn at the Guild and physically in the center's gorgeous glass building. It is a structure that says to students, in Strickland's words, "Hey man, you're worth something. Hey man, I care about you. You're going to college. Your life's going to change. We're going to turn the sunshine on and let it bathe you. . . . Sunshine is free, it doesn't cost nothing. You don't need to be rich to walk in the sun; you can be anybody to walk in the sun" (p. 83).

From the passionate missionary voice of this inspirational entrepreneur, we hear about the very focused purpose that arts education plays at the Guild. Strickland explains, "I'm not into art for art's sake. I believe that art has a purpose in people's lives that can be very transforming. That's a good part of the reason why I do the arts because you can measure the improvement and change in people's lives as a result of the association with the discipline of the arts. And that's not to say that art in and of itself is not important because it is. I'm simply saying that I want to take advantage of the . . . good things that the arts provide" (p. 90). The measurable outcomes of admissions to college are certainly at the forefront of the "good things" provided by the arts to students at the Guild. Impressively, with the at-risk population that the Guild serves, the rate of application and acceptance to college was almost twice that achieved by the Pittsburgh Public Schools with the mainstream population of students. The Guild's ceramics instructor puts it simply: "The expectation I have is for each and every one of [my students] to go to college" (p. 87).

The Guild is connected to Pittsburgh's economic community through the vocational instruction provided by its partner organization, the Bidwell Training Center, which is also housed in the new building. It is connected as well to its immediate geographically defined community, especially in its invitation to community members to attend the world-class jazz concerts and art shows at the center. But the specific "community" that Manchester Craftsmen's Guild sets out to serve is clearly defined as the population of "at-risk" high school students in the Pittsburgh public schools. Director Bill Strickland characterizes these students as "struggling academically" and "feeling somewhat displaced in the public school environment. They don't belong." Perhaps unsurprisingly, the Guild does not turn away self-selected students who do not apparently fit the "at-risk" profile and Bill Strickland has repeatedly pointed out that all "kids are at risk." The otherness of the Tonio Kroeger/George Seurat image emerges in this context as an attribute of disenfranchised youth as surely as it has previously as an attribute of the outsider artist.

The Guild's curriculum is structured to serve the specific needs of the target community, focusing on life skills training, including the self-presentational strategies of "winning the right to be heard" (another theme) as well as the acquisition of marketable skills in ceramics or photography. Summer programs take students and their families (who are unfamiliar with the college scene) on to college campuses. Students who are disenfranchised from school recognize or discover an affinity with these artists, many of whom share the disenfranchisement, calling themselves "counselors" instead of "teachers" and definitely not "parents." But these individuals "care" when others may not. "Relationship" is a virulent theme resonating through the fabric of the Manchester Craftsman's Guild. Addressing some students who lacked parental support, Strickland expressed this theme, saying: "If no one comes for you, if you do not have a parent who comes . . . what you need to know is I am Bill Strickland and I will serve as your parent." Explaining that every faculty member at the Guild will similarly serve, Strickland says, "We care about you, think of us as the persons who care "(p. 107).

The administrative partnership with the Bidwell Training Center was a real boon to ascertaining initial funding for arts education at the Guild, but the Guild, at the time of our study, had begun to see its dependence on grant funding as unfeasible. Saving itself from an "at-risk" status, the Guild began to increase its sources of earned income, including ticket sales from jazz concerts and investments in Bidwell Food Services. Looking to the future, Strickland at that time planned to build a multi-industry park around the Guild and to endow the institution; his plans always change, but his entrepreneurial spirit never fails. Strickland was kept from failing out of school and introduced to college by his ceramics teacher, Frank Ross, a self-appointed mentor who found a way to keep Strickland working at school in the studio all day and amass a body of work to present in his application to college. Now Strickland works to replicate this transformative experience for his students. Speaking of the students he serves, mostly from poor neighborhoods, Strickland says: "They're all with spiritual cancer. They're all dying, every one of them. It doesn't matter whether it's a Black neighborhood or a White neighborhood or a mixed neighborhood, they're all dying. This is an alternative to dying for a lot of these kids" (p. 86). Introducing students to a beautiful setting like the Guild and to people who say they are "something" is what the Guild is all about: "The idea of the program is to get them addicted to living like this, so they want to live like this for the rest of their lives. To do that you've got to go to college, you've got to grow up" (p. 86).

Strickland's clear-cut objective of college admissions provides a measurable outcome in a field in which immeasurables abound. Dollie McLean's measurables can be found in attendance (that students show up and show up again) and progress (that they move from beginner to advanced levels). But how do we measure the impact that art classes at MollyOlga had on the little child that perished in the fire or on her mother? And how can we estimate the impact of tireless nightly rehearsals in dance and discipline on a Hartford youth training for the Yaboo Ceremony? There are as many different outcomes for the arts in education in these centers as there are students who self-select and participate fully. Students individuate their success in these centers even as these centers individuate what institutional success looks like in a diversified educational community that prioritizes a range and multitude of objectives.

Principles of Effectiveness

From the resonance within and across the themes that emerged at these different centers, however, we were able to derive statements descriptive of overall educational effectiveness in settings where educational effectiveness is being created and recreated with the attention to process that artists know so well how to meter. These statements both speak to the heart of the matter of these inspirational sites of arts learning even as they leave room for a range of realizations, perhaps in a range of settings.

1. *Educationally effective centers espouse and engage the power of art to transform, and/or to articulate personal identities.* This phenomenon is apparent in the theme and the process of "becoming somebody" at the Artists Collective through which students acquire such habits of learning and living through the performing arts as discipline and self-presentation. These abilities not only enable students to realize their potential as dancers or musicians but also to transform behaviors in such other arenas as school or street. At MollyOlga, the theme of "the model of the professional artist" guides the process of becoming an individual who makes his or her own choices, mixes his or her own colors, and takes responsibility for completing what he or she has started. "Winning the right to be heard" is a process of self-transformation evident at the Manchester Craftsmen's Guild through which students acquire the tools with which to express themselves in ways that will be heard and understood and ultimately entitle them to their place in the sun.

2. *Educationally effective community art centers cultivate strong re-lationships among center constituents (teachers, students, parents, staff).* This feature is evident in the theme of "relationship" as mentorship and collaboration at the Manchester Craftsmen's Guild and the theme of "family" at the Artists Collective. At MollyOlga, "realistic accessibility" speaks to the faith, wel-come, and rapport the center has with its community. One com-munity arts educator in our study faulted schools for not pro-viding time and opportunity for teachers and students to form and develop strong relationships. Community art centers have the freedom and space to cultivate bonds of familial support and mentor/mentee relationship as agents to development in if not self-transformation through the arts.

3. *Educationally effective community art centers know and carefully attend to the changing interests and needs of the communities that they serve.* "Realistic accessibility" at MollyOlga results from a knowledge of what community members do and do not feel comfortable with, just as the process of "winning the right to be heard" at the Manchester Craftsmen's Guild builds on the cen-ter's knowledge of the particular challenges and frustrations that face the at-risk students that the center serves. The Artists Collective is closely familiar with the needs for positive rewrit-ing of the inescapable stereotypes that confront the children of color they serve. In "the process of becoming somebody," these needs are specifically addressed through broad exposure to positive Black role models from actually knowing Jazz great Jackie McLean to admiring the images of black movers and shakers that are plastered all over the walls of the center.

4. *Educationally effective community art centers provide durable oases for students and families.* One of MollyOlga's emergent themes is the notion of the center as a "constant survivor," a place within the community on which residents can rely no matter what happens on a community or individual level. This durable con-nection between the center and the community seems parallel to the theme of oasis or "safe haven" at the Artists Collective. An oasis of African-American culture in a larger sphere in which the traditions and promise of that culture are ignored or devalued and a place for artists is nurtured and secured. At the Manchester Craftsmen's Guild, the theme of "a place in the

sun" not only speaks to the future the center strives to provide for its students, but as surely to the place that is the Manchester Craftsmen's Guild: a sunlit oasis of promise in a sphere of low expectation. Effective community art centers create space and place for the important relationships that they foster.

5. *Educationally effective centers carefully attend to their own process of development and transformation.* At the Artists Collective, the center as well as the students has experienced a rite of passage in the center's long-range planning and realization of its transformational move to Upper Albany Street. In the fund-raising efforts of MollyOlga, which maintained its status as a constant survivor, and in the careful day-to-day records that were scrupulously kept to enrich the educational scene, the center's deliberate motion was carefully monitored. Through their entrepreneurial efforts and track record with achieving their educational objectives, the Manchester Craftsmen's Guild has won its own right to be heard as a voice in the community. A careful attention to the limits and potential of overall center direction and growth is a resonant marker of effectiveness in these community-based centers for the arts in education.

REVIEWING ARTS IN EDUCATION IN THE COMMUNITY— SAFE HAVEN

The features we've identified as salient in these settings are reminiscent of the characteristics found in the educational settings of schools that focus on the arts. The qualities of process and reflection seem reflected in a view of the arts as agents to the transformation and/or articulation of personal identities as well as a center-wide attention to the organization's process of development and transformation. The activities of cultivating relationships among center constituents and knowing and catering to the interests and needs of the community seem reflective of the characteristics of connection and community that were associated with schools that focus on the arts. Indeed, passion and industry and difference and respect seem to be at the heart of the institution and maintenance of durable oases, alternative enclaves that respect individuals and their needs for and interests in artistic development.

In the austere setting of the mighty muse, objects are the recipients of conservation and cultivation and learning has a decidedly "connoisseurship" cognitive bent. The more passive activity of contemplating and talking about art seems remote in comparison to the hands-on active practice of offering art-making as a medium through which students can actively recreate circumstance and self. In the relationship-rich context of the community art center, acceptance and support dominate the scene. In the art museum, though curators work to contextualize the art works they present, decontextualization prevails. The art works are displayed out of the context in which they were made. The visitors are away from their daily contexts. Even education struggles for place in a setting in which it is both a priori and barely defined.

Community art centers know and care about the communities they serve. The mighty muse is often located incidentally in a given community and, rather than seeking out the needs and interests of that community, it may as often set an agenda that community members can take or leave. Where community art centers provide durable safe oases, art museums may seem forbidding and monolithic. Where museums house great works of art that stand the test of time and human attention, community art centers are in themselves vibrant works of art, actively engaged in—rather than physically representing—the possibilities for social reconciliation. The alternative experiences that both settings provide hold great promise for mutual enrichment, and at this moment the boundaries between museums and community as we have known them are being traversed and renegotiated. Such exchange, determination, and redetermination of meaning are reminiscent of the ever-changing dialogue between the producer and the perceiver of a work of art.

As Octavia marvels at the ability of the artist who fashioned *La Grande Jatte*, her wall-painting friend is working with artists at the Boulevard Art Center. As Octavia tries to understand the mysterious group and individual behaviors of the graceful crowds moving in and out among the works of art at the Art Institute, her wall-painting friend is experiencing firsthand what it means to participate in a collaborative group of artists turning their thoughts to things that speak to and for the neighborhood in which they live.

5

Framing Education as Art

OCTAVIA FIVE

Octavia, now 17, is daily ensconced in piles of heavy books at a table in the school library. She finds the situation somewhat amusing. Of all the seniors in her high school, she is the one to have chosen for her honors project the mounting of a show. Her friends were astonished that Octavia, an excellent student in every academic subject, would "take the easy way out" and select the art option for a senior project. They were equally astonished that the faculty approved Octavia's proposal and granted her request for a small amount of funds with which to put up her version of Stephen Sondheim's musical, *Sunday in the Park with George*. As the director/producer, Octavia has lots to do. She wants to know everything about the work so that she will be able to put the parts together well. When she used to make paintings, putting the parts together in a work of art involved deciding how the colors, lines, and shapes would go together on a page. Now Octavia is considering which actors will bring her characters to life, how they will articulate the words and music, how she will build and light a set, and how it will all come together into one powerful aesthetic whole.

At one point in the first act, Sondheim's George points out to his mistress, model, and muse: "I am what I do" (Sondheim & Lapine, 1991, p. 75). Octavia has read that Sondheim said of this passage: "I feel that all creative artists reveal themselves more in their work than in their conversations. An artist isn't only what he does. He is also a human being, but the core of a serious artist is what he does" (Gottfried, 1993, p. 161). Octavia believes this is true. For this reason, she feels she needs to learn as much as she can about Sondheim, who created the lyrics and music for this show; and about Seurat, who created the painting that is this show. And somehow, since this is her creative rendering of the show, she suspects that in studying these artists and their work and creating her own version thereof, she will learn something about Octavia who is now "putting it all together." *I am what I do*, she reflects with some gratification and excitement.

Octavia's research into Sondheim takes her into the realm of literature. She is encountering 19th-century melodramas (like *Sweeney Todd, The Demon Barber of Fleet Street*) that inspired Sondheim's musical of the same name (1979). She is reading psychology, specifically Bruno Bettleheim's *The Uses of Enchantment* (1975) and the work of Carl Jung (1964), both of which informed Sondheim's musical *Into the Woods* (1987). When she encounters Sondheim's *Assassins* (1991), Octavia is considering history—specifically the individuals throughout the past who have killed or attempted to kill American presidents.

Throughout them all, she is considering how controversial this work can be—how for Sondheim the charge of "romanticizing" reality through music has plagued him throughout his career. Can an audience laugh at murder in the case of a demon barber like Sweeney Todd, or sing about villainous assassins, or admire the gang members in *West Side Story* (1957)? Octavia feels a kinship with Sondheim, who faced the suspicion of his audiences and peers by taking the risks he did in making his edgy musical creations. She faces similar suspicion from her peers as she bravely tackles art while others write "easy" research papers.

In researching Seurat, Octavia realizes she is learning a lot about science. She discovers that Seurat called the dot dot painting he was doing "chromoluminarism"—not "pointillism," as it has come to be called (Gottfried, 1993, p. 156). The roots of this amazing word have to do with color and light, which so preoccupied the impressionist and neoimpressionist painters of the 19th century. These artists studied color theory and they must have studied optics, a field of science Octavia discovers that is concerned with all aspects of light.

As she prepares for what her audience will see on the stage, Octavia collects another set of resources from the books and Web sites she can access in the school library. Now she is interested in the clothing that her actors will wear. What did folks wear in 19th-century France? And what class of people does she see in Seurat's painting? She must consider wealth and class as elements in costume selection and design. She and her mother will be buying fabric and creating the costumes that her fellow students-turned-subjects in a painting will wear.

This managing of a budget is new to Octavia and makes her grateful for the math she has studied in school. She also finds herself exploring new mathematical terrain when she thinks about designing the set for the show. If she recreates a version of the original set, she will need to know the dimensions of Seurat's painting and to think about the scale at which she will have it reproduced. Mixing colors that approximate the original painting will involve chemical considerations. And what about the lights? In a show that is all about color and light, Octavia needs to learn quickly about the aspects of technical theater that will help her to realize her vision. Thank goodness for the "techies," those smart outsider kids who seem to know all this stuff.

Indeed, Octavia is becoming very skilled at knowing whom to turn to for the expertise she needs to put this show together. Her friends at the Boulevard Art Center have volunteered to paint the set. The local hardware store will donate the paint. Her friends from the band will play the music, and their peer director will help Octavia select actors whose voices seem most right for the parts. Sondheim had originally wanted a lyrical soprano to play Dot, but he adjusted the music for the "belt it out" stage voice of musical theater icon Bernadette Peters who ended up being the perfect selection. Octavia was beginning to realize that she had neither a lyrical soprano nor a Bernadette Peters trying out at her school, and that, like Sondheim, she would adjust her vision to the talents that were available. This making and communicating hard decisions as to who would be in and out of the show was testing and stretching Octavia's interpersonal skills. She felt herself in this monumental senior project, growing and learning on almost every front.

This, she thought as she worked away, *is the most challenging learning experience I have ever had at school. I need and find knowledge in all*

areas, literature, history, math, science, and even personal communica-
tion. I am learning about leadership and administration. It's funny, she
thought, remembering her mother's many efforts to get more arts
into Octavia's school, *that the arts are always kept out of school—as if*
they are about something else than learning and knowledge. The opposite
is true. The arts give me a reason to learn, make my learning my own, and
help me to put together in one enormous piece of work, the things I know
from so many different subjects. When I am through with this, Octavia
thought, imagining as complete the production scheduled now for
the day before her graduation, *I will have accomplished what Sondheim's*
George longed to do: "to get through to something new, something of my
own—something I can be proud of."

INTRODUCTION

Returning to where we began, the relationship between the arts and
education is in many ways comparable to the relationship between
the artist or the arts and society. Societal ambivalence toward the arts
renders them simultaneously revered as the best that humans can produce and dismissed as the least necessary of activities. So is it with the
arts in education. The arts are applauded for putting students in touch
with their humanity even as they are derided for distracting students
from the business of education. On the one hand, arts classes are recognized for the high levels of engagement and creativity they evoke and
for the opportunities they provide for students to synthesize learning,
interpret experience, and give shape to meaning that matters to them.
On the other hand, arts classes are questioned for the level of noise and
activity they generate, the difficult topics they dare to confront, the
mess and space they require, and the alternative skills and attitudes
they inspire. Envisioning the arts in education as the artist among us,
we confront in this context the duality of world forsaker and world
mover—unwanted outsider and at the same time precious keeper of
the heart of the matter.

   Do the arts provide a reason and a way for students to make sense
of their experiential and academic learning? Isn't what Octavia discovers—that arts production creates a need for and interest in disciplinary
and interdisciplinary learning—an ideal goal for any educational activity? Do the arts provide windows not just on learning as an "integrated

whole" but also on the individual student as the owner and legislator of his or her own learning? If these possibilities have mettle, why do so many educators regard the arts as tangential and find it challenging if not an imposition to make connections between learning in traditional subjects and learning in the various venues of art? Is it possible that a history of defensive arguments for the extrinsic benefits of arts learning has so compromised and clouded the scene that it has become more difficult to uncover the real nature and promise of arts learning's intrinsic benefits? And is it possible that that real nature of arts learning lies just where Octavia has found it, in the opportunities the arts provide for all of us to make sense of the many strands of experience, emotion, and thought that we take in all at once, strive over time to comprehend, and ultimately present to an audience of ourselves and others as who we are and what we know.

The discussion is invariably reduced to "art for art's sake" versus "art for non-art's sake"—in this context, studying art because it is important in itself, judging progress in terms of achievement in arts learning versus studying art as important to non-arts subjects, measuring success in terms of improvement in those areas. What does it look like when we consider the possibilities of "art for education's sake"— studying art because it is essential to making education whole, gauging its imprint on students' developing ability to put together or make coherent the diverse strands of what they are learning. The arts provide students with the tools to make sense of their learning, to weave together in theatrical or musical performance, visual arts production, or written poem or story the education that they are encountering in but also out of school.

In this spirit and in this final chapter, I attempt to do some weaving of my own and in pursuit of an alternative that arts education advocates I believe have for too long thought unacceptable to political, social, and mainstream educational forces. Turning the lights and action to a positive, chest-beating, self-congratulatory view of the arts as indisputable agents to effective education, I revisit the various aspects of the arts and the arts in education that we have explored and reconsider them as sources of inspiration for enlivening non-arts education. For example, from early discussions of the making of art and the child as artist to the exemplary models we have reviewed in arts-focused educational settings, attention to the elements of process and reflection invariably looms large.

Process attributes are frequently identified as key to an arts-related approach to education, as is evident in arts-education champion Professor Eliot Eisner's John Dewey Lecture (2002), entitled, "What Can Education Learn from the Arts About the Practice of Education?" Eisner describes a "culture of schooling" that is based on the model for experience that the arts provide. It is a culture of schooling, he says, in which:

> more importance is placed on exploration than on discovery, more value is assigned to surprise than to control, more attention is devoted to what is distinctive than to what is standard, more interest is related to what is metaphorical than to what is literal. It is an educational culture that has a greater focus on becoming than on being, places more value on the imaginative than on the factual, assigns greater priority to valuing than to measuring, and regards the quality of the journey as more educationally significant than the speed at which the destination is reached. (p. 16)

Eisner eloquently advocates the process-based approach to education, which is espoused by community arts educators who purposely view their centers of learning as works of art in process. One veteran director described her active approach to making of the education she provides an aesthetic whole: "As an artist and administrator, I look at it as a kind of painting. It's like in a painting where one puts down a gesture and then responds to that. And eventually, one may change her whole perspective through that growth process of question and answer . . . sometimes I may disagree with myself, but by the time it's all done with . . . hopefully I will have a better understanding of who I am and what the problem is" (Davis, 1993a, p. 32).

The field of education struggles continuously with the question of what it is and what problems it faces. In colleges and universities, the subject of education is often and ironically estranged from the principal disciplines of study and research. While they may do the most important work in our society, teachers in our schools are rarely regarded or compensated at a level commensurate with their responsibilities. In what sense are all teachers and the field of education writ large, like artists and the arts, both valued and doubted for the world-changing work that they do? Like artists, teachers are thought to play, to do work that has intrinsic value such that extrinsic rewards should not matter, and to have power that can motivate or defeat future generations. Why not embrace as central the virulent connections that persist on an illusory and practical level between education and art, and mine the examples that the arts in education writ large can provide?

Like the veteran community arts educator, general educators sharing an arts-based approach to teaching and learning seek out the "problems" and mistakes as places to begin, and reflect continuously on developing process, as Eisner suggests, with less of an eye to measurable product. This attitude may seem self-indulgent (a word often applied to artists) in an educational climate in which accountability is test-driven, and especially with regard to subjects that are thought to "matter." But what if the scales of mattering were suddenly reversed and the arts were situated in foremost place as enviable examples for the reshaping of non-arts subjects and the rewriting of the larger educational scene? How might the efforts of all teachers and learners change and the alternative efforts of maverick educators come suddenly to the center? Artists we've reviewed reflect continuously on what they do even as they reconstruct their struggle as inspiration. Following the artist's lead, I reflect not only on the features that characterize the processes of learning as well as making and finding meaning in the arts but also on the struggles that confound the process-based, artist-driven, self-adjusting, self-promoting field of arts in education. In these reflections, I reconstruct them all as admirable entities from which even the broadest spectrum of educators might learn.

Throughout our discussions, "either" and "or" have served as means not ends, as generative tensions for moving on rather than alternatives for tying off. With an eye to the space that lies "in between," in this last section, I'll revisit separately and in kaleidoscopic interaction each productively oppositional tension. While each set of views generates delimited perspectives, encountering them all together in succession helps to frame one view of the whole. Most importantly, in these final reflections I attempt to demonstrate the critical opportunity that the arts provide to initiate sense-making across the curriculum—to put things together and to make of individual and collective education an aesthetic whole.

Perhaps unsurprisingly, I offer these reflective examples as questions that educators embracing an arts-related approach might ask of themselves or of their students. I do this hoping that the reader will find through these queries specific suggestions for the arts-based reshaping of non-arts education and in the activity of open-ended self-questioning, a means toward that end. I know that in the exploration of this final territory, I enjoy the good company not only of educational researchers and philosophers who have inspired and informed my thinking, but also of the many artful non-arts educators who have already broken this ground. I celebrate their efforts as I brave this final terrain.

A Cautionary Tale

I was excited to share my "art for education's sake" phrase with a small group of arts advocates who met recently to plan a series of conferences to help educators network around schools that focus on the arts. How might these meetings be of most use? One of the participants liked the new expression and considered its implications. Sounding as if she'd been communing with Tolstoy, she suggested that we might even represent the arts as being in some way associated with virtue. "Truth, beauty, and virtue," she told me, "they're back in vogue. Why not education?"

We seemed in agreement that the time was now for holding our heads up high and saying to others, "We've been doing something special for a long time. Let's reflect on what it is we do so we can share the news with educators who are interested in making the 'core' subjects they teach have the appeal and energy of the arts. Let's stop looking for a way to get our foot in the door and start looking at the way we move our feet! Let's not worry about how what students learn in the arts 'transfers' to other subjects; let's consider how the arts 'transform' the learning and living of students who pursue them!"

Another of my colleagues, whom I assumed was swept away by the palpable self-congratulatory spirit that seemed to prevail, agreed but said that we needed to stage a conference that would "teach" assessment because arts educators did not have the vocabulary of evaluation that non-arts teachers employed regularly. "They have to learn how to do evaluation; they really don't like to or know the dominant ways to evaluate student work." "Wait a minute!" I protested. "Don't art teachers assess student work all the time? Do they not in fact teach students to assess their own work as an important part of learning in the arts? Might evaluators forcing the process of learning into the product-driven measures of standardized tests have something to learn from the role of assessment in the creation of a work of art? If they were taken more seriously, might the artists' skills of self-monitoring ongoing assessment serve as a model for assessing student progress in all subjects? Could we envision assessing a student's ability to assess her own work, to self-critique with purpose and candor, as one measure of educational effectiveness?

The veteran administrator looked strangely put out as she turned to me and said, speaking very clearly: "Arts educators need to learn the vocabulary that other educators are using. They need to be able to talk about how learning in the arts transfers into other areas." "What about inventing new vocabularies?" I pressed on. "Perhaps all teachers worry as much as art teachers do about the damage that evaluation might have on the spirit and creativity of their students? Isn't this just another way in which we can learn from what arts educators do?" Now my collaborator looked at me as if I was out of my mind, stuck in the comfort of the progressive era in which arts education was truly celebrated or lost on some Utopian planet far from the realities of selling the arts as hard-edged arenas as robust as any of the other "thinking" disciplines.

If the greatest supporters of the arts in education were so ensconced in the values and vocabularies of those who doubt, change would be difficult. It would take hard work, real risks, the loss of the comfort of familiar responses, and the turning of new ways of thinking into performance. Deep-seated devaluation and suspicion of those beloved outsiders—artists, arts educators, and arts education—is hard to reverse. Fearing a view of the arts as mushy compassion-laden arenas, advocates have seriously bought into the need for the arts to be as quantifiable as any worthwhile kind of learning—catering to what Socrates had called "the part of the soul which trusts to measure and calculation." The advocate who would "teach" assessment referred to a recent study that demonstrated "critical links" between the arts and other subjects (Arts Education Partnership, 2002), shared some final comments about what teachers need ("We all know the arts are important, but . . ."), and made a hasty departure. It became clear to me that although deference and defeat hadn't served the cause of art education very well, arrogance and action would have to be metered carefully.

THE ARTISTIC PROCESS—FEELING/THINKING

Revisiting the Tension

Our earliest theoretical considerations were of arts production and perception as both the communication of feeling and the comprehension of thought—the coexperience of emotions and the coconstruction of ideas. When we applied a lens of infected or transmitted emotion to the activity of producing and perceiving art, we saw that the arts provide fertile ground for the articulation, appreciation, and alteration of human experience from unity to catharsis to social reconciliation. We noted the prevalence of a playful attitude both in the flexibility of attitude inherent in artistic expression and in the engagement involved in making meaning through art. We saw that the boundaries of the various terrains of art are constantly rewritten and challenged by artists, stretching art's definition and objective from creative physical composition to active human interaction. Artful teachers (those who fill and refine their teaching with art) have the same vision and power and persistently challenge the norms, rewriting the boundaries, definition, and objectives of education.

Understanding the artistic process writ large and over time as a growing vital organism, we reviewed examples of changes in attitude and style from romantic to modern to postmodern perspectives. Beyond that, we exercised the room there is in reflection on art for multiple perspectives and understandings. Expression, communication, and intention emerged for us as salient features in a feeling approach to the artistic process just as reflection, symbolization, and interpretation appeared as significant to an approach based on thought. All of these features hold sway in an artful approach to education—one that values and cultivates the multiplicity of arts-related experiences and understandings that teachers and students bring to the making and finding of meaning in any subject area.

We were aware that the artist's choice and use of symbols result in important differences in the impact and clarity of artistic statements, inviting differing responses from those who make sense of art. A thinking perspective reveals works of art as manipulated symbolic constructions whose referential integrity is transient. Art in this light is not a fixed concept; it is a sometimes state decided upon not only by the way in which things are made, but also by the kind of attention that they require of the viewer or audience. External contexts (which clearly change) and/or inherent properties (that can be noticed or not) determine an object's status as a work of art.

The portability of this perspective on art makes way for a view of teaching and learning as an aesthetic process. What contexts and properties prevail in an artful approach to education? Under what circumstances can education be regarded as art and/or art as education?

Postmodern artists mine the educative aspects of art; artful educators mine the art like aspects of education. When is education about thinking and when is it about feeling and is it, like art, arguably and always about both? When we take a non-art subject and attend to it as if it were art, what aspects do we notice that are otherwise overlooked?

Fundamental questions like what or when is art never seem to be resolved, but are instead repeatedly addressed by new artists and audiences. From a thoughtful perspective, ambiguity and interpretation are central aspects of the artistic experience even as the reexperiencing of a particular emotion may drive a feeling approach. But the apparently dichotomous territories of thought and feeling are everywhere seen to overlap and to expand an understanding of the multiplicity of art's purview. We found emotion framed as an intellectual construct and cognition as an emotionally mediated process. Lines become fuzzy and in the messy edged porous boundaries between art and what it represents and/or conveys, a certain truth emerges, more layered and familiar than factual detail. Do we reach in education for what thinking teaches us about feeling and feeling about thought? What place is there in schools for the discovery and celebration of the ambiguity, overlap, layers, and fuzz? Can we reach beyond public fact to personal truth in every discipline?

The relevant features of our thinking and feeling approaches serve as different facets or lenses admitting a variety of illuminations that both clarify and complicate our understanding of the nature of the artistic process. How might they stimulate a practitioner's perspective on a non-arts domain and thereby on the connections that persist (and the differences that obtain) between that domain and the arts—between that domain and any others considered by her students. The application of lenses from one domain to another is at the heart of interdisciplinary learning. When the lenses are taken from the arts, they promise to muddy the scene in the important ways in which the arts make the familiar unfamiliar, the falsely simple richly true. What roles do emotion, communication, and intention play in the processes involved in regions of human production such as science or math?

Why or when do mathematical equations and scientific discoveries make the individuals who find them weep? What emotion drives the intellectual pursuit of scientific queries or investigations? What does play look like in the domain of math or science or history or social studies? Do we provide opportunities for playful encounters with the meaning-making processes of these non-arts domains and do we count intense engagement as a marker of effectiveness? Should the difficulty of measuring such engagement deter us from valuing "flow" as a symptom of effective education?

Is intention fixed or changing in a scientific experiment? Fixed or changing in a work of art? Can we experience firsthand the similarities and differences around intention in discovery in science and discovery in art? Does knowing what you're going to find make the process more clear-cut or less honest? Artists often say they did not know what they thought until they saw it in the work that they created. Is there a counterpart for this element of discovery in production in non-arts arenas? A concept like intention, so virulent in discussions of art, is the sort of thread that can serve a student in the weaving together of an education made of disparate parts. This is true as well of emotion and of communication. These active concepts not only inform different perspectives on the purpose and function of art, they also serve as and exemplify porous boundaries for the consideration of non-arts domains.

From Arts to Non-Arts

What conditions need to be in place for non-art subjects to invite the close interpretive attention associated with the aesthetic? To what extent do, can, or would non-arts educators reach in their teaching for the sort of presentation that requires of the student attention to the smallest detail? While a discussion of a painting, poem, or story demonstrates to students that there is room for different "takes" on the same source of learning, it may be less clear that the different aspects of an historical record are also "read" in perhaps importantly differing ways by different constituents. Borrowing theatrical technique, some artful teachers encourage students to play different roles and to interpret documents that are apparently clear presentations of facts from the perspectives of various constituents who may be variously affected by the content. What is gained when we ask students to participate as artists in their learning? What is gained when we view our teachers as artists and texts as works of art?

Considering Ptolemy and Copernicus as astrological artists, why and how did their interpretation of what they saw differ and how and why did each of them make different sense of the same phenomena? Comparing the processes of Abbott Handerson Thayer drawing what he saw of animal coloration with Kepler's drawings of vectors and orbital ellipses, what are the similarities and differences between their efforts? What are the respective roles that drawing plays in art and in science and in learning writ large? What might that have to do with the idea we seem to have of children as artists? Is it possible that children's nascent understandings in science have the same sort of power and clarity as their nascent understandings in art?

Researchers with different agendas make sense of the same sets of data in very different ways. Students who know and experience this artful reality may come to understand that in science as in art, they have a real voice in determining and prioritizing what they learn. Some contemporary educators think it important for students to consider that facts may just be symbols for current knowledge and, like artistic symbolization, be transient. Determining who is telling a given story or framing an apparently nonnegotiable cadre of information is an important consideration in making sense of what we read and learn at any level of education. Readers of a business school case may attend to the perspective of the subjects in the presentation who apparently tell their own stories without recognizing that the author of the case, the business school professor is curator of the show deciding what direct quotations or data points will be included. Reciprocally the reader of the case has her own perspective that is drawn to the retelling of some aspects over others. The interaction between production and perception prevails across arts and non-arts domains. Interpretation is not just the province of the artist and art perceiver (see Parsons, 1991).

The romantic notion of communication through art may find contemporary and relevant realization in the recognition in social science that has recently been given to Voice—the preoccupations, experiences, and biases of the investigator exploring any issue. In our attempts to interpret what we see and experience in any realm, we are all like artists constructing and perceivers recognizing their shared humanity. How does interpretation serve as a thread across disciplines for the student who is weaving of it all some kind of balanced whole? Will my education be as valid as yours if the sense I make of it differs? And if there is so much room for individuating education, for making different and personally relevant sense of what we learn, why do educators turn to standardized measures for evaluating educational effectiveness? Is there no way to assess sense making as an important educational outcome even if it finds different realizations in the work of different students? Are there other skills—like asking real questions or constructing coherent interpretations—that can be assessed across a range of manifestations?

Building on the cognitive approach to the arts, a consideration of fundamental questions in every discipline (What is science? What is math? What is history?) serves students well not only in coming to know the different terrains of various subjects but in understanding as well that those subjects' boundaries, like those of the arts, are constantly being renegotiated. The students' attempts to define and redefine these arenas are part of a real and not just a "school" conversation. Building on the feeling approach to the arts, what does it look like when an educator considers the emotional aspects of his or her subject (perhaps attending to expression, communication, intention) as well as the emotional impact of the teaching of that subject? What does it look like when the non-arts discipline is likened to art and the teaching of that discipline to the artistic process? How are thought and feeling manifest as differing in whatever non-arts discipline and how do they overlap? And at the level of school values, how, if at all, might such emotive considerations jeopardize the profile of mainstream subjects? Can we take the discussion to that level of context and talk with students about what values have held sway in educational settings? What do *they* value most about their education? Why do they think that non-arts subjects are rarely considered or described as arenas for expressing emotion?

Surely the association with emotion has rocked the security of the arts in the value systems of school. A consideration of the struggles associated in any domain with prioritizing feeling, impression, or instinct could therefore be informed by a study of postcognitive revolution arguments for the centrality versus extraneousness of the arts in education. How can the arguments that confront defenders of art's connection to emotion inform our perspective on the role of emotion in a non-arts domain? When do intimate and moving stories of historical figures make history more engaging and when, if at all, do they distract from detecting the chronological spine of historic information? Students writing a well-documented fictive entry into a slave's journal for American history class might be asked whether they thought the emotional aspects or the human connection they experienced in their writing made their work more or less important, valuable, or intellectual. Did it attach or distract them from their study of history? While considering the emotional aspects of the assignment in this way sets the stage for the reflective activity of metacognition (thinking about thinking), it also encourages students to encounter within the domain of the study of history a traditional and controversial aspect of making and appreciating art: the notion that feeling may be the agent and/or product of thought.

Experiential Considerations

At one point I was a decorative painter, mostly creating murals on the walls of comfortable homes. I would paint apple orchards filled with caricatures of the children of a family collecting apples in a back hall, or animals and alphabet words on the walls of a nursery. It was interesting illustrating walls instead of pages and coconstructing the ideas for what went on them with my clients. For his 50th birthday, an actuary was given as a gift from his wife one of my hand-painted rooms. The actuary and I met to discuss what would be on the walls of his bathroom. Beyond stylized depictions of his wife and children, a rendering of himself as a knight in shining armor, the actuary wanted his favorite actuarial symbols glazed on the tiles of his shower and his favorite actuarial equations painted on the shower curtain. I wondered as I produced them whether the actuary would enjoy the color and balance involved in the rendering of these symbols—the use of stylized outline to attach their presentation to the faux castle effect of the room. Or would he see through the artistic presentation to what the symbols denoted, which was what he held most dear?

This recollection comes to me at this juncture because painting those symbols, experiencing them as art, brought back to me so vividly the pleasure I had taken in drawing circles, equilateral triangles, all kinds of angles, and even parallel lines in school geometry. Attending as I did for the actuary to the details of color and presentation introduced me to the symbols in ways that necessarily went beyond their literal representation. I remembered as well the thrill of drawing in biology the details of the human heart and the motion of the blood through it. The act of drawing attached me indelibly to my understanding. I remember my decisions of how to add dimensionality to the rendering of the arteries and veins and am reminded of them when I see their treatment in medical drawings that I encounter today. I had always thought these were private pleasures reserved for me because I liked to draw, but other "non-artist" students seemed as well to find the aesthetics of representation in these areas a source of great pleasure.

How I wished we could have stayed with those images a while, wondered not just whether all the parts had been included or the lines had been drawn just right. What an opportunity to consider aspects of reference. How did my drawing of the heart relate or not to the actual structure and function of a real human heart? What things in the world or the life of the mind did our geometrical proofs represent? And what if we looked at these representations differently and thought instead of the colors that we'd chosen to use or the scale or texture of our work? Did we change what we had created from diagram to art just by attending to them differently? What new perspectives on the science we were learning might artful approaches allow? Might we, applying the artist's eye, see more than we expected in a given phenomenon, perhaps even discover something new that a less artful perusal would overlook?

As a college student of biology, I had the horrifying experience of holding in one hand the body of a vivisected frog while its heart, separated, beat slowly in my other hand. The question we had to answer when the unforgettable experience was over was, "When did the frog die?" and "Is the whole organism more, less, or equal to the sum total of its parts?" What are the connections between that visceral experience and the moments in which I try to decide if a drawing or a piece of writing or a day in my life is a complete aesthetic whole? What are the similarities and differences between the frog as an organism that is greater than the sum of its parts and the unity in art that Aristotle describes with exactly the same language? The lines between art and life, part and whole, and almost anything we study are thin and porous and the crossing over, for a while at least, available to our students. Why don't we ask students in the science class to draw flowers that are art? How will those renderings differ from drawing flowers that are science? Where from the past might we find examples of both?

How does symbolization work in non-art domains? Do we ask our students to consider the nature and effect of the symbols that they are using in math and science? How do these symbols affect the audience for the work? How might they be altered to achieve different effects? Is there the equivalent of representational and abstract reference in non-arts domains? How do modes of presentation change the ways in which we "read" and respond to meaning? Is the letter *a* a different kind of symbol when it is used in an algebraic equation than when it is used in a word? When we create a balanced unified aesthetic whole in math or science, what does that look like and how does it "speak" to those who take it in? What does that unity have to do with the greater scene and how we make sense of it? To what extent is there universality in the language of that symbol system and how does it change across context and culture?

Artful teachers reflect with students on the non-arts domain as serving a transformational role in the arenas of human experience and consider what happens when we look at math or science as communication among individuals. Is there a sort of recognized and shared humanity in that discourse? What are the ways in which non-arts domains shape and change the world? How have our definitions of math or science or history changed over time? In what way, if at all, are mathematicians and/or scientists romanticized or derided as world-moving outsiders and what does that tell us about the what and the why of the boundaries we draw? What are the student's personal definitions of math and science and history and how and why are those definitions likely to change? How are they changing now in the broader context and because of the individual efforts of the student? How different are our personal understandings of it all? And who can say which of these personal understanding will be right or wrong?

Embracing Ambiguity

If I ask my student how tall she is, she can give me a truthful or untruthful, right or wrong response. But if I ask her what tree she would be if she were a tree, whatever response she provides is beyond such judgment. A mural of student selves as trees can be the beginning of a conversation in which students reflect together on self and other. What comparable activities abide in non-arts subjects? Artful educators exploit the room for generative ambiguity and multiple interpretations that persist in any discipline. Conversations about these constructive process-based aspects of non-arts subjects invite a different, more artlike engagement on the part of the student. Moreover, they help students see that useful discussions persist across subjects, and it is the organization of their own learning that makes what they learn useful, representative of their own understandings, and whole. Students in community art centers, disenfranchised from school and other mainstream expectations, are said to overcome their personal sense of not mattering through the tactile and immediate sense of consequence that they experience in aesthetic decisions. "I can see how the addition of this red changes the balance of this image." "I can experience the difference in effect if I read this line louder than the rest." Artful educators know that that sense of student mattering needs to be an objective of or agent to any educational experience.

The recognition that students are actively defining the domain with their every contribution changes the discourse from one of acquiring and accurately demonstrating knowledge of information to one of selecting and using information to fuel different questions and equally valid alternative points of view. What does metaphor look like in science or in math? The more you know about drawing, the more apt and surprising the metaphoric referential connections you can make on paper. This must be true of math and science as well. How might metaphor making in art inform and differentiate metaphor making in other domains? How much must we know of feeling and of thinking to recognize a felt thought?

The arts are synthetic and can be taken apart without compromise into non-arts-specific components such as scale and measure, psychology and history, balance and disruption. Do non-arts subjects decompose as well? Why or why not? Is it as difficult to point to what is not science or what is not math as it is to say for certain what is not art? Is there a way in which whatever we are studying is art? Why and why not? Do or can you own the work you are doing in this non-art class the way you own whatever you create in art? Why and why not? Is there a counterpart in non-arts productions for the interdisciplinary feast that Octavia experienced in her oversight of the Sondheim show?

All of these considerations, associated loosely and directly with issues around feeling and thinking in art, remind students that the lines between non-arts and arts subjects are not as firm as we appear to draw them. Allowing the student to redraw the lines between and across disciplines helps to shift the ownership and direction of his or her learning. While the considerations that obtain in the producing and making sense of works of art are many and diverse, they represent and align with the unique ability of the arts in education to lead the way simultaneously into a deeper understanding of a particular work and to a broader understanding away from that work into any number of non-arts disciplines and experiences. The opportunities that arts or arts-related learning provide for synthesizing what students learn may be that illusive unique although completely apparent quality that arts educators struggle so hard to identify.

Throughout these reflections, and with little direct attention, I am assuming that the more opportunities students have to experience arts learning as thinking and feeling in as many artistic domains as possible, the more opportunities they will have both to apply and to make sense of what they are learning in other subjects, from life skills to foreign language. Similarly, the more art-related considerations are applied to non-arts learning, the richer and more complex that learning will be. Underlying and at the heart of this thinking is a view of the student as artist, as the mover of her own world, the maker of her own understandings, ready and able to confront and to contribute to whatever discipline she is learning. Artful teachers may provide the opportunity for artful thinking across disciplines; but students as artful individuals in this world come equipped to individuate that thinking and to make it real.

THE CHILD AS ARTIST—ROMANCE/REASON

Rewriting Boundaries

As a nascent art teacher in the early 60s in New York City, I organized my summer curriculum for 200 children from ages 6 to 12 around the great books. I based my approach on the non-arts winter curriculum that I enjoyed at St. John's College where, although we all struggled and soared mightily with diverse and coherent interpretations, every student read the same books: Plato, Sophocles, Newton, Thucydides, Kant, Dostoevsky, and other icons of Western Civilization. Far from tests and right answers, the curriculum was metered through seminars in which our teachers were presented as expert learners introducing the processes of inquiry and reflection as students forayed back and forth through open-ended questions, ultimately arriving at new and better questions.

Coming to college from a cookie-cutter secondary school in which each of us scrambled in our choice of courses for faux individuality, determined largely by our assigned intellectual abilities and with an eye to acceptance at an Ivy League college, I was amazed to discover that in this extraordinarily structured scenario in which course selection was predetermined, I encountered, and with authenticity: difference, inquiry, self-initiated discovery, self-conscious participation in a continuum between the unique and the universal, and an appreciation for the variation and value of others' points of view—everything I would have hoped for in the learning of my students in the arts and crafts barn at the Hoffmann School.

I developed a camp-wide weekly curriculum that was shared by all the students, defined uniquely by each child artist. Each week of the 8-week program, we explored a particular theme. One week it was people; on other weeks the circus, nature, outer space, and animals. Each class began with seminarlike group reflection (all stemming from open-ended questions) on the particular theme and, although the media changed every day, every day every camper explored the weekly theme through the same medium. The freewheeling and enthusiastic 5-year-olds approached finger painting from a different perspective from the sophisticated and initially outraged 12-year-olds. But regardless of medium, both these age groups explored the same topic and marveled at the different ideas and representations of ideas embodied in their respective work.

Murals, ultimately joined so that they wrapped around the art barn, presented colorful displays of collective work—expanses of animals interrelating in tempera and texture, simultaneously individuating themselves and their creators. Ten-year-old Jeremy's orange hound scratched at the base of a tree on which 6-year-old Lisa's red monkey was swinging from the branch on which sat 8-year-old Michael's nest of blue birds. No two representatives of the same animal were exactly alike despite the dedicated efforts for sameness of some children in the middle grades. My children were learning about difference, inquiry, self-initiated discovery, self-conscious participation in a continuum between the unique and the universal, and an appreciation for the variation and value of the points of view of others—everything that I had been learning in the particularly non-arts related arena of St. John's College.

My teaching was my bridge between arts and non-arts curricula, just as my students applied that framework to the considering, making, and sharing of images. I intend no irreverence or trivialization in the alignment of revered selected texts from Western literature with everyday arbitrary themes in child experience. My intention is only to suggest that students, like artists, see beyond the content to the structures of their education. Because these structures are portable and can sustain arts and non-arts learning, they deserve the attention of the arbitrators of their success: the teachers who breathe life and excitement into their actualization. Some educators think that "transfer" needs to be taught—that students will not make connections between their learning in different domains unless we show them how (see Perkins, 1992). I contend that students naturally make, need, and want connections across their learning and that school too frequently and wrongheadedly teaches boundaries, cuts up learning, and suggests to students that they select and settle for one piece of the pie. The arts can break the boundaries and artful teachers set us free.

Artful teachers of all subjects, like sculptors and painters, study and find creative ways to expand their discipline. Like dancers on the stage, artful teachers attend to their audience and the ways in which it will most fruitfully be engaged. Like actors in a theater, artful teachers are aware in the classroom of the space in which they move and the many roles and faces of adulthood that they represent to their students. Like writers facing a blank page, artful teachers choose their language carefully and work toward effective communication. And of course like jazz musicians, artful teachers know well the baffling skills of improvisation and will, in a single class, abandon their intended melody to explore in-depth an unexpected theme.

The great vibraphonist Gary Burton tells a resonant artist story when he speaks of the moment in his development as a musician at which he no longer needed to think about which notes he was playing. He described the "high" he felt watching his hands move almost from a distance, without connection to his deliberation or intention, inventing and playing music that "blew him away" (1998). Veteran teachers in any domain know that high when the class comes alive and the teacher almost seamlessly moves through the coconstruction of learning both at the center and on the edges of the moment, like artists standing back at a distance from which vision is direct to the center of it all.

Revisiting the Tension

In our discussion of the child as artist, we considered artists and the traditional contradictory image of them as both world movers and forsakers. Do artists leave the world in order to change it? Do artists align themselves with children in order consciously to leave the adult world? Do they reach for the child within in order to regain the fresh-ness and clarity of vision of the young child—that quintessential out-sider who works hard in the domain of school to learn the ways and means of the adult world that she strives to enter? Romantic images of the child as the artist whom adult artists want to be sets the stage for a more rational cognitive view of the young child arriving at school with artistic attitudes and abilities that can be reasonably compared with the artistry of adult artists.

A view of the child as artist can in itself inspire non-arts educators to rethink their understanding of their students and the approaches that they use to reach them. What if I consider every child in the room to be an artist—a maker of meaning who has vision and skills that bring special perspective to her work? The comparison between teachers and artists is ripe. But the view expands further when it is of student as artists. How do I engage this artist student? The incorporation of the arts into my curriculum is an obvious and important response. But can I also find ways to present my non-arts subject as artistic media and to authentically invite my student artist into a new arena for making and finding meaning—as I assume (romantically or rationally) she already does in the arts? The languages of art have porous boundaries. We can-not say for sure when poetry becomes music, dance becomes theater, or visual arts become performance. How can I extend arts' boundaries to include the language of whatever discipline I am teaching? When does math become poetry, physics become drawing, history become theater, or chemistry become painting?

In our considerations of the child as artist and the tension between romance and reason, we noted three child virtues that adult artists sought to reclaim: connection, freedom, and distance. From a romantic perspective, connection was viewed as a seamless attachment to ideas and emotions; from a reason-driven perspective that connection was un-derstood as a lack of differentiation—that "I am what I do" perspective that Sondheim attributed to the artist Seurat. From a romantic perspec-tive, freedom was viewed as a disregard for or ignorance of the rules or conventions of the domain; from the reason side of our discourse we saw freedom as a developmental stage at which the very young child is unaware of audience either as a perceiver trying to make sense of her art or as a critic intending to judge it. From the romantic perspective, distance involved the purview of the aching outsider either as the artist rejected or rejecting the norm or the child looking in at what might and should be. From a rational or cognitive stance, distance was understood as what was crossed through the work of artist and child in the making of metaphor and its inherent bonding of symbol and meaning.

A director of an arts-focused school, embracing what I am now calling an "arts for education's sake" perspective, told me that she has just assigned to her academic dean the challenge of making the academic courses more like the art courses. "The kids love the arts classes and endure the academics. What will it take for us to realize that we need to figure out what makes the art courses work and how we can adopt those features into our non-arts teaching and learning?" In an arts-based school, the discussion begins with the realization that students who have self-selected the arts at the secondary level have arts-related skills and perspectives on learning that can enliven the non-arts classes. But these self-identified young artists hold attitudes, abilities, and points of view of value to all teachers who choose to consider their students as artists. What appeals to these students should appeal to all.

The three child virtues from our earlier considerations provide useful tools for meeting this educator's challenge. The artful teacher can ask: What might connection look like in my non-arts activity? Are there ways I can encourage my students to express themselves directly—individually and collectively—through the medium of math or science or whatever non-arts discipline I am teaching? Regarding my discipline as a medium for meaning making, how can I encourage students to have an interactive relationship with their work in which they pursue self-exploration through the medium of history or math? Can they view their study, as artists do, as works in progress—and understand that change and growth and new perception hold greater promise than anything that's fixed and right? Where will they find and where will there be room for them to declare voice in their efforts in this arena?

How do I in my non-arts classes encourage my students to feel freedom from the very rules and conventions that I also want them to learn? What does rule-breaking look like in math or science and what discoveries have emerged from breaking a convention or rule? How will I discuss this phenomenon with students and how might it relate to a view of mistakes as opportunities and the road not taken as full of worth. What does "right" look like in art, in philosophy, in science? How do I provide opportunities to invite and respect multiple ways for students to devise and understand the implications or possibilities for their experiments or problems? Can my students, like artists, see answers as the beginning of a conversation and not the end? Can they own their work like artists do and learn physics or science or math in order to make better their creative constructions? What part will self-assessment play in their independent processes of bettering their work? How might I turn to that important self-regulating activity as a measure of my students' learning instead of applying a set of rigid product-related grades?

Responding to the Child Artist

How differently will I relate to my student if I envision him or her as an outsider? Can I help the student find a place on the inside that honors the importance of distance? Can I celebrate the not knowing that is at the heart of distance from a domain or subject? (See Duckworth, 1987.) What can my students see from their distant perches of a subject about which I sometimes think I know too much. How can I celebrate their outsider status and convince them that theirs is a useful and new perspective that I celebrate and from which I can learn. If only I could attend to a scientific phenomenon with the eyes of a child, as if I were a stranger on the planet Earth, meeting this equation or that chemical reaction with the wonder of a first encounter.

How can I keep that perspective alive in my students and let them know that I do not see them as empty slates on which school will write the stories that they must know. If my student is an artist, how will I make sense of his or her work? How many different ways in must I consider? What will I see in the work that transcends the narrow lines between right and wrong? How will I come to know and celebrate what is different about this child's work since difference is at the heart of what I do with these world-moving outsiders? Throughout it all, I might reflect with them on all these considerations in order to share with and learn more from them about the artful possibilities inherent in any domain (see Davis, 2000). Let me know the ways in which this learning is, for you, art.

Can I design an activity in my non-arts subject that, like mural making, captures the imagination of my students, increases their respect for each other's work, and enlarges their collective pride in creating a product that others will admire? What activities can I engender that similarly engage my students in collective inquiry, reflection, imagination, and production? Artful teachers have responded to the challenge. In history, students write their own history books and critique class texts from the expertise they have gained. With the critical eye of a fellow artist historian, they consider what topics are missing in the class texts. Students collectively assemble a dictionary of key words associated with geometry, selected by them for inclusion, for which they research and write definitions. On what basis do they prioritize the terms they include? How will that collective effort be displayed and/ or distributed for the use and enjoyment of others? What issues of design and illustration need they consider in their presentation? How are these choices informed by convention and/or invention? What role do images play in clarifying or expanding text? Artful teachers activate production and perception as agents to critical curriculum.

How will I assess my students' work and what care will I use in discussing it when I buy into the possibility that for my student artists, they are what they do? Child artists working collectively on dramatic productions and/or writing and performing music critique each other with excellence as an objective and mutual respect as a guiding principle (see Soep, 1996). What can we learn from these child artists working together to constructively evaluate each other's performance with an eye to collective success? How do the balances, incentives, and results change when the purpose of assessment is collective improvement rather than individual judgment? What do students in non-arts classes gain when artful teachers ask them what modes of critique feel most comfortable to them? How often do we ask them to assess assessment? How do student attitudes toward evaluation change when they learn from adult artists about the important part of the artistic process that is played by ongoing reflection on developing product?

If our children are artists and they turn to their work for what's wrong as a place to begin, they may be more able to weather whatever range of evaluative measures schools put in place. As standardized tests are appraised for their reliability as true measures of performance or relevance to content material, too little time is devoted to the well-being of students who must survive the harsh results these tests often deliver. Can we not mine the resources of artist attitudes toward assessment as a part of their working process (as opposed to the hard criticisms of product from critics in the field) as a means through which our students can better understand what measures matter most in terms of the development of their work. Can failure be reconstructed as a means and not an end? Can the developmental trajectory of the u-Curve be repopulated with more students, like artists, ascending after the fall? From a view that acknowledges the loss inherent in gain, those undifferentiated early understandings that are necessarily dislodged by development seem not so far from the coherent "put together" education that artful teachers hope their students will achieve.

Artful teachers in any domain recognize and hope to cultivate rather than rewrite the experiences and abilities of their students. They search for ways to preserve the early sense of the whole even as knowledge of each part is gained. Like artists, artful teachers attend to part and whole all at once in one united effort. Like artists, artful teachers introduce the ways and means for sense making across the curriculum even as they recognize that sense making is the natural proclivity of the child, that "transfer" is a word invented in response to the slicing and dicing of learning that would be better off whole.

Considering the developmental paradigms that cognitive psychologists have uncovered, does it matter that children come to school expressing themselves like artists and, for the most part, leave without seeing themselves as such or apparently caring one way or another? What are the implications for their learning in other subjects of the loss of artistic proclivities that most schoolchildren are expected to endure? Artful teachers strive to keep that artistry alive and to reconstruct the trough of the u as a passageway rather than a destination. Creative individuals in any domain rewrite the boundaries of artistry and demonstrate how thinking and feeling like an artist enriches any and all human activity.

THE ARTS IN EDUCATION IN SCHOOL— JUSTIFICATION/CELEBRATION

Revisiting the Tension

Reviewing the history of the arts in education, we saw the fluid octopuslike movement of the arts, assuming whatever pose was most in demand, addressing whatever mainstream curricular issue would justify its movements. There are some that say that the arts can be flexible in how they serve education because of their naturally synthetic nature. Encompassing all disciplines in aesthetic and cultural expression, the arts can be sliced and diced and linked accordingly. But in our efforts here to turn this outsider field's struggle into fodder for insider subjects, it is useful to consider the extent to which other subjects could emulate the arts in self-reflecting on reasons for their inclusion in educational fare and in redefining themselves regularly in order to meet multiple and alternative needs and goals. To what extent is the ongoing need to identify and showcase different possibilities as important an impetus for all areas of education as it is for the realm of the arts?

Responding to various prevailing ethics in general education, historical justifications for the arts in education include better use of leisure time, the promotion of democratic ideas, the enhancement of community life in the classroom, the cultivation of creativity, the development of the whole child, and the cultivation of such cognitive capacities as critical thinking and problem solving. The ways in which art educators have responded to these changing demands holds promise for artful teachers and students in non-arts classes. How will my artful teaching of history help to create adult citizens who attend with art-like acuity and aesthetic judgment to the details of historic and current events? To what extent am I developing in any subject area an arts-like reflective connoisseur who knows how to take in, assess, and make constructive use of information?

While arts educators are now conspiring to find ways to make of their students critical consumers of visual, popular, and media culture, artful math teachers, science teachers, history teachers, English teachers, and foreign language teachers also recognize the influence that current cultural contexts have on their students' meaning making in their respective domains. Artful teachers in any domain join the arts education front in thinking through the various languages of their disciplines about the content of and the ways in which contemporary culture delivers meaning to students. With the media's promulgation of racial stereotypes, economic imbalance, and artificial values, students need to "own" and be able to negotiate both the making and receiving of such meanings. No school subject is unaffected by the climate of the times; no contexts of learning exempt from contemporary culture; no student out of reach of media influence.

One way in which the arts have tried to integrate themselves is through the application of the "aesthetic" (variously defined) as a universal applicable to all disciplines. Aesthetic understandings may be gleaned from reading poetry, listening to music, or viewing great art, but they open the doors to reflection on the many different areas of thought that throughout time have been affected by art. Similarly, other disciplines can benefit from thinking beyond themselves to their imprint on other subjects. What are the ways in which beauty in math can be apprehended and applied to other subjects? To what extent is the learning of structure in a Euclidian proof applicable to the development of an argument in creative and academic writing? How will the scientific method help students to find their way through works of art or literature, media representations, or music? Might more of our outsider artist students come in to acquire these skills if their applicability to arts-related activities were made clearer?

Many of us have questioned, albeit facetiously, why math teachers aren't asked to demonstrate how their teaching of math enhances students' ability to express themselves in any arts media. After all, arts educators are repeatedly asked to demonstrate how studying the arts will enhance student performance in math and other academic subjects. The question is usually posed to point to the irony of asking so much more of the arts than is asked of other disciplines. But in the context of these last reflections, I ask that question without irony. Why shouldn't the math teacher be thinking of how what she is teaching will help her students make sense of art or history or science? And why shouldn't she share those considerations with her students so that she can help the student make sense of his or her learning as an integrated whole, and not a set of separate areas in which he excels a bit less or more. If we can celebrate a view of art for education's sake, why not celebrate a view of education for art's sake?

The notion of value, knowing good art when you see it, has been promoted in some arts education approaches. Indeed, the value of value as a measure for art in itself invites lively student discussion. Does that concept work its way into other domains? When is a mathematical argument or a scientific proof or an analytic paper successful as an aesthetic whole? How do students express themselves in unique ways and with relative effectiveness through these different media? Artful teachers invite individual expression as an objective in science and history, as well as in art. Can we study history to find ourselves as we do in art? Can we study science as a new language through which we can speak, as we do in art? What is unique about these different languages? What can I say through the symbols and conventions of science that I cannot say in writing or in dance? What are the relative definitions and values of right or wrong across disciplines?

And what of the disciplinary experts that have played such a role in the teaching and learning of art in schools, whether as models for foundational content areas or in the framing of practice? What of the visiting artist who brings the arts to life for students in school? Visiting artists were originally invited to keep alive a space for the arts in schools that were eliminating arts specialists. What can other subjects learn from the benefits that have been accrued from this fallback strategy for the arts? What is the impact of bringing a scientist on a mission into the science classroom? How moving is it to meet an historian making sense of a contemporary challenge? How like the artist telling a story is the historian recording events? Artful teachers expand their curricula through interactions with artists from all fields.

What is considered creative today in the art world will be de rigueur, uninteresting, or obsolete in the future. Is this as true for new plateaus in science, math, technology, and history? The question of creativity is worth consideration by artful teachers and students in every domain. Like Seurat inventing pointillism, Newton invented the calculus to make sense of phenomena he couldn't otherwise effectively explain. Artful teachers draw on connections and introduce various branches of mathematics and science as mutually informative with rather than disjunctive from the languages of art. In this vein, artful teachers consider across disciplines concepts like "suspension of disbelief," so obvious in theater but just as salient when we are asked for the moment to conceive of an impossible possibility such as infinity. The arts, those sorry outsiders looking for ways to come in, can be found at the center in every context. Artful teachers mine the opportunity to find in all subjects various and new ways to make sense of and represent experience.

A frequent reason for dismissing the arts in education has been because so few students will grow up to be artists. We do not dismiss other subjects because so few students will grow up to be mathematicians or scientists or historians or writers. Against a backdrop of suspicion and ambivalence, it is possible that we dismiss the arts because we'd just as soon not have our students grow up to be artists. We mentioned that the playfulness, magic, emotive power, and alternativeness of the arts keep them from the center of the curriculum. Do the arts become more central when artful teachers in every subject reach for the playfulness, magic, emotive power, and alternativeness of their domains?

Eight Ways

We looked at eight ways in which the arts are included when they are celebrated in mainstream education. The first was arts-based, in which all subjects were taught through the lens of the arts. How does that approach differ from math-based or science-based or history-based approaches to curriculum? How is it similar? The arts-based model is an example of a discipline being more than an end in itself but providing a window onto learning in other disciplines. Artful teachers in any domain consider their subjects as windows or doors and not just rooms.

The arts-infused approach covers that visiting expert coming into the classroom, but also a range of imprints of the injection of a discipline into another setting. Can we call on the chemistry teacher to help us with compounds in photography or ceramics, the math teacher with scale in painting, the art teacher with propaganda in history, the music teacher with ratios in math? Obviously time is needed to keep up with what is happening in each other's classes and to consider the potential connections or cross threads in the weave. The work of putting it together bit by bit is the work of a community of learners, not just the responsibility of a lone teacher or student.

The arts-included model, in which the arts are simply given as much time in the school day as any other discipline, may hold less apparent inspiration for subjects that are regularly prioritized. But there's something for all subjects to learn from the angst of being excluded and all subjects might benefit from their facilitators thinking: Why does whatever subject I teach deserve a place in the daily life of every child at school? What can I do to make it more deserving? What current priorities call for the exploration of new aspects of what I teach? Artful teachers across the curriculum do not sit on the laurels of what is; they question the given and think beyond now.

The arts-expanded approach, through which the arts take students out of school and into the community, holds clear implications for the direction and activity of non-arts subjects. What are the institutions where my discipline is being pursued or explored in the community? Artful teachers bring their students to the lab, where process prevails; or the science museum, where curators arbitrate knowledge; or the brokerage office, where technology and numbers abound; or the local newspaper, where history is being recorded; or the library, where the newspapers of the past give testimony to the conversation over time in which their history students are involved.

My youngest son, an artist, was in the ninth grade at an independent school. He had been sick and missed quite a few classes, but was determined to get well in time for his science class's trip to the Museum of Science in Boston. The excitement of the move from the regular classroom to the world outside, the delight in seeing both classmates and teacher in another setting, and the opportunity to be surrounded by science in a setting in which science was the raison d'être—the thrill of this sort of learning was something he would not miss. I was relieved and delighted that he was well enough to go to school the day of the trip and devastated for him and furious on my own part when a sorrowful Benjamin called to say that his teacher had not let him come along. The teacher felt that since he'd missed so much school, it was more important for Benjamin to be in study hall and review his missed lessons than to go with the class on a "field trip."

Without a field trip to an art museum or a gallery or a studio, students rarely have firsthand encounters with works of art, those originals that in so many ways demonstrate the hand, heart, and skill of the professional artist. Along with other arts-related activities, field trips to art museums do not happen as often as they might. Nonetheless they demonstrate, in what they hold and have to teach, what trips out of the classroom can mean in any domain. Ben's science teacher saw the field trip as an extra, not an essential. He saw it as made up of another and clearly lesser set of experiences than studying from a science text. The arts-expanded model should serve to encourage non-arts teachers to take their children into the community where the art of their discipline is being practiced and to acknowledge that that encounter is a privileged and powerful and not extraneous and dispensable opportunity for learning.

In an arts-professional model, teaching and learning holds that vision of the work of the artist and a life as an artist as a viable and desirable outcome. Artful teachers throughout time have enjoyed treating their students as if they were expected to become scientists, writers, mathematicians, or historians. How does this attitude affect the dynamic in the classroom—even when working with elementary school children? What activities and preprofessional adventures does this artful approach engender? Artful teachers explore roles and possibilities in order to gain the earnest engagement that social play invites and to open doors for student development within and across arenas.

The prevalent arts extra model in which arts learning is relegated to extracurricular time has always served as a model or parallel frame for non-arts subjects. Math clubs, science clubs, technology workshops, school papers, and history trips all represent non-arts educators' value of added time and space that for the arts may be the only venue for their teaching and learning. When art is regularly prioritized during the school day—when theater is taught during the school day or painting is part of the curriculum—the arts extra model moves from compensatory to enriching. Artful teachers mine the resources of extra school time in the precious few hours of in school learning.

In considerations of justification, aesthetic education, with its cadre of texts, artworks, and philosophical ruminations enriching student learning inspires the artful teacher of any course to incorporate classics of her field and works of art that speak to the subject. Students benefit from philosophical reflection on the aesthetics of any field, as many prior considerations have suggested. Our last framework, the Arts Cultura model, perhaps holds the broadest range of possibilities for non-arts learning.

How many of us remember a teacher explaining whether the mathematical symbols we were learning were unique to our cultures or universal and how and why. Were we asked how we found math in our home and our community and to consider how it might access discourse across nations and time? I'd have liked to understand math more as a language for communication since I liked to speak and less like an arena for accuracy since I didn't like to fail. Are all the disciplines prioritized in schools in the United States taught across cultures, and how do they differ in content and approach? Do French philosophers consider the same issues as American philosophers and are they trained to be philosophers in the same or different ways? What are the cross-cultural implications of whatever non-arts subject is being studied and what new understandings of culture in all its iterations do these subjects make possible? How, if it is, is the wheel of culture differently motored by math or science or history or technology? Why and how does art speak differently across place, time, and circumstance?

Passion and Industry

When we looked for examples of celebration of arts learning to those schools in which the arts were intrinsically valued, schools that focus on the arts, we discovered a set of descriptors that artful educators embrace in any non-arts setting: process and reflection, connection and community, difference and respect, and passion and industry. These qualities, so resonant across exemplary settings of arts learning, inform the critique of artful teaching and learning in any class and school.

When it comes to process and reflection, we repeatedly find in schools that focus on the arts a view of the educational scene as a work in carefully attended progress. Artful educators in any setting ask to what extent their teaching and learning is authentically enriched by constant review and revision. They struggle for time in the school day to reflect like artists on the work-in-progress that is the teaching they provide. With regard to connection and community, as we have considered, the exploration of connections between student and subject and across other disciplines enriches the teaching and learning of any discipline. These connections include personal connections beyond school walls to a community of local, national, worldwide, and cross-cultural disciplinary experts. To what extent are such external connections fostered among students of math and science in schools that do not focus on the arts in education? Artful educators cultivate their students' sense of identification with a broader population of experts in order to increase the breadth of the reach of in-school learning and to demonstrate to students its relevance in a broader sphere.

The sense of difference as a given and respect as handmaiden to diversity seems particularly generative in these contexts. To what extent do or could non-arts-related schools see themselves as safe havens from more predictable institutions, braving the challenge and suspicion of breaking new ground and providing a place for students who may not feel they fit in in other settings? It is, of course, not just those students who are self-proclaimed artists who feel alienated from much of what goes on in mainstream education. How might all schools, no matter their academic priorities, find a way to embrace a maverick position and assume difference as a given to be embraced and respected? To what extent are different points of view overtly valued in non-arts-related classroom settings? How do we demonstrate in those subjects that different approaches and understandings are celebrated and respected?

Finally we come to passion and industry, perhaps the most resonant of the identified characteristics echoing throughout all the themes in our portraits of schools that focus on the arts. To what extent is passion recognized as a key word in schools that do not focus on the arts?

Surely industry prevails throughout education; teaching and learning is hard work and the level of passion that educators have for their students and for their work may be taken for granted in too many settings. But what are the passions beyond the classroom of teachers in non-arts settings? To what extent do their students know these passions and identify with them? What can we all learn from these hard-working groundbreaking teachers and learners who take the risk of industriously following their passions?

ARTS IN EDUCATION IN THE COMMUNITY— MIGHTY MUSE/SAFE HAVEN

Revisiting the Tension

Our explorations of the world of the arts in education took us beyond school walls to two settings for arts learning that I juxtaposed: the art museum and the community art center. The educational content and promise, as well as the struggles and triumphs of each of these environments, as with the rest, provide opportunities and paradigms for non-arts learning. In these out-of-school settings, we see situated integrations of the threads of an artful approach that by now resound throughout these final reflections.

Muse Opportunities

In the setting of the mighty muse, the venerable art museum, we explored the way in which interactions with arts can provide students with that experience of "owning" their learning that artful educators value so greatly. In this setting, students encounter firsthand the power that their life experiences have in helping them structure understandings and create and respond to open-ended questions. Open-ended questions are the kind that art uniquely asks, the kind that defy right or wrong, begin rather than end conversation, and open the door for different and equally valid perspectives and responses. As it is with original works of art, there is a special quality about encountering these questions in the setting of the art museum. What makes them special is readily apparent. But the experience that they provide is transferable across settings. The art museum also abounds with factual information (to which, of course, right or wrong attends), but students framing questions, harnessing facts in service of inquiry, take leadership in their learning and turn the empty-vessel image into one of a brewing pot.

In the learning that they do in the museum, students identify with makers of art and reconsider the range of problems that faced creators from the content referenced in the work to the constraints of the media that is employed to the nature of the emotions that are expressed. Artful educators in non-arts classes strive for similar empathetic and active connections between student and domain expert. Beyond school walls in the potentially elite environment that is the art museum, we see students having the chance to build meaning actively and to lead their own active journeys through the vast and object-laden walls of the museums. Artful educators often incorporate cultural objects into their classrooms and strive to create the opportunity for student-directed adventures.

What if schools thought of themselves as art museums? What does it look like when children navigate their own way through the resources of their schools? Artful educators repeatedly consider this possibility and respond with a range of alternative options. What if non-arts texts and subjects were thought of respectively as works of and arenas for art? Could we consider them with the attention to detail, care of presentation, and other curatorial considerations that are applied to works of art? How would that honoring resemble or differ from what experts in any domain do? How would students curate a show of their own learning? Which of my drawings in biology would I include in a presentation of my developing understanding of the motion of the blood? What labels would I attach to each element of my learning? What information would those labels include? Would I base the label's text on inquiry and ask the viewer questions about my work or would I provide direct information? And in either case, what issues would I address and what sort of language would I use? What difference does context and self-direction make in the thoughtful display of a student's understanding?

Artful educators encourage students to consider that, as it is with interpreting works of art in a museum, there are many and equally valid ways into any text and multiple and different entry points emerge in different contextual settings. Their students learn in non-arts courses that good questions set the stage for more good questions, and that the posing of a question is a powerful opportunity not only for organizing information but also for mining the rich messy edged layers of meaning. As a clearly resonant refrain in artful teaching and learning, the understanding of oneself as the able poser of open-ended questions rather than the hopeful provider of right answers changes the balance of power in teaching and learning. Artful educators set the stage for and mine the promise of this rearrangement.

The art museum serves as an encounter and an example, a unique place to visit and a replicable context for learning. The incorporation into any classroom of some of the ways of seeing, moving though, and learning in the art museum prepares students for a range of other out-of-school scenes of learning. We have considered the artist image of the student as Spiderperson weaving a web from subject area to subject area, from individual personal experience to multiple perspectives, from texts and teachers, from the receipt and display of learning. The art museum provides an opportunity for the spidering to extend across broader contexts. The close observation, respect for place, and encounter with self-directed inquiry are tools that can be actualized in that august setting and alternatively provided in a range of artful contexts for learning.

Haven Goals

While art museums tend to the presentation and contextualization or decontextualization of objects, community art centers, those safe havens that abide in challenged communities, attend to the preservation and cultivation of young makers of art and performance. When reviewing the range of goals of effective community art centers, we came up with objectives for teaching and learning that artful teachers in any setting pursue in whatever subjects they teach. Artful teachers of non-arts subjects prioritize, as we have already considered, personal and interpersonal goals that obtain to their discipline. The artful non-arts teacher may think of the way that recording history can play a role in the personal life of the student, or how expertise in the discipline of physics can set the stage for mentoring roles and the sense of self-mattering needed for self-esteem, self-confidence, and self-expression. These resonant refrains in artful teaching and learning resound across settings.

Cognitive goals, prioritized in community art centers, are obvious objectives of non-arts courses in schools. But in this context, artful teachers of non-arts subjects who follow the lead of community arts teachers consciously develop skills and knowledge of how to be productive (even as entrepreneurs) within the discipline. What does it take to create or perform and find audience for a work constructed out of the media of math, science, or social studies? Other "arts-related" cognitive objectives that artful teachers of science or history aim for include subject-specific skills of appreciation, the cultivation of the ability to innovate, concentrate, find and solve problems, and complete what one has started. These habits of learning, often evoked as justifications for arts learning, serve equally well as curricular goals for non-arts subjects. While their realizations may differ, they resound across settings in which artful teaching and learning reside.

Multicultural and culture-specific goals are embraced by artful non-arts teachers in any setting, and they are explored as they are through the arts. Foundational concepts like scale and rhythm take on meaning when they carry appreciation across different cultures' approaches to visual art and music. Learning in any discipline can purposely shape a vocabulary that can not only carry a student across intercultural understandings but also can scaffold considerations of the extent to which all kinds of language are translatable or not across the various understandings of culture. An Arts Cultura approach goes beyond school and discipline. In community art centers, these goals are actively explored by and through the intercultural learners that comprise the center's populations. Artful schools attend as well to what cultures are represented by their students and to the active exploration of and forging links among the cultures of neighborhood and the culture of school.

Community goals, directly tied to schools that focus on the arts, are highly prioritized in the safe havens that we reviewed. These goals range from the improvement of buildings in a neighborhood to the reduction of violence on the streets. Artful non-arts teachers in any setting consider with their students the ways in which their subjects can foster social reconciliation or the improvement of daily community life or even the beautification of community buildings. How do elements of math and science play into architecture and design? In what ways do historical events foreshadow possibilities for contemporary social justice? What do students think are the uncharted possibilities for whatever non-arts subject they are studying? As it does across artful educational settings, the sense of responsibility to community abides in these centers and projects on an institutional level that aspect of individual artistry we encountered at the start.

Community is as central a word in the naming of these places, as is *art*. And throughout the goals and their realizations or attempts for realization at these centers, there is a visceral connection to what it means to be an authentic member of the community. Students at these sites of arts learning speak to the authenticity of the work that they do there—the knowledge that the dance recital is not just an opportunity to display their talents, but as much or more an opportunity to bring in resources for the center and the continuation of the teaching and learning that these students self-select.

In this vein, when it comes to the area of professional goals as they are prioritized at community art centers, a certain authenticity also prevails. We have considered the benefit that artful teachers derive in any setting from envisioning their students as gifted child scientists, child mathematicians, and child historians. In this light, the gifts these nascent experts bring to class are valued and their understandings thought of as poignant and fresh instead of naïve and deficient. But in a community arts center, professional arts opportunities are valued as ways for students to gain employment and recognition that will help them move forward to college scholarships and/or monetary rewards that they would otherwise not know. The seriousness with which skills are modeled and acquired takes on new meaning in these settings. But artful teachers in school also recognize the importance of this "real-world" component, and also bring it into their classes.

With an eye to developing professionalism, artful educators construct learning scenarios designed more authentically to emulate and connect to the professional arena, including considerations of the ways in which artists (or other domain experts) market their art, represent themselves responsively in the field, and forge careers that bring them security even as they remain socially responsible to others. What are the fiscal and moral realities of living the life of a mathematician, or historian, or politician? Artful educators know that students value their learning when they can appreciate and/or experience the challenges and possibilities that abide in the world of work and service beyond school walls.

Principles of Effectiveness

Educationally effective community art centers have been observed as engaging the power of art to transform and/or to help articulate personal identities. How might expertise or facility in any domain be directed toward such self-defining efficacy? What role does the content and style of non-arts educators' teaching play in the articulation of their students' identities? How does their teaching frame their own personal identity? Strong relationships are a marker of effectiveness in the cultures of community art centers. Artful teachers of any subject dare to connect with students and with parents, creating familylike learning cohorts and encouraging mentorship relationships. Artful schools make time and space for relationship.

Community art centers prioritize a strong knowledge of their communities in order to be responsive to their interest and needs. Artful schools and non-arts teachers similarly consider their students as clients whose requirements and interests have real voice in the direction and shape of teaching and learning. Furthermore, this notion of durable oasis so central to the purpose and function of these centers of art provides an example and possibility for all artful schools. Is or can this quality of shelter and celebration be a goal in the building of any community of learners? Artful educators make of schools safe havens for individualized and collective personal and intellectual growth—a canvas for thinking and feeling, so many possibilities.

Finally, like artful teachers and learners and schools that focus on the arts, effective community art centers attend scrupulously to their own process of development and transformation, the purpose of that ongoing and active process of self-reflection. One vivid gift that arts making, teaching, and learning offers is an understanding of the how and why of a thoughtful process orientation. From an artist's approach, the subject and the class in which it is taught is constantly being attended to and revised by both the teachers and learners whose performance and perception conspire to make sense of it all. Reflection is a means and an end, agent to and a measure of effectiveness. This we have seen on an individual and institutional level. The questions of intention, communication, connection, reflection, symbolization, and interpretation that informed a feeling-thinking view of the artistic process emerge full blown at the overall process level of producing and perceiving artful sites of learning.

A FINAL WORD AND IMAGE

The recurring issues across the artistic contexts that we have revisited speak, I believe, to the certainty of the firm and flexible models that

the arts provide for teaching and learning and for making and finding meaning in any discipline. However, I don't believe that we have
begun to exhaust the range of alternatives that the arts in education
provide as inspiration for learning in non-arts domains. There are
many more questions to be posed and possibilities to be considered
than any one interpretive voice can provide. My hope is that the reader
will extend the discourse with new and better questions and identify
and explore whatever generative tensions help most in the tireless and
never-ending work of taking apart and reassembling the whole. What
the arts do in and for education is not extraneous, not dispensable, and
worth emulating in every arena.

*   *   *

As the overture played and the curtain rose, Octavia looked with
wonder and pride at the vista she had created and the actors and action that she had choreographed into production. There on the stage
was her version of Seurat's painting made out of color and light with
all her friends in perfect place and proportion, transformed by their
roles into visible elements of a work of art—the lyrics throughout reflecting the dot dotting of pointillism, the music so gracefully embodying the harmony of the image. There at the center was pitiful and irre-
sistible George, isolated by and heroic in his "mission to see." Octavia
felt her heart swell as she considered the show's repetitive articulation
of the artistic process: "putting it together, bit by bit." That, she and I
thought, is what the arts do in and for education.

References

American Association of Museums. (1984). *Museums for a new century*. A Report of the Commission on Museums for a New Century. Washington, DC: Author.

American Association of Museums. (n.d.). *What is a museum?* Retrieved August 17, 2002 from http://www.aam-us.org/resources/reference_library/3careers.cfm

Anderson, R. (1982). *Abbott Henderson Thayer*. Syracuse, NY: Emerson Museum.

Aristotle. (1951). *Aristotle's theory of poetry and fine art with a critical text and translation of the poetics* (Butcher, S.H., trans.). New York: Dover Publications.

Arnheim, R. (1962). *The genesis of a painting: Picasso's Guernica*. Berkeley: University of California Press.

Arnheim, R. (1966a). *Art and visual perception*. Berkeley: University of California Press.

Arnheim, R. (1966b). *Toward a psychology of art*. Berkeley: University of California Press.

Arnheim, R. (1969). *Visual thinking*. London: Faber & Faber.

Arts Education Partnership. (2002). *Critical links: Learning in the arts and student academic and social development*. Washington, DC: Author.

Arts Journal (n.d.). *Museum Attendance Down, Los Angeles Times 10/02/01*. Retrieved August 9, 2002 from http://www.artsjournal.com/Artsbeat/ab%2001-10-07.htm

Aspin, D. N. (1991). Justifying music education. In R. A. Smith & A. Simpson (Eds.), *Aesthetics and art education* (pp. 215–225). Urbana: University of Illinois Press.

Becker, C. (Ed.). (1994). *The subversive imagination: Artists, society, and social responsibility*. New York: Routledge.

Benton, M. (2001). *Interpretation of object and audience: Exploring relationship between museum educators and curators*. Unpublished Independent Study, Harvard Graduate School of Education.

Berleant, A. (1991). *Art and engagement*. Philadelphia: Temple University Press.

Bettelheim, B. (1975). *The uses of enchantment: The meaning and importance of fairy tales*. New York: Alfred A. Knopf.

Bever, T. G. (Ed.). (1982). *Regressions in mental development: Basic phenomena and theories*. Hillsdale, NJ: Lawrence Erlbaum Associates.

Boal, A. (1979). *The theatre of the oppressed*. New York: Urizen Books.

Boal, A. (1992). *Games for actors and non-actors*. New York: Routledge.

Broudy, H. (1987). *The role of imagery in learning*. Occasional Paper 1. Los Angeles. Getty Center for Education in the Arts.

Bruner, J. (1977). *The process of education*. Cambridge, MA: Harvard University Press. (Original work published 1960)

Burton, G. (1998, September). *The art of improvisation*. John Landrum Bryant Lecture/Performance. Harvard Graduate School of Education.

Burton, J. (1996). Natural allies: A trilogy. In J. Remer, *Beyond enrichment: Building effective arts partnerships with schools and your community* (pp. 309–329). New York: American Council for the Arts.

Burton, J., Horowitz, R., & Abeles, H. (2000). Learning in and through the arts: The question of transfer. *Studies in Art Education, 41*(3), 220–257.

213

Burton, J. M., London, P., & Lederman, A. (Eds.). (1988). *Beyond DBAE: The case for multiple visions of art education.* New York: University Council on Art Education.

Catterall, J. (2001). Commentary. In Winner, E., & Hetland, L. (Eds.), *Beyond the soundbite: Arts education and academic outcomes. Proceedings from beyond the soundbite: What the research actually shows about arts education and academic outcomes.* Los Angeles: J. Paul Getty Trust.

Catterall, J., Iwanaga, J., & Chapleau, R. (2001). Involvement in the arts and human development. In E. B. Fiske (Ed.), *Champions of change: The impact of the arts on learning.* Washington, DC: Arts Education Partnership; The President's Committee on the arts and Humanities; The John D. and Catherine T. MacArthur Foundation; and the GE Fund.

Caws, M. (2001). *Virginia Woolf.* Woodstock and New York: Overlook Press, Peter Meyers Publishers.

Celant, G. (Ed.). (1992). *Keith Haring.* Munich: Prestel-Verlag.

Chiu, S.-M. (2000). *The work of Leonardo da Vinci as a natural integration of art and science.* Unpublished qualifying paper, Harvard Graduate School of Education.

City of Sacramento, Crocker Art Museum. (2002, April). Job posting for curator of education. Retrieved March 14, 2003 from http://www.cityofsacramento.org/personnel/classes/01728.txt

Clark, G., Day, M., & Greer, D. (1989). Discipline-based art education: Becoming students of art. In Smith, R. (Ed.), *Discipline-based art education: Origins, meaning, and development* (pp. 130–193). Urbana and Chicago: University of Illinois Press.

Cleveland, W. (2000). *Art in other places: Artists at work in America's community and social institutions.* Westport, CT: Praeger.

Cockcroft, E., Weber, J. P., & Cockcroft, J. (1998). *Toward a people's art: The contemporary mural movement.* Albuquerque: University of New Mexico Press.

Collingwood, R. G. (1958). *The principles of art.* Oxford, UK: Oxford University Press. (Original work published 1938)

Congdon, K., Blandy, D., & Bolin, P. (2001). *Histories of community-based art education.* Reston, VA: National Art Education Association.

Consortium of National Arts Education Associations. (1994). *National standards for arts education: What every young American should know and be able to do in the arts.* Reston, VA: Music Educators National Conference.

Corbett, W. (1994). *Philip Guston's late work, a memoir.* Boston: Zoland Press.

Csikszentmihalyi, M. (1990). *Flow: The psychology of optimal experience.* New York: Harper & Row.

Csikszentmihalyi, M. (1996). *Creativity.* New York: Harper & Row.

Cuno, J. (1994). *Defining the mission of the academic art museum.* Occasional paper, Harvard University Art Museums. Cambridge, MA: President and Fellows of Harvard College.

Damasio, A. (1994). *Descartes' error.* New York: G.P. Putnam's Sons.

Davis, J. H. (1986, April 10). Interview with Rifat Chadirji as part of Independent Study on Creativity. Unpublished transcript.

Davis, J. H. (1989). *The artist in the child: A literature review of criteria for assessing aesthetic dimensions.* Qualifying paper, Harvard Graduate School of Education.

Davis, J. H. (1990). *Games for museum-goers to play* [Harvard Project Zero Technical Report #38]. Cambridge, MA: Harvard Graduate School of Education.

Davis, J. H. (1991a). *Artistry lost: U-Shaped development in graphic symbolization.* Unpublished doctoral dissertation, Harvard Graduate School of Education, Cambridge, MA.

Davis, J. H. (1991b). Co-arts interview with Katherine Dunham. Unpublished transcript.

Davis, J. H. (1991c). *Sketch of the children's art carnival.* Unpublished manuscript. Cambridge, MA: Project Co-Arts

Davis, J. H. (1993a). *The Co-Arts assessment handbook.* Cambridge, MA: Harvard Project Zero, President and Fellows of Harvard College.

Davis, J. H. (1993b). Museum games. *Teaching, Thinking, and Problem Solving, 15*(2).

Davis, J. H. (1993c, Winter). Why Sally can draw: An aesthetic perspective. In E. Eisner (Ed.), *Educational Horizons, 71*(2), 86–93.

Davis, J. H. (1996a). *The MUSE BOOK (Museums uniting with schools in education: Building on our knowledge).* Cambridge, MA: Harvard Project Zero, Presidents and Fellows of Harvard College.

Davis, J. (1996b, October). Why must we justify arts learning in terms of other disciplines? [Commentary]. *Education Week.*

Davis, J. H. (1997a). Drawing's demise: U-shaped development in graphic symbolization. *Studies in Art Education, 38*(3), 132–157.

Davis, J. H. (1997b). The u and the wheel of c: Development and devaluation of graphic symbolization and the cognitive approach at Harvard Project Zero. In A. M. Kindler (Ed.), *Child development in art anthology* (pp. 45–58). Reston, VA: National Art Education Association.

Davis, J. H. (1998). Everything old is new again: Self-assessment as tradition in community art centers. In R. E. Stake (Series Ed.), K. G. Congdon, & D. Boughton (Vol. Eds.), *Advances in program evaluation: Vol. 4. Evaluating art education programs in community centers: International perspectives on problems of conception and practice* (pp. 117–132). Stamford, CT: JAI Press.

Davis, J. H. (1999, May-June). Nowhere, Somewhere, Everywhere: The Arts in Education. *Art Education Policy Review, 100*(5), p. 3.1.

Davis, J. H. (2000). Multiplicity and metacognition: The arts as agents to different hues of thought. In M. Shaughnessy (Ed.), *Educational Psychology.* New Haven, CT: Yale University Press.

Davis, J. H. (2002). Balancing the whole: Portraiture as methodology. In P. Camic, J. Rhodes, & L. Yardley (Eds.), *Qualitative research in psychology: Expanding perspectives in methodology and design.* Washington, DC: APA Books.

Davis, J. H., Ackerman, J., Anisko, E., Bernard, R., Brody, A., Gatzambindes-Fernandez, R., Hamovit, L., Kennedy, S., Lehmann, A., Pruyne, E., & Sidoli, E. (Eds.). (2001). *Passion and industry: Schools that focus on the arts.* Cambridge, MA: President and Fellows of Harvard College.

Davis, J. H., Eppel, M., Galazzi, M., Gonzalez-Pose, P., Maira, S., & Solomon, R. (1996). *Another safe haven: Portraits of Boulevard Arts Center, then and now.* Cambridge, MA: Harvard Project Zero, President and Fellows of Harvard College.

Davis, J. H., & Gardner, H. (1992). The cognitive revolution: Its consequences for the understanding and education of the child as artist. In B. Reimer & R. A. Smith (Eds.), *The arts, education, and aesthetic knowing: Ninety-first yearbook of the National Society for the Study of Education, Part II* (pp. 92–123). Chicago: University of Chicago Press.

Davis, J. H., & Gardner, H. (1993). The Arts and Early Childhood Education: A Cognitive Approach to the Young Child as Artist. In B. Spodek (Ed.), *The handbook of research on the education of young children*. New York: Macmillan.

Davis, J. H., & Gardner, H. (1997). Creativity: Who, what, when, where. In A. Montuori (Ed.), *Unusual associates: A festschrift for Frank Barron* (pp. 138–147). Cresskill, NJ: Hampton Press.

Davis, J. H., Soep, L., Remba, N., Maira, S., & Putnoi, D. (1993). *Safe havens: Portraits of educational effectiveness in community art centers that focus on education in economically disadvantaged communities*. Cambridge, MA: Harvard Project Zero, Presidents and Fellows of Harvard College.

Davis, J. H., Solomon, B., Eppel, M., & Dameshek, W. (1996). *The wheel in motion: The Co-Arts assessment plan from theory to practice*. Cambridge, MA: Harvard Project Zero, President and Fellows of Harvard College.

Dennis, S. (1991). Stage and structure in children's spatial representations. In R. Case (Ed.), *The mind's staircase* (pp. 229–245). Hillside, NJ: Erlbaum.

Dewey, J. (1958). *Art as experience*. New York: Capricorn. (Original work published 1934)

DiMaggio, P., & Pettit, B. (1998, Fall). Surveys of public attitudes toward the arts: What surveys tell us about the arts' political trials—and how they might tell us even more. *Grantmakers in the Arts, 9*(2), 26–30.

Dissanayake, E. (1988). *What is art for?* Seattle: University of Washington Press.

Dobbs, S. M. (1992). *The DBAE handbook: An overview of discipline-based art education*. Santa Monica, CA: The J. Paul Getty Trust.

Dobbs, S. M. (1997). *Learning in and through art: A guide to discipline based art education*. Los Angeles: The Getty Education Institute for the Arts.

Dobbs, S., & Eisner, E. (1987, Winter). The uncertain profession: Educators in American art museums. *Journal of Aesthetic Education, 21*(4), 77–86.

Dow, A. W. (1899). *Composition: A series of exercises in art structure for the use of students and teachers*. (13th ed.). New York: Doubleday Dunn & Co.

Duckworth, E. (1987). The virtues of not knowing. In E. Duckworth (Ed.), *"The having of wonderful ideas" and other essays on teaching and learning*. New York: Teachers College Press.

Duncum, P. (1986). Breaking down the alleged "u" curve of artistic development. *Visual Arts Research, 12*(1).

Duncum, P. (2002). Clarifying visual culture art education. *Art Education. 55*(3), 6–12.

Dunning, D. (1999). Gender differences in the drawing of elementary school children [Unpublished raw data]. Harvard Graduate School of Education.

Efland, A. (1990). *A history of art education: Intellectual and social currents in teaching the visual arts*. New York: Teachers College Press.

Efland, A. (1992). History of art education as criticism: On the use of the past. In S. Aburgy et al. (Eds.), *The history of art education: Proceedings from the second Penn State conference, 1989* (pp. 1–11), Reston, VA: National Art Education Association.

Efland, A. (1996). The threefold curriculum and the arts. *Art Education, 49*(5), 49–56.

Eisner, E. (1988). *The role of discipline-based art education in America's schools*. Los Angeles: Getty Education Institute for the Arts.

Eisner, E. (1997). *Educating artistic vision*. Reston, VA: National Art Education Association.

Eisner, E. (2002). What can education learn from the arts about the practice of education? *Journal of Curriculum and Supervision, 18,* 4–16.

Eisner, E., & Dobbs, S. (1988, July). Silent pedagogy: How museums help visitors experience exhibitions. *Art Education, 44*(4), 4–15.

Fineberg, J. (1997). *The innocent eye: Children's art and the modern artist.* Princeton, NJ: Princeton University Press.

Fish, S. (1980). *Is there a text in this class?: The authority of interpretive communities.* Cambridge, MA: Harvard University Press.

Fowler, C. (1996). Strong arts, strong schools: The promising potential and shortsighted disregard of the arts in American schooling. New York: Oxford University Press.

Freud, S. (1900). *The intepretation of dreams.* New York: Macmillan.

Gablik, S. (1991). *The re-enchantment of art.* New York: Thames & Hudson.

Gardner, H. (1973). *The arts and human development: A psychological study of the artistic process.* New York: John Wiley & Sons.

Gardner, H. (1980). *Artful scribbles: The significance of children's drawings.* New York: Basic Books.

Gardner, H. (1982). *Developmental psychology.* Boston: Scott, Foresman & Co.

Gardner, H. (1985). *The mind's new science: A history of the cognitive revolution.* New York: Basic Books.

Gardner, H. (1989). Zero-based arts education: An introduction to ARTS PROPEL. *Studies in Art Education, 30,* 71–83.

Gardner, H. (1993). *Creating minds.* New York: Basic Books.

Gardner, H., & Perkins, D. (1989). *Art, mind and education: Research from Project Zero.* Champaign, IL: University of Illinois Press.

Gardner, H., & Winner, E. (1982). First intimations of artistry. In S. Strauss (Ed.), *U-shaped behavioral growth* (pp. 147–167). New York: Academic Press.

Geahigan, G. (1992). The arts in education: A historical perspective. In B. Reimer & R. Smith (Eds.), *The arts, education, and aesthetic knowing.* Chicago: University of Chicago Press.

Geller, D., & Goldfine, D. (Producers). (1996). *Kids of survival: The art and life of Tim Rollins & K.O.S.* [video portrayal].

Giroux, H. (1994). World without borders: Buying social change. In C. Becker (Ed.), *The subversive imagination: Artists, society, and social responsibility* (pp. 187–207). New York: Routledge.

Golomb, C. (1991). The child's creation of a pictorial world: Studies in the psychology of art. Berkeley: University of California Press.

Gombrich, E. (1960). *Art and illusion.* Princeton, NJ: Princeton University Press.

Gombrich, E. (1977). *Art and illusion: A study in the psychology of pictorial representation.* London: Phaidon Publishers.

Gombrich, E. (1995). *The story of art* (16th ed.). London and New York: Phaidon Publishers, distributed by Oxford University Press. (Original work published 1950)

Goodman, N. (1976). *Languages of art: An approach to a theory of symbols.* London: Oxford University Press.

Goodman, N. (1978). When is art? In *Ways of worldmaking* (pp. 57–70). Indianapolis, IN: Hackett Publishing Co.

Gottfried, M. (1993). *Sondheim.* New York: Harry N. Abrams.

Greene, M. (1995). *Releasing the imagination.* San Francisco: Jossey-Bass.

Greene, M. (2001). *Variations on a blue guitar.* New York: Teachers College Press.

Haskins, J. (1990). *Black dance in America: A history through its people.* New York: HarperCollins Publishers.

Heath, S. B., Soep, E., & Roach, A. (1998). Living the arts through language learning: A report on community-based organizations. *Americans for the Arts, 2*(7), 1–20.

Herbert, D. (1996). The national policy window for arts education. In J. Remer, *Beyond enrichment: Building effective arts partnerships with schools and your community* (pp. 432–442). New York: American Council for the Arts.

Heron, R. E., & Sutton-Smith, B. (1971). *Child's play.* New York: John Wiley & Sons.

Hirzy, E. C. (Ed.). (1992). *Excellence and equity: Education and the public dimension of museums.* Washington, DC: American Association of Museums.

Horsley, C. (1998–1999). Silence is so accurate. Mark Rothko exhibition. Retrieved March 16, 2003 from http://www.thecityreview.com/rothko.html

Housen, A. (1983). *The eye of the beholder: Measuring aesthetic development.* Unpublished Ed.D. Dissertation, Harvard University, Cambridge, MA.

Housen, A. (1987). Museums in an age of pluralism. In P. Banks (Ed.), *Art education here* (pp. 27–39). Boston: Massachusetts College of Art.

Housen, A., Yenawine, P., & Miller, N. L. (1993). *Reports on audience research 1991–1993.* New York: Museum of Modern Art.

Ives, S. W. (1984). The development of expressivity in drawing. *British Journal of Educational Psychology, 54,* 152–159.

Jung, C. G. (1964). *Man and his symbols.* New York: Doubleday.

Karp, I., & Wilson, F. (1996). Constructing the spectacle of culture in museums, In R. Greenburg, B. Ferguson, & S. Naime (Eds.), *Thinking about exhibitions* (pp. 251-267). New York: Routledge.

Kennick, W. E. (Ed.). (1964). *Art and philosophy: Readings in aesthetics* (pp. 7–18). New York: St. Martin's Press.

Kern, E. J. (1985). The purposes of art education in the United States from 1870 to 1980. In *The history of art education* (pp. 40–52). Philadelphia: The Pennsylvania State University College of Arts and Architecture School of Visual Arts.

Kim, H. (2001). Art education in the Museum of Modern Art. In K Congdon, D. Blandy, & P. Bolin (Eds.), *Histories of community-based art education* (pp. 19–29). Reston, VA: National Art Education Association.

Kindler, A. (Ed.). (1997). *Child development in art.* Reston, VA: National Art Education Association.

Koch, K. (1973). *Rose, where did you get that red: Teaching great poetry to children.* New York: Random House.

Koch, K. (1980). *Wishes, dreams, and lies: Teaching children to write poetry.* New York: Harper & Row.

Koch, K. (1998). *Making your own days: The pleasures of reading and writing poetry.* New York: Scribner.

Korzenik, D. (1973). *Children's drawings: Changes in representation between ages five and seven.* Unpublished doctoral dissertation, Harvard Graduate School of Education, Cambridge, MA.

Korzenik, D. (1985). *Drawn to art: A nineteenth-century American dream.* Hanover, NH, and London: University Press of New England.

Korzenik, D. (1987). Why government cared. *Art education here* (pp. 60–73). Boston: Massachusetts College of Art.

Lacy, S. (Ed.). (1995). *Mapping the terrain: New genre public art.* Seattle: Bay Press.

Langer, S. (1942). *Philosophy in a new key: A study in the symbolism of reason, rite, and art.* Cambridge, MA: Harvard University Press.

Langer, S. (1953). *Feeling and form.* New York: Scribner.

Lawrence-Lightfoot, S. (1983). *The good high school: Portraits of character and culture.* New York: Basic Books.

Lawrence-Lightfoot, S. (1988). *Balm in gilead: Journey of a healer.* Boston: Addison-Wesley.

Lawrence-Lightfoot, S. (1994). *I've known rivers: Lives of loss and liberation.* Cambridge, MA: Perseus Publishing.

Lawrence-Lightfoot, S., & Davis, J. H. (1997). *The art and science of portraiture.* San Francisco: Jossey-Bass.

Leeds, J. (1989). The history of attitudes toward children's art. *Studies in Art Education, 30*(2), 93–103.

Lowenfeld, V., & Brittain, W. L. (1970). *Creative and mental growth* (5th ed.). New York: Macmillan. (Original work published 1947)

London, P. (1988). J. Burton, A. Lederman, & P. London (Eds.), *Beyond DBAE, the case for multiple visions of art education.* North Dartmouth, MA: Art Education Department, Southeastern Massachusetts University. (Sponsored by University Council on Art Education.)

Madeja, S. (2001). Remembering the aesthetic education program: 1966 to 1976. In K. Congdon, D. Blandy, & P. Bolin (Eds.), *Histories of community-based art education* (pp. 117-127). Reston, VA: National Art Education Association.

Mann, T. (1989). Tonio Kröger. In *Death in Venice and seven other stories* (pp. 75–132). New York: Vintage Books.

Markowitz, R. (1991). *Canonizing the popular.* A paper delivered at the conference Banality and Fatality, sponsored by the CUNY Committee for Cultural Studies. Retrieved August 19, 2002 from http://www.culturalstudies.net/canon.html

May, S. (2000). Abbott Thayer: The nature of art. Retrieved August 22, 2002 from http://antiquesandthearts.com/archive/thayer.htm

Museum of Contemporary Art. (n.d.). *Teachers resource. A cube is a cube is a cube.* Retrieved August 20, 2002 from http://www.mcachicago.org/MCA/Education/Teachers/Book/Lewitt-plan.html

Museum of Fine Arts, Boston. (n.d.). *Mission statement.* Retrieved March 9, 2003 from http://www.mfa.org/mission_statement.html

National Endowment for the Arts (2002, April) The Arts in the GDP: Consumers spend $9.8 Billion on admissions to performing arts events in 2000. Research Division Note #79. Retrieved August 19, 2002 from http://www.nea.gov/pub/Notes/79.pdf

National Guild of Community Music Schools Quarterly. (1940). Volume I, Number 1. New York: Author.

Newsom, B. Y., & Silver, A. Z. (Eds.). (1978). *The art museum as educator: A collection of studies as guides to practice and policy.* Berkeley and London: University of California Press.

Nicolaides, K. (1941). *The natural way to draw.* Boston: Houghton Mifflin Co.

O'Doherty, B. (1999). *Inside the white cube: The ideology of gallery space* (Expanded ed.). Berkeley: University of California Press.

O'Donnell, S. C. (1995). The New York City Museum School: A learning process. *Museum News, 74*(3), 38–41, 64, 66, 68.

O'Neill, E. (1964). *Ten lost plays.* All God's Children Got Wings. New York: Random House.

Paley, N. (1995). Finding art's place: Experiments in contemporary education and culture. London: Routledge.

Pariser, D. (1979). *The orthography of disaster: Children's drawings of wrecked cars* [Harvard Project Zero Technical Report No. 10]. Cambridge, MA: Harvard Graduate School of Education.

Pariser, D. (1989). Normal and unusual aspects of artistic development in the juvenalia of Klee, Toulouse-Lautrec, and Picasso. *Visual Arts Research, 13*(2:26), 53–56.

Pariser, D., & van den Berg A. (1997). The mind of the beholder: Some provisional doubts about the u-curved aesthetic development thesis. *Studies in Art Education, 38*(3), 158–178.

Parsons, M. J. (1987). *How we understand art: A cognitive developmental account of aesthetic experience.* Cambridge, UK: Cambridge University Press.

Parsons, M. J. (1991). Cognition as interpretation in art education. In B. Reimer & R. A. Smith (Ed.), *The arts, education, and aesthetic knowing: Ninety-first yearbook of the National Society for the Study of Education, Part II* (pp. 70–91). Chicago: University of Chicago Press.

Perkins, D. (1992). *Smart schools: Better thinking and learning for every child.* New York: The Free Press.

Perkins, D. (1994). *The intelligent eye: Learning to think by looking at art.* Los Angeles: Getty Education Institute for the Arts.

Persky, H., Sandene, B., & Askew, J. (1998). *The NAEP 1997 arts report card.* Washington, DC: U.S. Department of Education, Office of Educational Research and Improvement.

Piaget, J. (1962). *Play, dreams and imitation in childhood.* New York and London: W.W. Norton.

Piaget, J. (1985). *The child's conception of time.* New York: Ballantine Books.

Piaget, J., & Inhelder, B. (1948). *The child's construction of space.* New York: W.W. Norton.

Piaget, J., & Inhelder, B. (1969). *The psychology of the child.* New York: Basic Books.

Plato. (1953). Republic. In *The Dialogues of Plato* (Vol. II, 4th ed., B. Jowett, trans.). Oxford: Clarendon Press.

Putnoi, D., Olmsted, K., & Davis, J. (1994). *Two transcriptions of the generic game in action: A focus on facilitation.* Cambridge, MA: Harvard Project Zero, Presidents and Fellows of Harvard College.

Quiller-Couch, A. (1931). *The Oxford Book of English Verse 1250–1900.* Oxford, UK: Clarendon Press. (Original work published 1900)

Rauscher, F. H., Shaw, G. L., & Ky, K. N. (1993). Music and spatial task performance. *Nature, 365*(6447), 611.

Ravitch, D. (1983). *The troubled crusade: American education 1945–1980.* New York: Basic Books.

Reddy, M. (1979). The conduit metaphor. In A. Ortony (Ed.), *Metaphor and thought.* Cambridge, UK: Cambridge University Press.

Reimer, B., & Smith, R. A. (Eds.). (1992). *The arts, education, and aesthetic knowing: Ninety-first yearbook of the National Society for the Study of Education, Part II.* Chicago: University of Chicago Press.

Remer, J. (1996). *Beyond enrichment: Building effective arts partnerships with schools and your community*. New York: American Council for the Arts.

Ricci, C. (1887). *L'art dei bambini*. Bologna: Nicola Zanichelli.

Rice, D. (1993, January/February). The cross cultural mediator. *Museum News, 72*(1), 38–41.

Rood, N. O. (1879). *Modern chromatics with application to art and industry*. Chicago: F. Biren.

Rosenblatt, E., & Winner, E. (1988). The art of children's drawing. *Journal of Aesthetic Education, 22*(1), 3–16.

Rothstein, E. (1996, October 19). When teaching the arts becomes social work [review of the film *Kids of Survival: The Art and Life of Tim Rollins & K.O.S.*]. *The New York Times*.

Sayre, H. (1997). *A world of art* (2nd Ed.). Engelwood Cliffs, NJ: Prentice Hall.

Scheffler, I. (1991). *In praise of cognitive emotions*. London: Routledge.

Schiller, F. (1967). *On the aesthetic education of man, in a series of letters*. (E. M. Wilkinson & L. A. Willoughby, trans.).Oxford: Oxford University Press.

Seigesmund, R. (1998). Why do we teach art today? Conceptions of art education and their justification. *Studies in Art Education, 39*(3), 197–214.

Shipps, S. W. (1996, Spring). About thinking, about "art." *Journal of Aesthetic Education, 30*(1), 73–83.

Sloboda, J., & Rogers, D. (1983). *The acquisition of symbolic skills*. New York: Plenum Press.

Smith, N. (1972). *Developmental origins of graphic symbolization in the paintings of children 3–5*. Unpublished Ed.D dissertation, Harvard University, Cambridge, MA.

Smith, N. (1983). *Experience and art*. New York: Teachers College Press.

Smith, R. (Ed.). (1989). *Discipline-based art education: Origins, meaning, and development*. Urbana and Chicago: University of Illinois Press.

Soep, E. (1996). An art in itself: Youth development through critique. *New Designs for Youth Development, 12*(4), 42–46.

Sondheim, S., & Lapine, J. (1991). *Sunday in the park with George* [libretto]. New York: Applause Theatre Book Publishers.

Soucy, D., & Stankiewicz, M. A. (Eds.). (1990). *Framing the past: Essays on art education*. Reston, VA: National Art Education Association.

Sparshott, F. (1993). The future of dance aesthetics. *The Journal of Aesthetics and Art Criticism, 51*(2), 227–235.

Spolin, V. (1986). *Theater games for the classroom: A teacher's handbook*. Evanston, IL: Northwestern University Press.

Stern, W. (1924). *Psychology of early childhood*. (A. Barwell, trans.). New York: Henry Holt & Co.

Stiles, K., & Selz, P. (Eds.). (1996). *Theories and documents of contemporary art: A sourcebook of artists' writings*. Berkeley, Los Angeles, and London: University of California Press.

Strand, M. (2000). *The weather of words*. New York: Alfred A. Knopf.

Strand, M. (2001). *Hopper*. New York: Alfred A. Knopf.

Strauss, S. (1982). *U-shaped development*. New York: Academic Press.

Sutherland, D. (producer/director). (1986). *Jack Levine: Feast of pure reason* [videotape]. Newton, MA: David Sutherland Productions.

Thayer, G. H. (1909). *Concealing coloration in the animal kingdom*. New York: Macmillan.

Tolstoy, L. (1995). *What is art?* London: Viking Penguin Books. (Original work published 1898)

Ulbricht, J. (1998, July). Interdisciplinary art education reconsidered. *Art Education, 51*(4), 13–17.

Victoria and Albert Museum Web site. (n.d.). *About the Victoria and Albert Museum*. Retrieved March, 8, 2003 from http:/www.vam.ac.uk/visiting/aboutvanda/?section=aboutvanda&view=Mainframe

VUE Institute Information Web site. (2003). *What is VTS*. Available: http://www.vue.org/

Weitz, J. H. (1996). *Coming up taller: Arts and humanities programs for children and youth at risk*. Washington, DC: President's Committee on the Arts and the Humanities.

West, S. (Ed.). (1996). *The Bullfinch Guide to Art History*. Boston: Little Brown.

White, A. M. (2002). *The effect of music learning on student leisure time*. Unpublished doctoral dissertation, Harvard Graduate School of Education, Cambridge, MA.

Wilson, B. (1993, June). *Popular art and school art: Comic books and Japanese children's graphic narrative constructions of reality*. Paper Presented at the Jean Piaget Society, Philadelphia, PA.

Winner, E. (1983). *Invented worlds: The psychology of the arts*. Cambridge, MA: Harvard University Press.

Winner, E. (1988). *The point of words: Children's understanding of metaphor and irony*. Cambridge, MA: Harvard University Press.

Winner, E., & Gardner, H. (1981). The art in children's drawings. Review of research in *Visual Arts Education, 14*, 18–31.

Winner, E., & Hetland, L. (Eds.). (2000). The arts and academic achievement: What the evidence shows. *The Journal of Aesthetic Education, 34*(3–4).

Winner, E., & Hetland, L. (Eds.). (2001). *Beyond the soundbite: Arts education and academic outcomes. Proceedings from "Beyond the soundbite: What the research actually shows about arts education and academic outcomes."* Los Angeles: J. Paul Getty Trust.

Wolf, D., & Gardner, H. (1980). Beyond playing or polishing: A development of artistry. In J. J. Hausman (Ed.), *Arts and the schools* (pp. 47–77). New York: McGraw-Hill.

Wolf, D., & Perry, M. (1988). From endpoints to repertoires: Some new conclusions about drawing development. *Journal of Aesthetic Education, 22*(1), 17–34.

Zessoules, R., Wolf, D. P., & Gardner, H. (1988). A better balance: Arts Propel as an alternative to DBAE. In J. Burton, A. Lederman, & P. London (Eds.), *Beyond DBAE, the case for multiple visions of art education* (pp. 117–130). North Dartmouth, MA: Art Education Department, Southeastern Massachusetts University. (Sponsored by University Council on Art Education.)

Zucker, B. F. (2001). Anna Curtis Chandler: Art educator nonpareil at the Metropolitan Museum of Art. In K. Congdon, D. Blandy, & P. Bolin (Eds.), *Histories of community-based art education* (pp. 8–19). Reston, VA: National Art Education Association.

Index

About the Author

Jessica Hoffmann Davis, Ed.D., founded and was the first director of the Arts in Education Program at the Harvard Graduate School of Education. A cognitive developmental psychologist with an abiding interest in children's artistry and arts learning, Dr. Davis held Harvard's first chair in the arts in education as the Patricia Bauman and John Landrum Bryant Senior Lecturer on the Arts in Education. Davis has worked as a teacher, practitioner, and administrator in the visual arts. She holds the persistent belief that arts learning should be part of every child's every day at school.